Praise for
Colorado Phantasmagorias

"*Colorado Phantasmagorias* is an apt title for a highly imaginative work about some of the Centennial State's most notable men and women. What Joan Jacobson has done is what historians seek to do but rarely achieve – evoke empathy for historical figures. The dialogue may be fictional, but the characters are very real. She captures the essence of some truly remarkable Coloradans."

> **William Wei**, Professor of History, University of Colorado at Boulder, **Colorado State Historian**, 2019-2020

"What a fun way to learn about characters from Colorado. This book is packed with stories to guide you to many exciting adventures where the action took place."

> **Rich Grant**, co-author with Irene Rawlings of
> *100 Things to Do in Denver Before You Die*

"I can't think of a more enjoyable way to learn our state's history than to spend a few hours in the company of this remarkable writer."

> **Don Morreale**, author of *Cowboys, Yogis, and One-legged Ski Bums: The Extraordinary Lives of Ordinary Coloradans*

"Often when we read about icons of Colorado's past—like path-breaking medical scientist Dr. Florence Sabin, enduring Ute leader Chipeta, and survivor Margaret Tobin Brown—we wonder what they'd make of their former stomping grounds today. Women's historical experiences in particular leave us with as many questions as answers. *Colorado Phantasmagorias*–a mix of real history, time travel, speculative fancy, and practical tour guide–explores Colorado from a fresh 'then and now' perspective. Joan Jacobson grounds her biographies in scholarly research, mixing in imagination to reveal the human aspect. I highly recommend this fresh trip through our state's history."

> **Dr. Marcia Tremmel Goldstein**, Past President of **Denver Woman's Press Club**

Colorado Phantasmagorias

A mashup of biography, fantasy, and travel guide

By Joan Jacobson

COLORADO PHANTASMAGORIAS. Copyright © 2020 by Joan Jacobson. All rights reserved. Printed in the United States of America. No part of this book may be used or reproduced without written permission except in the case of brief quotations embodied in critical articles and review. For information, address Words and Pages LLC, 1836 Dover St., Lakewood, CO 80215.

Cover Design by Craig Rouse, R Design LLC
ISBN (Paperback) 978-1-7345884-0-8
ISBN (eBook) 978-1-7345884-1-5

Photography Credits
The author gratefully acknowledges the following for use of their photographs:

History Colorado Photography Collection:
Felipe Baca Family
Chipeta and Ouray
Barney Ford
Coors Brewery
Florence Sabin
John Denver and Dick Lamm

Denver Public Library, Western History Collection:
Chipeta at Tunnel Dedication, Thomas McKee, Z-12037
John Brisben Walker, C62-21 ART
Margaret Tobin Brown, X21691
Ralph Carr, RMN-045-1574
Mount Sopris, MCC-1739
Stanley Biber, RMN-021-9942

The Atlantis Community: *1978 Bus Protest*

Grand County Historical Association: *Carl Howelsen*

University of Wisconsin-Milwaukee: *Golda (Meir) and Morris Meyerson*

iStock Getty Images: *Geode*

About web links: Website addresses were verified for efficacy. The author apologizes if changes over which she has no control render them ineffective.

DEDICATION

To my son, the native Coloradan.

Phantasmagorias:
Dreamlike images, illusions created by magic.

TABLE OF CONTENTS

| Today | Genie in a Geode | 1 |

1868	Felipe Baca, Leader & Legislator	3
1909	Chipeta, Peacemaker & Bead Artist	17
1912	John Brisben Walker, Developer & Dreamer	34
1913	Golda Meir, Nation Builder	53
1927	Margaret Brown, Feminist & Survivor	65
1942	Ralph Carr, Governor with Guts	80
1978	Wade Blank, Disability Rights Radical	96

1889	Barney Ford, Entrepreneur, Civil Rights Pioneer	115
1889	Ora Chatfield & Clara Dietrich, Ladies in Love	131
1915	Adolph Coors, Brewer	145
1917	Carl Howelsen, Ski Pioneer	158
1946	Florence Sabin, M.D., Public Health Pioneer	177
1969	Stanley Biber, M.D., Gender Confirmation Pioneer	192
1973	John Denver, Singer & Songwriter	206

Author Notes, Bibliographies 219
Felipe Baca 220
Chipeta 223
John Brisben Walker 226
Golda Meir 230
Margaret Brown 233
Ralph Carr 236
Wade Blank 239
Barney Ford 244
Ora Chatfield and Clara Dietrich 247
Adolph Coors 250
Carl Howelsen 253
Florence Sabin, M.D. 257
Stanley Biber, M.D. 262
John Denver 265

Acknowledgments, About the Author *268*

History in the Making

This book was researched, proofread, and in the final stages of production when the 2020 Coronavirus pandemic reached Colorado. It is being published while we are sheltering in place under the governor's order. If you are reading this before the 2020 Coronavirus pandemic has retreated into history, please enjoy these biographies from the safety of your home.

Virtually all of our museums and attractions are currently closed. I hope they reopen soon, as I'm sure you do, too. In the meantime, stay in your own neighborhood and use travel suggestions in the 'Just for Fun' sections to plan for—and look forward to—exploring the great state of Colorado when it is safe to venture out.

Joan Jacobson

> *"Coming events do cast shadows."*
> Iris Murdoch, *The Black Prince*

> *"There were hints and intimations of the shape of things to come."*
> Dexter Palmer, *The Dream of Perpetual Motion*

> *"Foreshadowing is like playing cat and mouse."*
> Mary Sage Nguyen

GENIE in a GEODE

A time-traveling genie in a geode links past to present in this book.

At the start of each biography, the character touches the crystals inside a broken geode, setting off a phantasmagoria (vision) that foreshadows the future.

If the word 'foreshadow' gives you nightmares of high school English, rest assured: *This is all fun and games.*

The visions portend their legacy in today's world. It's confusing to them, as you might imagine, to see a flash of images out of the far future.

But you, dear reader, have an advantage. You know something of how the world has changed, what things look like today. Enjoy a bit of fun puzzling out what the hallucinations signify.

Or not. The meaning of the phantasmagorias becomes clear later when a genie springs from the geode, revealing each character's legacy. (Can't wait? Check out Key to the Visions in the Author Notes.)

Then hop out of your chair and experience these legacies in person. Each chapter concludes with suggestions for outdoor activities, museums and tours, sometimes even crafts and recipes. Enjoy . . .

Felipe Baca
1829 – 1874
Latino Leader, Legislator

A ROCK RICOCHETS off a post, smacking Felipe Baca in the head. *What is the meaning of this?* The town founder is minding his own business, literally, jiggling the lock on his store, making sure it's secure, the store being closed this New Year's Day. The offending article lies in two pieces, its glittery crystals exposed. *La geoda.* He picks it up.

Then the bullets fly.

Not again.

Baca jabs his key into the lock, thrusts the door open and ducks inside. Blasts of gunfire assault his ears, even through the closed door. He checks for wounds, rubbing the bump where the geode hit, feeling his clothes for blood or bullet holes. None. *Gracias a Dios.*

He leans back into a safe corner, keeping a view out the window. Main Street is clouding with gunsmoke. His peaceful Trinidad is in tumult, the second time in a week.

Los idiotas.

His head throbs. The rock didn't hit that hard, but he feels *poco loco* nevertheless. He stumbles. Still gripping the rock, he tries to steady himself. The dizzy feeling—*el vértigo*—spirals into a hallucination. His store transforms before his eyes.

Unaccountably gone are the familiar barrels and crates. Standing in their place are men in black suits and high collars exhorting each other—in English. One waves a document. Baca squints to read the title: *Constitucion Estado de Colorado.*

Is this my life passing before my eyes? No, that can't be. I've not experienced this in my life.

Which is worse, *la alucinacion* ringing inside? Or bullets zinging outside? Losing one's mind or losing one's life? The outside is transmogrified as well. Main Street is altered from adobe and wood into brick and stone. That's what it looks like through the smoke anyhow.

His throat catches and his heart stops. Dolores stands amidst the danger. *Or does she?* An apparition looks just like his wife, but she's on the balcony of a two-story house he does not recognize, on a lot he knows to be vacant. It can't be her. *Gracias a Dios.*

He looks eastward, desperate for a familiar sight. Past the town limits rushes a blur of shiny metal. Otherworldly conveyances rip through ranchlands at unimaginable speed. What is the means of locomotion? Where are the horses? The oxen?

He must get ahold of himself. He sets the two halves of the broken rock on the sales counter, steadies himself with both hands. *Las ilusiones* fade. Reality returns, and it's still ugly out there.

He cracks the door open just a sliver, smells the sulphurous stink of black powder. Never mind the melee, *la pelea confusa*, he flings open the door. He must run as fast as he can to his hacienda. He has a family to protect.

୨୧

Trinidad
January, 1868

"ARE THE CHILDREN safe?" the patriarch demanded as he entered the courtyard of his *hacienda*. Felipe Baca had run home faster than a man half his age. His heart pounded like stampeding horses, but he slowed his pace and controlled his voice so as not to alarm his household. It would be unwise to incite panic among women and children. He put on the persona of a man in charge, portraying a calm he did not feel.

The pandemonium and the explosions of gunfire still resonated from Main Street. But here, down by the river, inside thick adobe walls with the gate pulled tight, the tumultuous disorder sounded farther away than it was. The sour, metallic taste of fear slowly dissolved from his mouth.

His wife motioned him out of the cold courtyard into the warm *cocina*. "Juan Pedro is in the hills, checking the sheep. Our daughters and little Luis are here, safe."

"And the servants? Are they all accounted for?"

"The servants are enjoying their day off."

"If any of them gets shot to death, I'll fire him!"

Dolores tilted her head, her dark eyes studying him carefully. "Are you all right, Felipe? You speak insensibly. What is all the commotion?"

Before answering, Felipe Baca felt compelled to check on his family. In *la cocina*, the littlest children played with their Christmas gifts, Luis positioning toy blocks into the shape of buildings and bridges, Rosa cuddling her cloth doll. Luz rolled corn flour dough in her hands, forming tomato-sized balls, lining them up in preparation for flattening. There would be fresh tortillas for lunch.

His older daughters were occupied in an adjacent room. Apolonia carded wool for her sister's spinning wheel. Catarina's feet danced on the treadle, her delicate fingers pulling taut the fibers from their own Churro sheep, the flywheel spinning faster than a runaway wagon barreling down Raton Pass. His first-born, Dionisia, worked the loom, hands propelling the shuttle through the warp threads, battening the weft into a geometric pattern. The soothing, repetitive motions of rug-making were a balm against the chaos in town.

Satisfied these children were safe within the impregnably thick walls of dried mud and hay, he worried only for Juan Pedro. His eldest son was sensible enough for a young man. Juan Pedro would ensure the well-being of the family's flocks on this winter day, then find a safe route home. At least, that was his father's prayer.

"Not here," Felipe said, finally, in answer to his wife's question. "Let us speak out of the earshot of the children."

In their bed chamber, he told her what he knew, which was little, and his speculations, which included many disparagements of *los idiotas*.

"Foolishness has disturbed the peace again," he told Dolores. "We must all stay here, God willing that Juan Pedro returns home safely, until the violence is over."

"Is it once again on account of that stupid wrestling match?" she asked.

"That's my conjecture as well," he sighed. "Frank Blue was spoiling for a fight and he got it. Even after Sheriff Gutierrez locked him away for trial, the ruffians and drunkards are keeping the fight going."

Last week, on Christmas Day, a stagecoach driver and gambler by the name of Frank Blue had issued a challenge to anyone within earshot. Wrestle or box, Blue didn't care, he just wanted a fight. A Hispano took up the challenge. Men crowded around, throwing cash into a hat for the eventual winner. The two went at it in the middle of Main Street Trinidad. The crowd whooped and hollered as their favored man took top position.

Then Blue picked up his opponent and slammed him onto the street. The crack of the snapping bone was almost loud enough to be heard over the hollers, but the shout and groaning of the injured man was more than loud enough.

Blue ran. His opponent's compatriots took chase. Men started throwing rocks and shooting off their guns. Another Hispano, not the wrestler, got shot, mortally wounded, probably shot by Blue, but maybe in self-defense, the scene in too much chaos to make sense of anything.

Blue hid. A mob climbed on the roof of the house where he was holed up and tore off the tin before the law arrived. Sheriff Guitierrez arrested Blue for assault and suspicion of murder and, there being no jail in Trinidad, locked him in a house under guard until trial.

Seeing that Anglos and Hispanos had already taken sides against each other, the sheriff appointed six Anglos and six Hispanos to guard the prisoner. The heavy guard presence and balanced approach did not prevent the dead man's brother and friend from shooting at the guard house windows. For three nights straight. But they were lousy shots, probably too whiskeyed up, so the prisoner stayed secure, the windows intact.

And now, after four days of relative peace, the rock throwing and gun shooting had started up all over again. *What new development was escalating tempers? Would Juan Pedro get caught up in it? Young men let excitement overwhelm good sense.*

The thunder of dozens of boots interrupted Felipe and Dolores. Into their courtyard ran ranch hands and household servants, bounding straight to their quarters.

"Ramon!" Baca said from the doorway to the kitchen, in a voice just loud enough to command attention amid the pounding feet. "Tell us the news. What is the cause of *la violencia?*"

Ramon skidded to a halt. He bent over double, heaving in air as deeply as he could, until he had breath to speak.

"Don Felipe Baca," he said, respectfully, "Señora Baca. There is bad trouble. A man—Dunn his name is—went and found some miners down in New Mexico and got together a posse. They marched on the guard house where the sheriff was holding Frank Blue. Scared the daylights out of Deputy Tafoya so bad that he released that murderer! The posse marched Blue to the Colorado Hotel. They're protecting him there!" Ramon stopped to catch his breath again. Still huffing, he continued, "Along the way everybody started shooting at everybody else. It's a war!"

"Outsiders stirring up trouble." Don Felipe Baca patted his servant on the back. "Do not leave our *hacienda* without permission. Until things settle down."

FELIPE WORKED on his accounts, or pretended to. Dolores paced continuously. They both hoped Juan Pedro was too busy tending sheep in the hills to notice the tumult on Main Street, much less get involved, but could not know for sure. Not until they saw him with their own eyes, and darkness was falling.

As the sun set behind the Sangre de Cristo mountains, their eldest son sauntered into the courtyard. Father and mother breathed a sigh of relief, and immediately gathered all their children in the room used for entertaining guests. A fire blazed in the corner fireplace, reflecting off the gypsum-white walls. Dolores and the older girls sat on chairs. The little girls sat cross-legged on the floor, Luis on his mother's lap. The patriarch stood to address them.

"The disorder at the hotel is not our business," he began. "You are to stay out of danger within these walls until peace is restored."

Juan Pedro stood behind his siblings, leaning against the wall, his fingers twitching against the weapon he carried to shoot wild marauders of his family's sheep. "*Padre!*" he objected. "*La Justicia!* Justice must be served! That man Frank Blue. . ."

The father held out his hand to silence his son. Juan Pedro's hand flicked away from his weapon in angry submission.

"You will not participate. Any shepherds who participate will be dismissed, and their duties will fall to you, Juan Pedro," said his father. "It's to your advantage to see they attend to my wool and not their weapons."

The father went about the room, touching each child in turn. "The Baca family does not take sides based on race," he said, firmly. "We take sides based on what is right and what is wrong. In this violence, all are wrong.

"Our family came here seven years ago to the fertile lands along the banks of *El Rio de las Animas Perdidas en Purgatorio* River. We came here from New Mexico to raise sheep, grow melons and squash, potatoes, pumpkins and corn. Together with the other twelve families from the Mora Valley, we founded this town. We dug ditches to water our crops. We worked hard. We have made good profit selling what we raise with all those who travel this way on the Santa Fe Trail. Mexicans, English, Germans, former slaves. They are all our customers.

"Our flocks thrive. The one thousand ewes we brought with us have increased by five times, soon ten times. In the spring we plant four hundred acres. Our store and the sawmill do good business. It is through our family's success that this town has a church and a school.

"There is no profit in violence. Dead men do not herd sheep. Widows cannot afford woolen rugs. Travelers skirt violence. Traders take their business elsewhere.

"Of course I believe in justice," he continued, looking at his elder son. "But justice does not come from the barrel of a gun.

"Listen well, my children." He looked over to his wife, her hand resting on her belly. "Even the child not yet born must hear this," he said. "Among civilized men, justice comes from laws, and men who study law, and men in black robes who adjudicate those laws. You will stay at home until law is restored. That is all."

BEFORE IT WAS OVER, the battle left two dead and five men wounded, 'moaning piteously in the street,' as the *Rocky Mountain News* described it. But the wish of Don Felipe Baca, founder of Trinidad, to stay out of the fray entirely, was not to be. It was his duty to join with his fellow Hispano Lorenza Abeyta and two Anglos, Dr. Michael Beshoar and County Commissioner James S. Gray, to calm the crowd and negotiate a truce.

The negotiators were quick to zero in on an opportunity. Both sides were firmly convinced their side was the side of law and order, so everyone agreed to call in federal troops to restore peace. Guns were confiscated, smoke dissipated, men who'd just gotten caught up in the fray were forgiven and released, and 'ringleaders' identified. Baca himself sheltered a small group of Anglo offenders in safety at his *hacienda* until the troops arrived. Once the militia galloped into Trinidad, martial law was declared, and all the Trinidad men were released. Only Dunn and his posse of roughs were prosecuted.

And then, Don Felipe Baca threw a party.

A GRAND FANDANGO was a fitting finale to this unfortunate incident. The Baca servants strung lanterns around the courtyard and set up a dance floor. Braziers warmed the chill out of the evening air. Trinidad's best musicians strummed melodies on their guitars, blared notes from horns, snapped rhythms with castanets. It was impossible not to dance.

The local men cleaned up in their Sunday best, except for *los judios*, Maurice Wise and his fellow religionists, who came in their Sabbath best. The women glowed in their most colorful dresses. Those who had settled from New Mexico came in their traditional mid-calf skirts and off-the-shoulder *camisas*, shawled against the cold. The Anglo women, what few there were, kept their shoulders and ankles covered, but their dresses swirled gaily nevertheless.

The air was redolent with the aroma of grilled mutton and spiced beans. Dried plum pies tempted those with a sweet tooth. Everyone was in a celebratory mood.

Impressed by it all were two honored guests, Acting Territorial Governor Frank Hall and a reporter from the *Rocky Mountain News*. Both had come to town to investigate, now that everything was safe.

His store clerk approached Don Felipe Baca and handed him the geode rock. "Señor, I found this on the sales counter. Mr. Maurice Wise told me this thing conked you on the head New Year's Day. Perhaps you want it as a memento? Now that peace is restored?"

Felipe Baca chuckled. "It was a minor occurrence. Barely a bump I got from it."

The clerk bowed and returned to dancing.

Felipe Baca opened the two halves. The purple crystals glinted in the lantern light of his courtyard. Like the Sangre de Cristos at sunset. He ran his fingers over the jagged points, and all dissolved before his eyes.

"BUENAS NOCHES, SEÑOR," says a strange man in a peculiar accent.

Felipe Baca has never seen this man before. Even though the fandango is open to all, this man is out of place. Baca feels out of place himself, weird. He can't hear the music anymore. The surroundings have changed; he stands not in his courtyard, but on the porch of a two-story house. He's wearing not his festive attire, but an Anglo-style black suit and high collared white shirt like the men in his New Year's Day hallucination. At least it's peaceful.

"My name is Mancio," the man says, extending his hand. "I'm a prophet. *Un Profeta*. A soothsayer released from that geode to show you the future, your legacy."

Another hallucination? Like when the bullets were flying on Main Street? Indeed, this balcony seems like where the apparition of Dolores had been standing. Baca has heard tales of religious rituals of *los Hermanos Penitentes* that supposedly bring on sacred visions, but he's neither priest nor brother, just a rancher who attends Mass. There's no sensible explanation.

"I can explain the hallucinations of last New Year's Day," the man says. "The phantasmagorias of that day portend your legacy."

Baca does not indulge in *las fantasmagorias*. Accounts, spring planting, bargaining the sale of sheep, all these activities are firmly grounded in the real world, where Felipe Baca prospers. He wishes to tell the strange man to leave. But he has welcomed all peaceable guests, even peculiar ones.

Because the man shows no intention of leaving of his own accord, Don Felipe acts the companionable host. Plus, he's curious. "What is my future then? My legacy?"

The stranger's face lights up, clearly pleased. "Your legacy is mixed, but your reputation revered," he begins. "Far into the future, you are remembered as a savvy cultural-broker, a negotiator of peace, a man who fights for the rights of Spanish-speaking people and bargains successfully with English-speakers."

Baca has a more intimate curiosity. "My children? What becomes of them?"

"Your babe in the womb becomes an attorney and judge. Felix. He is the black-robed adjudicator you described to your children. Another babe not yet born, Facundo, a doctor. Little Luis builds great things, a civil engineer. Dionisia, Rosa, and Catarina give you grandchildren. Luz becomes a nun, a Sister of Charity."

"Juan Pedro and Apolonia?"

"Apolonia dies soon after her wedding. Very tragic, I'm sorry, Don Felipe Baca. Juan Pedro superintends your flocks for some years, but does not heed your wise advice and dies in a gunfight."

Don Felipe shakes his head slowly. A man does not shed tears, but he is overcome. He lets his hands tremble. He sighs. If early death is their fate, he can't save them, just as he could not save baby Gregorita. But if not their fate, he will save them; he's the father. Prophet Mancio keeps respectful silence. Baca recovers his composure. This is just *fantasia*, after all.

"And what of Dolores?" he asks Mancio. "And myself? And what of this very strange house I don't recognize? Why does it seem as if I'm standing on a balcony?"

"A few years after the Grand Fandango, you and your wife trade twenty-two thousand pounds of wool for this Greek Revival-style house."

Baca approves of his future acumen. "What a good deal that is. It's like paying nothing. The sheep grow new wool every year. They're clever that way."

Mancio nods agreement. "Over a hundred years later, the house is still known as The Baca House. Two stories of shuttered windows, a widow's walk on the roof, but made from adobe. The merging of Anglo design and traditional Southwestern materials is symbolic of your life. It signifies a spirit of intercultural community."

"Hmmmph." A house as symbol? That barely makes any sense. Nevertheless, he has more important questions. "And Dolores?"

"She raises your children in this house."

"And myself? Why am I dressed in this suit and starched collar?"

"As the founder and Trinidad's top respected citizen, you are elected to represent this area in the Colorado Territorial Legislature. You go to Denver and fight for what's right and against what's wrong."

WITH NO FOREWARNING, Baca inexplicably finds himself standing in that room full of black-suited men shouting at each other, the vision from his store on New Year's Day. Indeed, he sees and hears his very self. It's like watching a stage play.

"One man, one vote." Baca's future alter-ego is not shouting like the others; his timbre of command gains attention through authority rather than volume.

The others quiet down. His hand pounds the lectern, not in anger, but with conviction. "It is wrong for an English speaker to have a greater vote than a Spanish speaker. We are all Coloradans. The proposed constitution is wrong in this regard."

A few "hear hears" are raised.

"And it is right that the state Constitution, once amended for equality, be published such that all Coloradans can read it. In English for the English-speakers. In Spanish for the Spanish-speakers."

"What about my neighbor and fellow rancher William Hoehne?" Baca whispers to Mancio. "That Prussian can't read English or Spanish."

"And in German for the German-speakers," the future alter-ego adds from the lectern. Baca nods approval.

"Unfortunately, you do not live to see statehood for Colorado," says Mancio in a normal voice. "Dolores does, though."

"Be quiet," Baca shushes him. He's more interested in his life than death.

"We can see and hear them, but they cannot see or hear us." Mancio does not modulate his voice at all. "A man cannot be in two places at once. So we're not really here. But know this, wisdom can outlive a man. Colorado does not become a state until the constitution is rewritten to provide for equal representation regardless of the language spoken. And the first state Constitution is published in all three languages."

"But you said my legacy is mixed," Baca reminds him.

"Alas, the English versus Spanish fight seems never to go away," says Mancio. "In 1988 English becomes Colorado's official language, but Spanish is still widely used. The good news is that more Latina and Latino legislators get elected. The number goes up and down of course. About a dozen Hispanic Senators and Representatives serve at any time. And then there are the Salazar brothers, John and Ken, descended from Colorado Hispano ranchers like you. U.S. Representative, U.S. Senator, U.S. Secretary of the Interior . . . They're a political power family in the twenty-first century."

"TWENTY-FIRST CENTURY?"

"That's where we're headed now."

Mancio leads Baca out of the crowded room into a city of fantastically-tall buildings. Denver, Mancio claims, but it looks nothing like the mining camp Baca knows. A swarm of those horse-less conveyances from his New Year's Day hallucination sit idle in rows. Mancio opens the door to one such contraption and, against his better judgment, Baca climbs in. The conveyance takes them through the streets at the pace of a gallop. It's not so bad. Then Mancio steers up a long, sloping bridge. They attain unimaginable speed. Felipe reveals no fear to Mancio, but surreptitiously grips the seat, closes his eyes, and silently prays to St. Christopher, patron saint of travelers.

Mancio jabbers away, speeding along a route he calls I-25, explaining the workings of the internal combustion engine and the development of the interstate highway system. None of it makes any sense.

"The journey that took you days and weeks, can be accomplished now in hours," Mancio says.

Baca's fingers ache from gripping, but Mancio hasn't crashed them into smithereens, so his prayers are answered for the time being. He masks the anxiety he still feels. "And what have these horseless carriages and this big road done to the Santa Fe Trail?" he asks in a steady voice. "All the traders and travelers that come through Trinidad along that route? The very lifeblood of *la economia*?"

"The railroad arrives in 1878. The Santa Fe Trail is instantly obsolete. Railroads still transport goods in the twenty-first century, but many goods and most people travel along large highways. The I-25 makes a beeline north and south from Denver."

They pull onto Main Street in a place Mancio insists is Trinidad. Very little looks familiar, as in almost nothing. Mancio opens the door for him. He climbs out, relieved to have his feet back on *tierra firme*. Baca scrunches his nose and opens his nostrils.

Mancio takes notice. "You're not going to smell black powder or manure, Rancher Baca," he says. "Horses stay on the ranches nowadays. Cattle and sheep are shipped by truck and rail, not herded through town."

Immodestly-clad twenty-first century people walk in and out of edifices made from brick and stone. The familiar adobe commercial buildings are gone. Considering how bullet-pocked some of them ended up after the troubles, perhaps that's a wise development.

Baca detects unfamiliar notes and rhythms. It's not coming from the fine musicians at his fandango, obviously, but it's unmistakably party music.

Mancio taps his foot to the beat. "Over the next one hundred fifty years, Trinidad has rich years and poor years, but through it all the people keep up the tradition of your fandango," he says. "There's no way I could explain to you the very weird ArtoCade festival or get you to appreciate the music at the Trinidaddio Blues Fest, but I'm sure you approve of the timeless goal—unity through music, dancing and good food."

Don Felipe Baca nods his head, still bewildered, but in agreement with the sentiment.

"So, my good man, with that I leave you to your present," announces Mancio. As inexplicably as he appeared, the soothsayer disappears.

It's as if no time at all has passed. Baca is back in his courtyard amidst family, friends and neighbors. The fandango is in full swing. He understands he has much left to do in his life, and if *El Profeta* is telling the truth, not that many years left to do it. But first things first. He takes his wife by the hand, and they dance.

Epilogue

Baca died in 1874, reportedly the richest man in Las Animas County. Two years later, Colorado became a state. Dolores lived until 1915. They had ten children, one of whom died in infancy, and at least 17 grandchildren.

In 1992 Felipe Baca was named one of the 'Colorado 100' by History Colorado and *The Denver Post*. He was inducted in the Colorado Business Hall of Fame in 1998 and in 1999 was listed among the fifty most influential Coloradans of all time by the Colorado Historical Society, *Rocky Mountain News*, and News4.

Just the facts, Ma'am

The one biography in book form is ***Felipe and Dolores Baca: Hispanic Pioneers*** by E.E. Duncan, one of the Great Lives in Colorado History series for young readers. His story is written, appropriately, in both Spanish and English. More about him and the Trinidad War of 1867-1868 is included in ***Trinidad, Colorado Territory*** by Morris F. Taylor. Taylor's book is long out of print, but can be read at the Carnegie Public Library in Trinidad, the Hart Library at History Colorado in Denver, or at a few other libraries in the state. Issue 1 of ***Colorado Heritage*** magazine (1982) featured 'Hispanic Pioneer: Don Felipe Baca brings his family north to Trinidad' based on the writings of his sons Luis and Facundo. In the winter of 2004 the same magazine published 'El Patron de Trinidad' by Paul D. Andrews and Nancy Humphrey. The online Colorado Encyclopedia includes a biography at https://coloradoencyclopedia.org/. The documentary ***Trinidad*** by **Rocky Mountain PBS** includes Baca's role in the town's history. It can be viewed at https://www.rmpbs.org/.

The 1865 proposed Constitution for Colorado was infamously discriminatory and opposed by African American Coloradans, such as Barney Ford (also profiled in this collection), as well as Latinos. Baca objected to it because the 2,500 Latino voters of southeast Colorado would have been represented by the same number of legislators as the 564 miners living in the mountain communities, not to mention that miners would be exempted from paying taxes that farmers and ranchers would have to pay.

His objections were recorded in the January 9, 1869 edition of the *Rocky Mountain News.*

Just for fun

Baca's original adobe *hacienda* is gone, but the Greek Revival **Baca House**, which Felipe and Dolores bought from John Hough in 1872, is part of The Trinidad History Museum at 312 East Main Street. Some of the furniture is original to the house, including a 'trail piano' and a bed with its shipping stamp 'Hough' still visible. The Baca ranch outbuildings are now the Santa Fe Trail Museum, with exhibits explaining the history of Trinidad. Next door, the impressive **Bloom Mansion** provides a dramatic contrast to the Baca House. Built after the arrival of the railroad, which made shipping building materials cheap and fast, the brick Bloom Mansion features many technological advances of the 1880s.

Colorado is an awe-inspiring place for scenic driving, but perhaps no route is so glorious as the **Highway of Legends** (Colorado Highway 12 and U.S. Highway 160 arching from Trinidad to Walsenburg). With its picturesque vales, spiny rock outcroppings and rolling hills fronting the stunning Sangre de Cristo mountains, it's no wonder the families from New Mexico chose this area for their homes. From Trinidad to Stonewall are several Hispano settlements from the late 1800s. Cordova Plaza is known to have been settled by families that came north with Felipe Baca from New Mexico. A historical guide to the highway is available free at the **Colorado Welcome Center**, 309 Nevada Ave., Trinidad.

A less scenic but also historic drive is the **Santa Fe Trail Scenic Byway** from Trinidad to Lamar. https://www.codot.gov/travel/scenic-byways Near La Junta along the remnants of the Santa Fe Trail is Bent's Old Fort, a National Historic Site: https://www.nps.gov/beol/index.htm.

Sheep ranching remains part of Colorado's agricultural economy. A number of **sheep ranches** welcome visitors, such as Desert Weyr in Paonia, Ewe Bet Ranch in Loveland, and Mayberry Farm in Byers. September is a month for **sheep festivals** such as the Jammin' Lamb Festival in Meeker and the Sheep Wagon Days at Villard Ranch near Craig. Enjoy lamb kabobs and demonstrations of spinning and weaving. For up-to-date information, search farm and ranch activities at https://www.colorado.com/.

No need to find a festival to enjoy lamb if you've got a grill or a crockpot:

BBQ'd Lamb Chops
Place meat on hot grill.
Season with salt and pepper.
Heat until they're done as you like.

Slow Cooked Lamb
In the morning, place leg of lamb in crock pot.
Sprinkle with your choice of salt, pepper, oregano, garlic, onions.
Add water to cover one inch on bottom of pot.
Cook on low all day.

Crafty? Add **weaving** to your repertoire of yarn skills. Classes are taught throughout the state at recreation centers, by arts & crafts organizations, and through yarn stores. Search 'weaving classes in Colorado' to find a teacher near you and get started on your own woolen rug.

Trinidad really is a town of quirky **festivals** that meld cultures, or are just weird. The annual ArtoCade, held the second Saturday in September, is the second largest art-car festival in the nation. Drivers deck their cars out in all manner of artistic mediums, from glass, to plastic, to fur, even teeth sometimes. Art, music, and food are celebrated throughout the year in Trinidad. To find out what fun is coming up visit https://visittrinidadcolorado.com/events/

Chipeta
1843 – 1924
Peacemaker, Bead Artist

THE TINY GLASS BEADS roll beneath her fingertips as they always have, their pressure comforting. So very few things don't change.

Chipeta grips the needle as she has for these many decades, nudging the beads into line, listening for the tiny tick, tick, ticks as the needle tip snatches each one by one. It's getting harder for her old ears to detect the tiny sounds. Harder for old eyes to discern the colors. Especially today, in this hotel room where heavy drapes conceal the faded September sunlight and noisy people gather outside on the street. A brass band is warming up. On the reservation she'd be beading under an open sky, with only the bleat of sheep and the laughter of small children. It's useless here in the white man's hotel.

She sets her sewing aside and picks up the rough geode on the table next to her beads. A young man gave it to her the day before. "Welcome back to Colorado," he said. She feels for the crack where it had been hammered in two. Inside, the crystals resemble mountain peaks. She discerns the hue even in the faint light. Purple mountain majesties, like in that white woman's poem. There's just enough light to glint off the crystals, shining like her people. 'People of the Shining Mountains' they are called. She runs calloused fingers over the purple peaks.

Suddenly, the room spins, brightening as if under the yellow sun of spring. A sweet aroma of burning sage replaces the hotel's stale cigar stink. The yammering of the crowd outside dims. In its place she hears the rhythm of sticks rubbing against sticks, the scuff of moccasins on dirt, the susurrus of dancing feet. *The Bear Dance.*

Scuffle sounds form into words. "Still here. We're still here and we will still be here, carrying on."

What on earth? The Bear Dance happens in the spring, when the bear comes out of his den. In an open meadow, with no walls but the branches and leaves of the *avi qui up* corral and the four horizons. At the end of each winter, the Bear Dance rejuvenates the spirit of the Ute people. It does not happen in a town hotel, in the fall, and the dancers' feet don't form words, certainly not English words. That's not a tradition. She is imagining things. Like in a sweat ceremony, but without the sweat or the ceremony.

She claps the geode halves back together, rakes a comb through her still black hair and laces up her moccasins. No time for the visions of an old woman. She has another president to meet.

Grand Junction
Late September, 1909

CHIPETA COULDN'T BELIEVE her eyes. William Howard Taft was as big as a buffalo. His mustache shaggy like buffalo whiskers.

He had come all the way from Washington, she from Utah, to celebrate the Grand Opening of the Gunnison Tunnel. Both were invited as honored dignitaries to watch the waters from the Gunnison River flow into the Uncompahgre Valley.

The event ripped her heart in two. The enormous tunnel was a great feat, because water is life, but her home in exile, the reservation in Utah, would stay dry as ever. The government had made exactly no effort to bring water to Utah. Another promise broken.

Meanwhile, this valley in Colorado, the home the white government had forced her to abandon, the beautiful Uncompahgre Valley she and her band had been made to leave forever, would grow green and lush. The injustice cut deep, the irony overwhelmed, but she was old, and she never turned down an invitation to come back home. By law, Chipeta was banned from Colorado, as were the other Tabeguache Utes here today. But that old treaty had never held much water for the white people, and nowadays white people considered Ute people colorful attractions. She chose not to examine their motives too closely.

The bushy-faced, buffalo-sized president stood on a grand stage beribboned with red, white and blue bunting, talking about something or other. Thousands of Coloradans stood behind her to see the big man from Washington. Some of the white people in the crowd had been born in Colorado, but more had moved here from the east. Even so, few had actually seen the great city of Washington, D.C. as Chipeta had. She had gone to Washington in person, by train, many years ago, at the invitation of Mr. Schurz, Secretary of the Interior. Rutherford B. Hayes had been president back then. He'd worn buffalo whiskers, too, but wasn't nearly so large as Taft. Chipeta was glad for today's front row seat. Her eyes were doing poorly. Although, to be honest, today's president was impossible not to see.

Impossible not to hear, either, although she didn't feel it necessary to listen. The talk of white presidents had never brought much good. He reminded her of the talkier chiefs who tried her patience at council meetings. Men, she had learned, whether white or brown or red, were fond of listening to their own voices.

Finally, the president stopped talking. The people applauded. She and her fellow Ute chiefs, honored guests, were ushered on stage. The utterly soft and huge paws of the president enveloped her own calloused and sun-spotted little hands. He invited her to ride in his motor car to the railroad station. From there they'd board a train for Montrose. Montrose was where the actual tunnel was, where the waters would gush forth. Chipeta nodded yes and smiled politely.

Nothing she ever did was without controversy. She knew that. Some of her people felt glad for peace, others were angry over the sacrifices that bought it. Wise people were both. Loss could not be avoided, which is why a person should not refuse occasions of pomp and fun.

The car and train ride were long. There was no reason to listen to the president yap. She smoothed the folds of her best dress, a blue dark as the Colorado sky when the first stars come out at night. She fingered the elk teeth on the bodice. Her husband had given her these as a gift. She'd sewn them on a buckskin dress when she was young, then clipped them off to sew onto this dress when she was old. One hundred twenty-seven in front, ninety-seven in back. They brought back a lifetime of memories.

HER FATE, indeed this very ride with President Taft, had been birthed out of great loss. Half a century ago, the death of beautiful Black Mare had left little Pahlone motherless. Pahlone's father, Ouray, was in his hunting prime then. Just as importantly, his intellect and ability to speak Apache, Spanish, English, and Ute made Ouray uniquely valuable when their little band went to the trading post to exchange tanned hides for beads and knives, rifles and ammunition. Ouray could not stay home to keep Pahlone fed and out of mischief. Chipeta had seen only fifteen summers when Black Mare died, but she loved children. When Ouray was gone, and even when he wasn't, Chipeta mothered Pahlone.

The first rumblings of the Great Avalanche were apparent even back then, the middle of the last century. The Ute, Nuuchuu in their own language, are mountain people, familiar with the devastating power of the avalanche. It starts with a crack, then the snow rolls off the mountains, growing ever wider as it crashes down. No one can stop the avalanche. It uproots and sweeps away everything in its path. But the Great Avalanche was like no avalanche the Utes had ever seen. It was far more destructive. It took years instead of minutes. It did not melt in the spring. And it never stopped. It was an avalanche of people.

Ouray's parents had been wise, or perhaps just more perceptive than others. They sent their sons to be educated by the Jesuits. That's where Ouray learned his Spanish and his English, and how to herd sheep and cattle, skills he brought with him when he left New Mexico to join her little band of Colorado Utes.

And then his wife, Black Mare, had died. Chipeta was happy to mother the apple-faced baby Pahlone. She sang him to sleep and comforted him when he skinned his elbows. She took on other tasks for Ouray. She knew how to lash together teepee poles and cover them with hide, how to weave a basket and line it with piñon pitch to hold water.

After a successful hunt, she roasted the elk or bison with hot stones sealed with damp grass over a pit. She knew how to preserve venison as pemmican, mixing it with wild plums and drying it in the sun so they could eat meat throughout the winter.

She could find and dig wild carrots and onions, pluck the nuts from piñon trees, make salad from cattail shoots and sorrel, soup from thistles and goldenrod, and tea from wild peppermint or rose hips. Best of all were the sweet thimbleberries and chokecherries. *Oh, to bite a sweet, juicy thimbleberry again, that would be heaven.*

In her youth, Chipeta had tanned deer hides as soft as silk. Countless times she had knelt on the ground, scraping fat and flesh from a hide with a chiseled bone scraper, scrubbing it with water, dragging it into the sun, massaging brains over it with her bare hands, stretching it and pegging it down to dry, curing it in the sun. She could sew moccasins and decorate them with tiny glass beads.

In those days, she had been too busy to think about the white people. That had not stopped the avalanche from coming. Ouray, though, could not stop thinking about all the people on their way. He'd return home from a trading trip, or even a hunt, every time more worried. He sat beside Chipeta in his teepee, Pahlone snoring beside them, and told her everything. Then he asked what she thought. A man asking a woman's opinion was not exactly a normal thing, but she had been too young to know better. She told him exactly what she thought. And he listened. And that's how they knew they had to be married.

Of course, it was more than just the listening. Ouray had been so handsome, his black braids flowing down his chest, undulating and shimmering like creek water flowing around river rocks. His face round as the moon, nose as straight as a Lodgepole pine, skin brown and smooth as cattails in summer, eyes shimmery and warm as mountain hot springs, his fingers long as summer grasses. Still, it was that he listened and took her counsel that made him irresistible.

There were too many white people coming, and more all the time, he worried, an avalanche. As the years passed, living alongside the white people became a bigger and bigger challenge. It wasn't just their numbers, it was that they kept changing what they wanted. First it was miners. Gold and silver they wanted. Just let us dig holes and build roads in peace, they said, keep your hunting grounds. Then the white ranchers came, cutting off game trails with their fences. Get out, they said, you can't hunt here! Next came the farmers, with wives and children, plowing up hunting grounds to grow wheat and beets. Then came the city people, chopping down trees for structures made of wood. Rows upon rows of houses. Denver, they called it. Quite grand, but not as grand as Washington, in the District of Columbia.

The first time Ouray went by train to Washington, Chipeta had not gone along, but her beaded buckskin had. Her handiwork ensured Ouray was outfitted befitting a Chief when he met the great President Lincoln. Then again Chief Ouray went to Washington, when it was President Johnson, and a third time, to meet President Grant. Never the same president, but always the same talking, listening, trying to make sense of what the white government wanted. Chief Ouray negotiated, signed papers, came home. And the avalanche kept coming.

The fourth time Ouray went to Washington, the last time, Chipeta went along. Yet another white man, Mr. Hayes, was president by then. She saw the great buildings made of white stone. Went on a shopping spree down Pennsylvania Avenue. Satin! Cotton! Cashmere! Buttons and thread! She experienced a nighttime brightly lit with lanterns along hard, straight pathways. She answered questions for the men in the great hall they called Congress. And she'd watched Ouray get sicker and sicker even as he was called on to negotiate peace.

Peacemaking in Washington was fascinating, even exhilarating, but always disappointing. Move here, move there. Hunt on this side of the line we drew on the paper, but don't hunt on the other side of the line. The lines from the paper are invisible on the land. Deer, elk, and mountain sheep can't read a map, nor can the hunters in pursuit. She recalled a childhood of plenty—deer and bear in the mountains, bison and antelope on the plains, trout and duck in the waters. Then every treaty bought peace at the price of smaller land, less game, starvation, humiliation and, ultimately, exile to the unwatered, unforgiving, unvegetated rocks of Utah.

But an avalanche can't be stopped. Painted horses with beaded saddles don't scare it. Braves in feathered regalia can't deflect it. Bows and arrows have no effect, not even rifles. Attacking makes the avalanche crash down harder and faster. Waving a treaty at it won't stop it, either, although not for lack of trying.

The world was harsh, as the elders always said, and as she said, too, now that she was an elder. Life was full of troubles, both for the Ute people and for Ouray and Chipeta personally. The kidnapping of Pahlone by a Plains tribe had been particularly hard, and the physical suffering of Ouray. He'd seen white doctors in Colorado and Washington, D.C. Ute medicine men burned herbs and sang songs. Nothing had helped. He hadn't even made sixty winters. He negotiated the treaty that sent their band to Utah, but didn't live to make the trip himself. Just as well.

TODAY, IN THIS new century, riding in the train with President Taft, Chipeta was older than Ouray had ever been.

Still, for all its difficulties, her life through all the changes had been beautiful, too, and she had a heart that savored the good. Fresh meat and tender herbs in the spring. The Bear Dance. A delicate blue columbine swaying on the forest floor, bright red paintbrush flowers speckling sunny hillsides. Butterflies flitting. Summer hunting parties on the prairie. Watching hawks and eagles circle the treetops. The rose glow of the mountains at sundown. The chirp of crickets. The sparkle of a fresh snowfall, like countless rhinestones lying on a bed of chalked deerskin. The warmth of a teepee on a cold winter night, telling the old stories around

Colorado Phantasmagorias

firelight. Catching the first glints of the rising sun from the teepee flap. Sinking her tired body into sacred hot springs. The love of family.

Chipeta's own belly had never grown large with child, but she'd mothered Ouray's Pahlone, and the other boys and girls they'd welcomed into their home. Adoption, the white people called it. She taught the girls how to soften hides, sew beads onto belts, how to gather and preserve fruits and vegetables, how to dry meat. Ouray taught the boys to care for and ride horses, make tools, string bows, clean guns, defend against enemies, and shoot game. Her family was as large as all the children she had loved.

The traditional ways had been hard, though. She recalled days of tramping through the woods, over the mountain passes, alongside the brown and white ponies pulling the travois, loaded with all their possessions. Usually with children in tow or strapped to her back. Men searching for game, the women seeking vegetables, there were days of plenty and days of hunger. In her youth she had been limber and strong, but it had been trying, even then. The sacred hot springs that dotted the mountainsides were essential for loosening exhausted muscles and worn joints. Back in her youth and even more now that she had weathered sixty-six winters.

She hadn't tramped over any mountain pass today, riding instead in a motor car and train, and didn't plan to tramp again anytime soon, yet still she hoped to sink into one of her favorite hot springs before returning to dry Utah.

FINALLY, SHE and Taft and his entourage arrived in Montrose. A motorcar, rigged out specially for her, idled in the street. A gentleman helped boost her into the rear seat. She felt the rumble beneath her

feet, smelled the gasoline. A banner, strung from the front to the back, proclaimed her name, Chipeta, in gigantic black letters. Ladies in white skirts sat along the parade route, sheltered by parasols, their men standing by their side, the children running to and fro, sometimes plopping on the curb, and all clapped as she passed.

A very different kind of crowd was seared into her memory. Angry, violent, insensible. In Pueblo. Thirty years ago. On that last trip to Washington. After the Meeker disaster. A lifetime ago, 1879.

Nathan Meeker had been the government Indian Agent for the White River band. An idiot, like so many of the white agents, though perhaps not all. Kit Carson wasn't so bad. Mr. Meeker, though, plowed up the band's horse meadow and race track and threatened to kill all the ponies. Outraged, the White River Utes fought back, but violence had not brought justice. Meeker was killed, along with other white men, maybe eight more, maybe ten, some said even more. Many Ute people died, too, but nobody bothered to count. The White River Utes kidnapped three white women, including Mrs. Meeker and her daughter, and two little children. Chipeta and Ouray knew first-hand the agony of kidnapping, on account of losing Pahlone to the Plains tribe. No good would come from kidnapping, they agreed. Ouray rode out and got the Meeker women and children released. Chipeta welcomed them into the safety of their home.

That rescue was not without controversy, as nothing ever is. A person can appreciate the innocence of a single snowflake while keeping aware of the danger of the avalanche. The women and children had nothing to do with the race track plowing and the pony threatening. But for three weeks they had been held captive. Who knew the fear they had endured? Chipeta had shown compassion is all. Still, some of her neighbors thought she was too kind. Perhaps they were right.

It's not like the white people gave Ouray any credit for the rescue. On their way to Washington to avert war and make peace, a violent mob attacked them at the Pueblo train station. White people hurled rocks and pieces of dirty coal at them. They pressed pale cheeks against the train windows, mouths contorted, screaming, "The Utes must go!"

They got their wish, too. That last trip to Washington brought peace, at the price of exile.

CHIPETA'S MIND TURNED again from the distant past back to the present, 1909. So much had changed. Instead of despised enemy sent away, now she was a beloved heroine invited home. She had not changed at all. Only the whites had changed, their opinions, anyhow, a little bit, thanks to a book by Mrs. Helen Jackson, plus a few decades time.

Mr. Eugene Field even wrote a poem about her:

She is the bravest and best of a cursed race —
Give her a lodge on the mountainside.
And, when she is gone, on a hill provide
The Queen of the Utes' last resting place.
She rode where old Ouray dare not ride —
A path through the wilderness rough and wild,
She rode to plead for woman and child —
She rode by the yawning chasm's side;
She rode on the rocky, fir-clad hill
Where the panther mewed and the crested jay
Piped echoless through the desert day —
She rode in the valleys dark and chill.
On such a ride as woman can —
By the Godlike pow'r that in her lies,
Or an inspiration from the skies —
Achieve for woman and son of man.
They live, and thro' the country wide —
Where'er they come, where'er they go,
Though their hairs grow white as the wintry snow —
They will tell of brave Chipeta's ride!
She is the bravest of a cursed race —
Give her a lodge on the mountain side,
And, when she is gone, on the hill provide
The Queen of the Utes' last resting place.
But give her a page in history, too,
Though she be rotting in humble shrouds,
And write on the whitest of God's white clouds
Chipeta's name in eternal blue.

The queen part was ridiculous. The Utes don't have queens. But the images of the fir-clad hill, the sounds of the panther and jay, she rather liked those lines.

Would she get a page in history? Would Ouray? They were now calling Ouray the greatest negotiator, friend and peacemaker. Maybe. He'd tried his best. She'd tried her best. They had looked toward the avalanche and steered their people out of its way. They wanted only for the Ute people to not get buried, to survive.

Her still-black hair blew wild as the motorcar paraded down the streets of Montrose. She waved at the ladies with their parasols, the children licking their lollipops, the men in black hats.

Soon she would go back to Utah, after a long soak in a hot spring.

PACKING UP later for the trip back to the reservation, Chipeta opens the geode again. Its jagged crystals reflect the light. Colorado's purple mountain majesties in miniature.

Suddenly she sees the bright yellow light again, hears the rhythm of the growlers, sticks rubbing against notched sticks, louder this time. Men are singing. *The Bear Dance.* The susurrus of dancing feet sound out words: "We're still here. We have survived. Our children our surviving. And our grandchildren."

Like a sweat lodge hallucination, she sees what's not there, hears sounds that cannot be. Her hotel room transforms into a meadow. She smells fresh spring air, the dust of dozens of feet, fresh juniper. She's standing at the entrance to a dance corral, an *avi qui up*, in the open air, facing east. Women pass by, anointing their hands with scent from the leaves of a juniper, rubbing the perfume into their hair, legs and feet.

The sticks growl like a bear in springtime. Women in jingle dresses dance to the beat, fringes flying, beaded moccasins kissing the earth. Their dresses sparkle with purples, pinks, blue, red, orange, gold and yellow, all creation's colors bobbing in the sunshine.

Where am I? This is not Grand Junction in September. It's not a sweat ceremony. It's confounding.

Men in blue jeans, black braids swinging beneath bowler hats and baseball caps, beaded medallions at their throats, accompany the women, the men's cowboy boots and colorful soft shoes stepping in unison with their partners. *These sights and sounds are out of place and at the wrong time.*

"*Mique*" says a women's voice. "Hello."

Who is she?

"Does this place look familiar?" says the woman.

A little familiar, and exceptionally clear. Chipeta's eyes and ears have not served her this well in a long time. Distant peaks look familiar, their slopes cutting the blue sky in sharp relief. The voices and the morache strumming ring crisp in her old ears. The people show the familiar round faces, strong noses and warm eyes of the Nuuchuu. Familiar and yet also strange.

"I'm Sybylla," says the woman. "A soothsayer, released from your geode to show you the future."

Chipeta is nonplussed. "Where am I?"

"The Bear Dance, of course," says Sybylla. "In the twenty-first century, over a hundred years into the future."

Impossible! Chipeta doesn't know what to say. She watches. It's too crazy to believe, but she is an old woman and old women are known to have visions, even outside the sweat. Perhaps that's all it is. She gives in to the vision, watches some more, recalling how she danced the dance herself, many years ago, but now her joints feel too stiff.

"They will dance like this until somebody falls down," says Chipeta. "It is the tradition. It could go on for a very long time."

"I am glad to use the time to show you more of the future," says Sybylla. She leads Chipeta away from the dance corral.

A woman Chipeta's age is sitting at a wooden table. The woman has spread a cloth and covered it with dozens of colors of tiny glass seed beads. A young boy and a young girl watch. Chipeta approaches, but they do not look up or greet her. It's as if she's invisible to them, which she supposes she is.

"The bead colors all have meaning," the woman teaches the children. The woman picks up a row of blue beads, her hands deft with the needle. "Blue can mean sky, but it can also mean fire, because the hottest part of the fire is blue. Yellow also means fire, or sometimes sun. Green is symbol for the earth." She lays the beads in an arc, tacking them down with her thread, continuing along.

"What about animals?" asks the little girl.

"Yellow reminds us of the mountain lion that roams the rocks in summer. Red is the weasel that hunts in the valleys in the spring," the woman tells her.

"What's the black for?" says the little boy.

"Ah, black is for winter, and the underworld, snakes, bad stuff," she says, swatting the boys hand away from her beads.

A hundred years forward, and my people still sew the beads. They celebrate the good and survive the bad. These future people are Nuuchuu. They are proud.

Chipeta's stomach rumbles. Sybylla must notice, because she takes Chipeta by the elbow and steers her toward the aroma of fry bread. Sybylla hands her a plate, a circle of dough glistening on it. She takes a bite, licks her lips. "My people can still cook," she says. "I am glad to see my people survive, and still dance, and know the meaning of the beads, and how to fry bread, but I have seen so much change in my own life, surely much has changed in a hundred years."

"You are wise, Chipeta. And very correct."

Sybylla leads Chipeta to the Sky Ute Casino and Hotel. It's an immense building colored red and tan like Colorado's mountain cliffs, an enormous five-story wall of windows welcoming in the sunlight. Here would be enough natural light for beading!

But inside, a clamor assaults her ears. Brilliant lights flash, roulette wheels twirl, playing cards snap against felted tables. It's the biggest white man's saloon Chipeta has ever seen, but there are women here, too. Gray-haired white women plugging coins into machines.

"Long ago the governments in Washington and Denver made gambling illegal, but people never stopped doing it," Sybylla shouts over the clamor. "The Ute people and other Native Americans reminded the government that the reservations are sovereign, not subject to laws passed in Washington and Denver. The tribes would offer legal gambling. To the white people. And make money from it."

The irony delights Chipeta. Get rich quick lured gold and silver miners into the Nuuchuu's mountains, and her people learned to exploit that frailty for their own profit. But the endless racket of dings and rings is overwhelming. She turns toward the door. Sybylla follows her out.

"What else do my people do?" asks Chipeta, standing again beneath the blue sky and real sun.

"Ranching," says Sybylla. "The Ute people raise cattle and bison for sale."

"Ouray was a skilled rancher," says Chipeta. "We had six hundred sheep, sixty horses and many cattle, too."

"Then there's the Red Willow Production Company, which hunts for oil and gas. Red Willow owns interests in eighteen hundred oil wells and is one of the country's largest private oil and gas production companies," says Sybylla. "Red Cedar Gathering Company transports natural gas that heats homes. They are different from other such companies. They care about human health and the preservation of the natural world."

It sounds very impressive.

"The people continue to make traditional crafts, jewelry, beaded clothing, pottery, which they sell in stores," says Sybylla. "And there is a museum of Ute history here and in Montrose, but we will not go there, because that is where your crypt is."

Of course. The prophetess says this is the twenty-first century. No one could live so long. "Tell me, then, how am I remembered? Kindly, I hope?"

"Kindly, yes, that is how you are remembered," says Sybylla. "You are remembered for your beauty and your big heart, your kindness, generosity, hospitality, intelligence, wisdom, and uncomplaining nature."

Chipeta laughs. "No person is all those things, least of all me."

"And humility," says Sybylla. "You're also remembered for that."

"But the loss of Ute lands in your time is a pain not forgotten. Some blame you and Ouray for your role in that."

"As should be expected. It was a hard time. We faced hard choices," says Chipeta. "Brave men buried are buried forever. Those who survive live to dance with pride. We survived."

"More than survived," says Sybylla.

They head back to the dancing corral. A woman falls. The dance is at its natural end.

WITH THAT, CHIPETA finds herself back where she had been before, in her hotel room, normal senses back intact, the strange woman gone. With her bags all packed, she asks the gentleman at the front desk to arrange a wagon ride to the nearest hot springs. He is helpful. The ride is not too far, and all along the route are views of her beloved home, where she tramped when she was young.

She sinks her old limbs into the water, leans her head back against a smooth rock, breathes in the familiar mineral aromas. Steam scuds across the surface, bubbles caress her skin, mist coats her hair. Water boils away the aches. Today she met a president, rode in a motor car and train, waved at folks in a parade, and saw into the future. *Unless I've taken leave of my senses.*

Normally she would leave a few beads by the pool to pay the spirits for their medicine. Today she leaves a larger gift. She sets the two halves of the geode beside the pool. Best for it to stay here, in Colorado, where it belongs. She must return to Utah.

Epilogue

Chipeta died August 20, 1924 at her home on Bitter Creek in the Uintah and Ouray Indian Reservation in Utah, which had been her home since the Tabeguache Ute, were 'relocated' from Colorado to Utah in 1881, after her husband, Chief Ouray, died. (Just to be clear, 'relocated' is a euphemism for banished.) She lived eighty-one years. Her crypt is near Montrose, Colorado, on the ranch where she and Ouray lived during their marriage. The property is now owned by the Ute Indian Museum, administered by History Colorado.

History has treated Chipeta and Ouray with respect, if not always accuracy. Ouray, for example, is often remembered as the 'Chief of All Utes,' which wasn't a real title. The Ute people had many chiefs, and important decisions were made by vote at large gatherings. Ouray's counsel would have been respected, but he was one of many. It was the white governments that treated Ouray as chief of all Utes. Unwilling to go to the trouble of figuring out and dealing with Ute decision-making customs, the U.S. and Colorado governments found it easier to deal with Ouray, primarily because he spoke English fluently. As you can imagine, the way the governments elevated Ouray's status was seen as both obligatory and infuriating by other chiefs.

Chipeta, like Ouray, is renowned for wisdom. Unique among women of her tradition, Chipeta was welcomed into her people's councils and was an active participant along with the male chiefs. This is historical fact. However, she was not 'Queen of Utes' as she was called by the poet Eugene Field and others. The Ute people had neither kings nor queens. She did have a regal bearing, though, based on old photographs.

Chipeta and Ouray's legacy of treaties and relationships with white people is not without detractors. Ouray urged his people to abide by the terms of treaties even as the U.S. government did not. He would seek out and punish treaty-breakers in his band. He and Chipeta counted as friends the roadbuilder Otto Mears, Indian Agent Kit Carson and Secretary of the Interior Carl Schurz. Whether Chipeta and Ouray were foolish or wise, heroes or fools, peacemakers or sell-outs, depends on a person's point of view. They were what they were, did what they did, and their people survived.

Colorado Phantasmagorias

Just the Facts, Ma'am

Native American history is infamously tragic and complicated. This is not the book for dissecting the terms of all the treaties or listing all the times they were broken, disregarded or just plain forgotten. It's also not the place for examining the interactions and relationships of the various bands in the Ute Nation. This story is as accurate as possible, without getting lost amid all the complexities.

But if complexity is your thing, ***Chipeta*** by Cynthia S. Becker and P. David Smith is a good place to start. It's about as readable a biography as could be written while including all the relevant dates and locations and treaty terms. Becker also wrote ***Chipeta: Ute Peacemaker***, published by Filter Press for young readers.

Just for Fun

The **Ute Indian Museum**, 17253 Chipeta Road, Montrose, Colorado, is one of the nation's most complete collections of the Ute artifacts, featuring exhibits and videos that let visitors experience the history, culture and daily life of the Nuuchuu of the Uncompahgre Valley. Located on the original eight-acre homestead site of Chief Ouray and Chipeta, the museum complex includes Chipeta's crypt, a native plants garden, shady picnic areas, walking paths, and teepees.

Chipeta is known to have enjoyed the many **hot springs** that dot the Colorado mountainsides. The Ute people consider these spots sacred. These were places where Ute, Cheyenne, Arapahoe and Navajo people would gather in peace. There are hundreds of hot springs in Colorado, many too small for a soak or on private land or just too remote, but about 45 popular sites are accessible to the public. A half dozen are primitive 'people's springs' on public land; the rest are commercialized to varying extents. You can find something for everyone. Want a place to show off your designer bathing suit and get a hot stone massage? Or watch the kids careen down a water slide? Or rest your naked behind on a pile of mossy rocks? To find a place that suits your taste, check out TripAdvisor or Google, or go the old-fashioned route and consult a guidebook such as ***Colorado Hot Springs*** by Deborah Frazier or ***Touring Colorado Hot Springs*** by Susan Joy Paul. Just make sure the advice you're taking is recent.

Colorado Phantasmagorias 32

Commercialized hot spring resorts are high maintenance real estate, so what may have been a beautiful place ten years ago could have deteriorated, and vice versa.

The Southern Ute band holds the traditional three-day **Bear Dance** on the Southern Ute reservation near the intersection of Bear Dance Drive and Ute Road in Ignacio every year on Memorial Day weekend. Visit https://www.southernute-nsn.gov/ for more information. Other Ute bands hold their own Bear Dance celebrations in May as well. The Ute Indian Museum in Montrose posts the various dates. Call 970-249-3098.

The Southern Ute band owns and operates the **Sky Ute Casino Resort** at 14324 Highway 172 North, Ignacio, Colorado 81137. There are hotel accommodations, popular music concerts, bowling at Rolling Thunder lanes and, of course, gambling. Slots, blackjack, roulette, craps, poker, whatever get-rich-quick scheme you desire! Even if you're not a gambler, the hotel offers upscale accommodations at a midscale price. The Sky Ute RV Park offers water and sewer hookups, showers, laundry, pool, fitness center, wi-fi. Call 888-842-4180 or visit https://www.skyutecasino.com/ for more information. Next door is the beautiful and fascinating **Southern Ute Museum**. Designed by the same architects as the Smithsonian's National Museum of the American Indian, it can be recognized by the metal tower that looks like a basket. Admission is free, donations are welcome. https://www.southernutemuseum.org/.

It's unclear where Chipeta stayed in Grand Junction. She is known to have stayed at **The Beaumont Hotel**, 505 Main St., Ouray, Colorado 81427, with other Utes in 1911 and in 1913. This lovely Victorian was closed for decades, but has been renovated and is welcoming guests again. Call 970-325-7000 or check out http://www.beaumonthotel.com/.

Colorado National Monument, Rimrock Dr., Fruita, CO 81521, offers lots of **hiking and biking** trails. Stop in at the Visitor's Center for a map and knowledgeable advice.

For authentic Native American **jewelry, pottery, sand paintings, rugs and beaded art**, go shopping at **Notah-Dineh Trading Company**, 345 W. Main St., Cortez. A free museum in the basement displays exquisite beaded gloves, art, obsidian knives and rugs from the nineteenth century.

Colorado Phantasmagorias   33

Waci-Ci Trading Company in Ignacio is another place to buy authentic handicrafts, in person or online: https://www.wacici.com. Ute handicrafts are also sold by the visitor gift shops at the Ute Indian Museum in Montrose and Mesa Verde National Park.

Crafty? Get yourself a bucket of **seed beads** at Notah-Dineh Trading Company, your local craft shop or online. There are excellent YouTube videos by modern Ute women showing how to do traditional **beading**. It's not difficult, but it does take patience!

Before the 'civilizing' Indian Agents took to forcing them to farm, the Ute people ate well by foraging for fruits, vegetables and herbs. You can, too, if you know what to look for, where to look, and how to avoid poisoning yourself. *Foraging the Rocky Mountains* by Liz Brown Morgan is a helpful guide for brave **foodies**. She tells where to find edible wild plants, how to figure out if they're safe and legal to pick, and then offers a **recipe** for every plant. Be sure to read the chapter on poisonous plants and the important warnings she sprinkles throughout.

Last but not least, if you're going to the Montrose/Ouray/Ignacio area you absolutely must detour to **Mesa Verde National Park** to see the spectacular cliff dwellings of the Ancestral Pueblo. Be sure to sign up for a ranger tour, and/or go off the beaten path to experience **The Ute Mountain Tribal Park**. Tribal members interpret tribal culture, pictographs, cliff dwellings, surface ruins, and artifacts. It has been selected by National Geographic Traveler as one of '80 World Destinations for Travel in the 21st Century.' Ute people did not live in the Mesa Verde cliff dwellings, but since the Ancestral Puebloans moved to New Mexico long ago, the Colorado Ute have adopted this sacred place. Go to https://www.mesaverdecountry.com/see-do/archaeology/ute-mountain-tribal-park/ to find out the details.

John Brisben Walker
1847-1931
Developer, Red Rocks Dreamer

THE PHANTASMAGORIAS are growing increasingly annoying. Out of the blue come visions of a never-ending line of vehicles, the likes of which he's never seen in reality, snaking through the red rocks of his beloved park. Then an ear-splitting cacophony of musical notes, flashing lights and the faint whiff of beer.

What in heavens name is the matter? John Brisben Walker does not drink alcohol in the morning, which is when these hallucinations intrude, and he is not a regular user of laudanum or hashish.

He nudges his spectacles up his nose, straightens his mustache with a forefinger. He replaces some papers on his mahogany desk, securing them beneath a paperweight, a geode his son found in the Colorado mountains. The rock's exterior is light brown, rough to the touch.

A vision of an impossible glass tower arises before his eyes. A Ferris Wheel like the one he once had built, but different somehow, surrounded by towers of no discernible use.

Perhaps he ought to consult a doctor about these hallucinations. He dares not. At sixty-five he is at an age where his mental faculties would be questioned. He cannot afford that. He shakes his head. The stone walls of his mountain manse reappear. It is time to head down the mountain. He has much work to do, projects to complete, another fortune to make.

༄

Denver
August, 1912

JOHN BRISBEN WALKER wedged one finger beneath his stiff collar, gently tugging his tie away from his Adam's apple. Just enough for a bit of relief, not enough to dislodge the neat knot. Sweat threatened to stain the white fabric and dissolve the starch.

Where is that damned artist?

His mind raced, as it was wont to do. All the designers and tailors in the world could not see fit to invent a proper businessman's collar that wasn't a torment? He should set his own mind to it. No, certainly not. A collar is a small thing for a small mind. Walker was a man of big ideas. He built big things.

Where is that damned artist, the sculptor?

He pushed aside the stack of photographs on his desk and swiveled his chair to face the open window. Sweet notes of women's voices rose up from the Denver street below. Late morning shoppers, showing off their purchases to each other, no doubt, sashaying prettily until it was time for luncheon.

The clip clop of horses' hooves provided a light percussion to the soprano voices. Then—vroom—the intrusive roar of an obnoxious gasoline-powered motor car interrupted. He could not wait until motor cars outnumbered horses as they had already overtaken them in speed, but surely the citizenry would rebel against the terrible din of gas engines. His fellow citizens would soon embrace the quiet dignity of the Stanley Steamer. It was inevitable. His investment depended on it. One of his investments, anyway.

At least the fermenting stench of horse shit ("No dear, we call that manure," his wife insisted.) was fast disappearing from civilized life. Still, some of it wafted through the window today, thanks to the heat and the occasional clip clop.

Who the hell was this artist to keep a man of his stature waiting like this? The deep rumble of a male voice came from the anteroom. *Finally.*

Walker's secretary tapped on his door, swinging it wide, her long skirt swishing against the tops of her shoes, her perfume veiling the animal scent from below. *Bouquet Nouveau*, he assumed, as that had been his Christmas gift to her. His wife had selected it, which was rather appropriate, as Ethel understood the wants and needs of a secretary, having served that role for him back in New York, before their marriage.

"Come in! Come in!" he greeted the artist, setting aside his annoyance. His secretary and her scent disappeared back into the anteroom. The door clicked behind her.

"It is an honor to finally meet you, Mr. Walker," said the artist, extending a calloused hand, his fingernails chipped. "The man building the Summer White House for the president. My children pester me for dimes to send to your fundraising for it."

The sculptor did not look like he could spare that dime. His suit required a more rigorous brushing. There was dust on it. And his shoes had not been shined in several days at least. Well, that just showed the man was doing a job, transforming stone into images that people would pay money to gawk at.

"Indeed, indeed. Ah, yes, my gift to the country. My other project. I have more than one iron in the fire these days. Please, sit."

"You did not ask me here to carve busts of the founding fathers for the courtyard of the presidential retreat?"

"Capital idea!" said Walker. The artist did not chuckle at the pun. "But, alas, no. I have something different—bigger—in mind for you."

Walker lifted the pile of photographs from his desk, spreading the black and white images in a row, one by one. "Diplodocus," he pointed to one photograph, "Stegosaurus," he pointed to another. "These are the giant, prehistoric reptiles called dinosaurs."

"So I see," said the artist. "There are no such creatures alive today. Where did these photographs come from?"

"A Mr. Carl Hagenbeck of Hamburg, Germany, commissioned these life-size replicas be made for his zoo. His Tierpark I believe he calls it. His reproductions are the talk of Europe, visited by hundreds of thousands annually. I want even better! The bones of the magnificent Stegosaurus were first discovered here at Morrison. It is appropriate they, and the other marvelous prehistoric beasts, should be reproduced here." He slapped his desk with a deliberation bordering on violence.

"At the Park of the Red Rocks," said the sculptor.

"The Garden of the Titans!" thundered Walker. A red rock could be puny, something you could hold in your hand. His park by Morrison deserved a name befitting its grandeur.

"My rocks are more than red. They are impressive, monumental, as if placed there by the hands of the gods themselves."

"God, you mean, placed there by the hand of God."

"Gods, small 'g.'"

The sculptor looked either offended or perplexed. Walker couldn't tell which and didn't much care.

"Aren't you the man who donated land to the Jesuits for Regis College on the northwest outskirts of Denver?"

Walker glowered at him. The artist squirmed in his chair.

Walker was no longer a fan of the church. He'd never make such a gift these days, but getting back that forty acres was futile. Even just trying would make him look small.

"Times change," said Walker. Success came from moving forward, not looking backwards. The church looked backward. Their dogma against divorce was tediously old-fashioned.

Emily had been a suitable enough wife in the past. Eight children proved that, but a time had come for him to move on. No sense dwelling now on all that wrangling over divorce. It had been accomplished. Ethel was the prize and she was his, now busy ably managing the staff and raising his children at the castle he had built on Mt. Falcon.

Forty acres was nothing. Now he owned four thousand acres of mountain land, studded with gigantic red monoliths. *Magnificent!*

Walker straightened his tie, which didn't need straightening. "I was speaking metaphorically, of course. My rocks came to be where they are through the forces of nature."

The artist studied the photographs. "What did you have in mind, sir?"

"To have my rocks carved into exact replicas of these gigantic creatures, the Stegosaurus and Diplodocus, Apatosaurus and of course the Duck-Billed. To commemorate their discovery. To educate, elucidate and entertain the masses."

"That is a bold vision, sir. I must see the rocks you intend me to carve."

Walker bounded from his chair, thrust open the door and hollered, "Tell Patrick to light the pilot on the Stanley. I'm taking the sculptor to the park." He paused. "And a lunch! Have the diner pack us a proper picnic to take along."

He turned to his guest. "Have you brought walking and riding attire?"

"No, sir, I'm afraid not."

"Get yourself to Joslin's, or Daniels & Fisher, for proper attire. Put it on my tab. You have twenty minutes. The Stanley's boiler will be warmed up and ready to go by then."

WHEN BOTH MEN were properly attired in riding dusters and sturdy shoes, they climbed into Walker's Stanley Steamer. A wicker picnic basket was stowed in the back. Walker pumped a long handle several times to build up the water pressure. With his large hand he squeezed the bulb of the side horn, to alert the lady pedestrians. A cloud of white steam billowed elegantly and car and the gentlemen floated down Arapahoe Street. Silently. Like riding on a cloud. Except for the occasional clinking of the Coors bottles nestled in the basket.

"IF MY AUTOMOBILE had an internal explosion engine, we would have to shout at each other," said Walker, congenially, as the Stanley Steamer rolled westward. He was a motor car aficionado eager to educate anyone who would listen. The sculptor certainly owned no automobile of his own, probably not even a horse and carriage. But every city dweller had experienced the racket of a gas combustion engine, or as Walker termed it, explosion engine.

"The Stanley Steamer is a fine piece of engineering ingenuity that allows us to converse like civilized men. The journey to the Garden of the Titans outside Morrison takes quite a long while, although the fifteen miles is not a great distance for a good automobile on a proper roadway."

The artist seemed to be a man of little words. Walker filled the void. "Did you know my son and I were the first men to drive a motorcar up Pikes Peak? Twelve years ago. We would have made the summit, too, if not for the fearfully washed out road. It was a harrowing experience, I tell you. That's the biggest impediment to progress in this country, terrible roads. I aim to change that. If the City of Denver would build a thoroughfare straight to my park, the time could be cut significantly. There would be fewer mishaps. A straight, macadam roadway will bring thousands to my park."

"You dream big, sir."

"That's the only way to dream, son."

THE WIND IN HIS FACE, invigorated, he steered toward the mountains in the distance, relating his life story to the artist, who had no choice but to listen: appointment to West Point, two years as a mercenary in the Chinese Army, his iron manufacturing plant in West Virginia, where he made and lost his first fortune. He told of his candidacy for Congress, which failed, thank god, followed by a stint as a journalist.

Then came a truly lucky break. His congressional campaign, plus his experience reporting and writing, brought him to the attention of the United States Secretary of Agriculture, who sent him to report on the arid lands of the west and prospects for farming with irrigation. Here, in Colorado, he discovered another fortune to be made, and it was not gold. It was alfalfa!

Once his report was duly filed, he packed up and moved his family to Colorado, buying 1,600 acres northwest of Denver that he dubbed Berkeley Farm. Alfalfa made his second fortune. Land he bought for $60,000 he sold for $372,000, a very tidy profit, not even counting all the money he had made selling the hay. The farm was long gone, of course. Replaced with homes and businesses.

"But life isn't all about profit, Artist," he continued, "As you surely know! People crave fun. All work and no play makes Jack a dull boy. Whatever I may be, I have never been described as dull. So I spent my fortune to buy land by Union Station, and built an amusement park."

"River Front Park. I spent many a fine afternoon there," said the sculptor. "My father took me to the racetrack."

Walker recalled the Ferris Wheel spinning beside the Platte River, the sweet smell of cotton candy, the crack of the bat at the baseball stadium, the dust billowing from the racetrack.

"The Castle of Culture and Commerce was especially impressive," said the artist.

"Ah, yes. I do love castles. The irony is that just three years after it opened, my competition went up on Berkeley Farm—Elitch's Amusement Park. No matter. People have an insatiable appetite for amusement. Even so, I had an opportunity to sell, and that is how I made my third fortune.

"Went back to journalism in New York City. Bought a magazine, but I couldn't even stand it ten years. Too miserable there in that city. By 1905 I was back, creating the Garden of the Titans."

"You build big, sir."

"That's the only way to build, son."

RED ROCKS STABLES, the wooden sign proclaimed. Walker parked his Stanley Steamer. There were too many places in the park an automobile could not reach. From this point they would tour among the red rocks on horseback, by foot, and via the funicular cable car.

"Sustenance, first," he announced, handing the wicker basket to a groom. A private table was being set up, upwind from the horses, of course. When the china had been laid, the sandwiches and pickles unwrapped from their paper, the Coors beer poured, he proposed a toast.

"To Stegosaurus!"

"To your Garden of the Titans!" They clinked glasses.

The pickle perked his taste buds, tender beef tongue and mayonnaise washed down easily with the frothy beer. When that was taken care of, the pair saddled up. Walker patted smooth the rough hairs of the horse, hoisted himself onto the horse's back and adjusted the reins. *These fellas still have some usefulness, for a few more years.*

They alternated riding and walking, examining various rocks as candidates for the sculptor's great endeavors. Walker never tired of his park. Or his rocks. Striated red, maroon, and pink. Encircled in greenery, thrusting mightily into the vast blue of the Colorado sky.

The view from Mount Morrison is not to be missed, insisted Walker, dismounting at the bottom of the funicular cog way. He caught the scent of grease as they clacked to the summit. There it was, eternity stretching past Denver onto the never-ending eastern plains. And then they descended, remounted their horses and continued the tour.

They dismounted again at the top of the natural amphitheater. "This," said Walker, "is the crown jewel of the park." Two massive rocks shouldered a slope descending to a third rock. It was impossible not to imagine a stage, an audience seated on the slope. "Creation Rock, or Rock of the Chronos," said Walker, gesturing to the largest of the monoliths, then, "Rock of Coios and, of course, Stage Rock. Stay there!" Walker took off down the slope on foot.

"Halloo!" he called out from in front of Stage Rock, in a more or less conversational volume. "This is the most superb amphitheatre in the world," he said, watching to make sure the artist understood.

He climbed up the slope more slowly than he had gone down. He wasn't as quick as he once was.

"Did you hear me clearly?"

"Yes, I did, sir."

"Pietro Satriano sang here, with a twenty-five-piece brass band. The famous Mary Garden sang here. She predicts someday twenty-thousand people will come here for concerts. I say a hundred thousand."

"I would not dispute her prediction, sir."

He ignores the slight. "And what do you think of my rocks? Which will you transform into dinosaurs for people to marvel at?"

"Apologies, sir, but to carve these rocks into dinosaurs would diminish them."

Walker didn't like that word, *diminish*. Not at all.

"And they would have to be carved here and there," the artist continued. "The appropriately-sized and configured specimens are not all in one place. It would be frustrating for large families to get their children from one to another."

The perils of pursuing entertainment with many children could not be denied. Walker knew that from personal experience, first with Emily and their children, now with Ethel and the little ones, never mind that the actual wrangling of tots he left to his wives and servants.

The artist continued, "And it would not be natural. Mr. Hagenbeck of Germany situated his creatures in natural settings such as if they were alive. It's the latest thing, and quite genius."

The latest thing. Genius. That's what he was after!

"How did he do it?"

"It appears from the photographs that he had fashioned them out of cement, sir."

"Cement is fine, if you say so, but bigger! Better!" bellowed Walker. "Beat that damned German!"

Mount Falcon
December, 1912

WALKER WAITED impatiently for Patrick to return from Morrison with the Sunday *Denver Post*. He would have driven down the mountain himself, he was so eager to see it, but Ethel insisted that Sunday was a day for rest. If not for church, to spend with her and the children. They were all dawdling over their breakfasts as he rambled from room to room, warming his hands at one fireplace after another—five in all, not counting the three in the servants' quarters. He peered out this window and that, watching for evidence of his valet coming up the road.

Finally!

"Is it there, Patrick?" he shouted out the front door. The valet waved the newspaper at him, bowing regally.

"I do not know sir! I rushed it up here without unwrapping it."

Walker bounded out the door, grabbing the paper, pounding Patrick on the back.

"Well done!"

A former journalist himself, Walker valued the power of the press and made certain to call upon it as often as possible. His projects achieved success partly through the renown brought by the newspapers. His name was regularly seen in print, his projects inspiring many articles. Even so, it was always a thrill to see his latest dream set forth in black ink. He strode through the courtyard on his long legs, burst through the door into the dining room, spread the paper flat on the table.

Plastered across the front page was an article about a pageant recreating Custer's last battle to be put on in three years' time. "Blazes," he muttered, so as not to attract the attention of Ethel. "What kind of foozlers edit this rag? A one-time reenactment of a losing—losing!—battle beats out my park? My park for the ages!" He flipped through the pages. Two entire sections of the newspaper had already blackened his fingers and still— nothing. Had that reporter lied to him? More pages of hokum. "Poor Children Make Appeal for Santa Claus at Christmas: Many Pathetic Requests Sent to Give Some Destitute Family Holiday Remembrance – Will You Drive the Reindeer?" *Oh for god's sake.*

Finally, there it was: "Walker Would Make Mount Morrison Greatest Show Place of the World." *At least the headline is accurate, if buried in section three on page five.*

The article described his business proposition for the City of Denver, that they build "a fine, straight-line road from the city to Morrison," where he, John Brisben Walker, would "reproduce in cement ten of the great prehistoric animals, ranging in length from 30 to 75 feet, whose home was formerly in this region."

Good that the reporter used the words giant prehistoric reptiles instead of Stegosaurus or dinosaur. Not everybody knew what those were. He wanted everyone to come to his park, not just the educated who knew paleontology. Far more profitable to attract a lot of people at a low price than a few at a high price, and even the common man appreciated quality. He had proven that at *Cosmopolitan* magazine. Back in New York City, people had called him crazy for improving the literature while dropping the price, but he'd shown them. His idea had multiplied subscriptions ten times over, until William Randolph Hearst handed over a mint to get his hands on that magazine, its readers and advertisers. Walker's fourth fortune, which paid the way for him to get out of New York and back to Colorado with his new bride.

Colorado Phantasmagorias

The *Denver Post* went on to describe the exact replica of the Egyptian sphinx the artist would carve from native stone. That was the demand he had insisted upon last summer, after he'd let the artist talk him into cement dinosaurs. A wonderful attraction, set off by itself, because Egyptology was all the rage.

The article also described how he would improve the natural amphitheatre for musical performances and athletic contests. He just needed that road.

Good writing, accurate, but damn, what lousy placement!

A year ago his plans for the Summer White House had gotten a full-page spread, on the back page, not as good as the front, but better than buried deep in Section Three. The presidential retreat was also part of a magnificent future for his four thousand acres. For his Summer White House, he would build soaring arches, peaked towers reaching into the clouds. None of that outmoded Jeffersonian understatement for today's presidents. *Breathtaking.* And just up the road from his own home on Mount Falcon. *Spectacular!* The cornerstone had already been laid. All of Colorado was excited for his plans. A legacy for the ages.

He wandered to his office, picked up his geode paperweight, put his feet up on his desk, juggled the rock gently between his hands. *A legacy for his grandchildren and great-grandchildren, a gift for the presidents of the future and all the citizens forever.*

A phantasm began forming again. He opened the geode, exposing the lavender crystals inside.

"You will not leave such a legacy, but your legacy will last."

ൟ

A VOICE? Sphinx-like. Where is it coming from?

He swivels his chair. The den is empty except for himself.

"Show yourself!"

"Go to your window. Look out."

Walker turns toward the window. The glass dissolves, the mullions collapse. He stands in the open air, his fireplace cold behind him. He hears a tangle of children's voices. *My family, thank God. No! It is a strange family, invading my courtyard, uninvited! Trespassers chattering as if I'm not even here. And what on earth are they wearing? How peculiar!*

His walls are gone, mostly, the roof as well. Only bits of the exterior remain standing, propped up inelegantly with rough timbers. His view is intact. Masses of evergreens undulating over the curves of the mountainside, meeting the blue sky as always.

"I'm your window to the future."

That voice again. He should consult a doctor about these phantasms after all. It would be terribly disappointing to live out his last years in an asylum. So much he will leave undone.

"You're not crazy, Mr. Walker."

Is it not crazy to hear reassurance that you're not crazy from a voice in your head?

"I'm not a voice in your head."

A man appears before him, dressed in something like miner's apparel. Work boots on his feet, blue jeans on his legs, a nappy purple jacket, the color of the geode crystals, covering his torso. "I'm here to show you your legacy."

"Where is my home?" Walker demands. "My family? The servants? Who are these interlopers?"

"You're seeing the world over a hundred years in the future. You're looking into the next millennium. Your home is gone, mostly, as you can see, as are you and your wife and children and servants, as is the way of things."

"Am I dead?"

"Well not at the moment, but in the future I show you, dead as a doornail. But your legacy lives. Once I have shown it to you, I will deliver you back to 1912, to your beautiful home and family, and you will continue your life to its natural end."

A breeze tufts Walker's thick hair. He stares. He stomps. He turns toward his view, taking it in. Moments pass. The parents head up the hill toward the Summer White House, the children skipping behind.

"Who the hell are you?" Walker demands.

"My name is Mancio. I'm a soothsayer, let loose from your geode. Like the genie in the story of Aladdin. As a literary type, you are familiar with that story."

Walker nods, hiding his bewilderment. "Why am I not shivering? It's December. And the fireplaces, what's left of them, are cold and empty."

"December is uncomfortably chilly for the out of doors, don't you agree? As long as we're viewing the future, I chose a fine spring day. More pleasant that way."

Colorado Phantasmagorias   45

Walker let that sink in. He would never, ever, tell anyone about this. "Who are the trespassers then?"

"Hikers, getting their fresh air and exercise, admiring your beautiful view. Your road is a hiking path, a gift to people who, like you, love the mountains and for all their busy business, need to get out and breathe the fresh air of the foothills. Your legacy. Part of it."

"My road was built for motor cars!" Walker exclaims, exasperated. "We raced on it! At top speeds!"

"Repurposed is all," insists Mancio. "A man once extolled the 'dry, bracing atmosphere of Colorado, living in the open air and forcing the oxygenation of his blood by plenty of exercise.' Who was it said that?

Walker harrumphs. "I may have said that, or something of that sort, I suppose." He starts marching uphill. "And what of the president and his retinue? Surely his motorcade is allowed, when he is in residence."

"The Summer White House did not get built."

"The hell!" Walker stops short. "I fast-talked Denver's best architect into designing it for no payment but the gratitude of his country! I opened the pockets of penny-pinching bankers for this! Not to mention parting small children from their dimes! Damn it!"

Walker stomps uphill, oxygenating his blood at a fast clip. Mancio follows. They catch up to the family at the spot where the Summer White House was meant to be. A Yule marble cornerstone is the only civilized bit, sitting hollow and forlorn amidst a pile of rubble.

The mountains spread out to the west before his eyes, remarkably unchanged except for the dots of houses here and there. The parents are reading aloud a placard that describes his dream.

He approaches the family. They act as if he's not there.

No castle in the clouds. His veritable palace of most original and picturesque design, a total bust. No president. Just a chiseled bit of white stone. His heart aches for all the dimes and dollars wasted.

"What happened?" he asks Mancio.

"The war. Every spare dime went to the war effort."

"What war? What a waste. How did we get into war? President Wilson is a pacifist, like me."

"Was, sir. Woodrow Wilson was a pacifist, and we don't have nearly enough time to discuss the origins of World War I."

One? World war one? What's a 'world' war, and why the numeral?

Before he can ask, Mancio waves his hands, dismissing the subject. "On the bright side, Big Head Todd and the Monsters are playing tonight at Red Rocks."

What on earth is there to say to that?

"There's much for you to see. Let's get going."

Mancio starts walking, Walker keeps up.

"Where are we going?"

"To Denver. Then to Red Rocks."

"Surely not on foot! What happened to my automobile? The Stanley?" Walker pleads.

Mancio laughs. "You can't believe your Stanley Steamer is running about in the twenty-first century. Regardless, no motor vehicles are allowed on these hiking trails. We will walk to the parking lot, easy hike, no problem, even in your shoes."

"I built this road for motor vehicles! I campaigned for fine roads! Roads are the key to progress. And a hundred years into the future and we're . . . we're *walking?*"

"Oxygenation, remember? And patience. It's not like you think."

Mancio takes deliberate strides. He means business.

"Here's the situation. When we come upon others, none can hear you," says Mancio, striding along deliberately. "Only I. And only I can see you, thank heavens, because your getup is outrageous."

My getup? The interlopers aren't even wearing collars! Dressed as if they had just spent a day panning for gold. Uncivilized.

At a macadam pad, Mancio gestures toward one of the vehicles lined up neatly, looking like the unreal assortment from his phantasmagorias. All enclosed. He would not be feeling the wind in his hair.

"I heard you like a quiet vehicle. I chose an electric for our adventure," says Mancio.

"A Fritchle?! Oliver won out in the long run, did he? I should not be surprised. His automobiles were renowned for excellence in mountain driving." He looks around. "None of these vehicles look like anything I recognize. Odd they are, very odd. Where's the Fritchle?"

Mancio looks very confused.

"A Fritchle!" Walker exclaims "That Titanic survivor gads about town in one. Mrs. J.J. Brown, the one they call 'unsinkable.' Fritchle builds his electric cars on Colfax Ave."

Colorado Phantasmagorias

Mancio shrugs. "I've never heard of Oliver Fritchle. This is a Tesla." Before Walker even opens his mouth, Mancio explains. "Named for, not made by, the famous Nikola Tesla."

"What about my Stanley Steamer? That's a quiet vehicle. What happened to my motor car company? Did my investment pay off?"

"The internal combustion engine won out for a century. Only recently has the electric car been reintroduced. Steam engines, I'm sorry, no. None are made today."

Walker shakes his head. His investment flopped.

Mancio opens the door for Walker, who slides in gingerly. And with that they take off, gliding downhill, in a silent car, like gentlemen, but without the cloud of steam.

WELL, NOW, INDIAN HILLS and Evergreen seem closer to what I imagined the future to be. By the looks of it, many thousands, maybe a million, people have moved to Colorado, and to the foothills. Why wouldn't they come here, with its dry, invigorating atmosphere, the most life-giving on the continent, water direct from the snowy ranges, cool nights in summer and bright, sunshiny days in winter? The roads are quite good as well, at least compared to that ghastly gravel 'hiking trail' my own road has deteriorated into.

Mancio swerves onto a curving pathway that empties onto a mammoth-sized highway. Multiple lanes are separated by a grassy ditch, an unending parade of motor vehicles. Hundreds, no thousands of every shape and size. House-sized trucks careening at high speeds. Baby-buggy sized bumps of speeding metal keeping the same pace. Sleek roadsters hug the road. Open-sided, two-man military conveyances in bright colors. He leans over to check the Tesla's speedometer.

"Oh, my God!"

"You were right, Mr. Walker; it was indeed poor roads holding us back. This is an interstate highway. Called I-70, a freeway."

This drive is exhilarating, and terrifying, in equal measures. He grips the door, his knuckles paling. *I must take my mind off the road or I'll go mad.*

"Did my magazine survive? Or did that idiot Hearst ruin it?"

"*Cosmopolitan* currently has a circulation of three million, published in thirty-five languages and a hundred countries."

"Well, then, Mr. Hearst made a success of it after all."

"Certainly. Be forewarned, in case you see a copy on our adventure. Mr. Hearst's heirs aren't as literary as you. Today it's less fiction, more sex and liberated women."

"Nothing wrong with sex and liberated women!"

THE TESLA CRESTS a rise and greater Denver fans out before his eyes, stretching north and south as far as he can see and all the way into the horizon on the east.

"Denver is larger than New York City!"

"No, sir! Although some complain it's on its way."

"Is there anything I will recognize?"

"Berkeley, the neighborhood built on your old alfalfa farm, the one you sold for such a profit . . ."

Walker interrupted, "A superb investment that was!"

Mancio continued, "Still thriving. Elitch's moved out though, to the Platte valley, where your River Front Park used to be."

They near the familiar riverbed at impressive speed. He sees a Ferris Wheel twirling in the distance, the image from his phantasmagorias. *I'll be damned.* Different though, surrounded by towers, presumably modern amusements. By the turn of the century, the nineteenth to twentieth that is, he'd already sold his city amusement park, then watched it degenerate into a soup kitchen for laid-off miners. A hundred years later the amusements are back, resurrected by Elitch's, his erstwhile competition. *What goes around, comes around. Good one. Just made that up.*

Mancio glides the Tesla into downtown Denver, descends into an underground cavern for cars. Ascending to the sunshine on foot, Walker experiences a place that, at first, bears no resemblance to the city where he once worked, where Emily then Ethel used to shop. For one thing, the air smells of—nothing. No manure. Not even exhaust fumes. And so many buildings! Astonishingly tall! He gapes, counting the stories, until his neck aches.

Then, here and there, he spots familiar shapes. The brick facades lining Larimer, Blake and Market look eerily familiar, though not the same at all. The Daniels & Fischer tower stands disconnected from its department store, looking lost. The building where Joslin's used to be seems vaguely recognizable. But where's the elegant Inter-Ocean Hotel? But then there, at his office address, an impossibly tall tower of glass, skimming and reflecting the sky. He listens, expecting any moment to hear the crack of glass, the tinkle of millions of shards shattering onto the ground. Nothing. *Surely this manner of construction is too fragile to endure!*

Colorado Phantasmagorias

"Please, Mancio. I am dismayed. It's too much to absorb. Let us escape!"

"To Red Rocks, then. It's wise to arrive well before the concert begins."

"To my Garden of the Titans! Straight away."

WALKER GRIPS the door handle and grits his teeth as he and Mancio zip along. Large green signs announce they're on Sixth Avenue freeway. They sweep onto I-70, or the interstate, as Mancio calls it. More signs instruct on the speed limit.

It's a relief when Mancio exits the divided roadway toward the park. Now signs warn of deer. Such a lot of information along these roads! Walker's road improvement idea is transformed into something far bigger than even he had imagined, and it's unsettling, although he's loathe to admit it.

Then the disappointments pile up, one upon another. A wooden sign is mislabeled "Red Rocks." *Garden of the Titans is the proper name. Why isn't that on the sign?* They keep driving.

Wait. No sphinx?

No magnificent cement dinosaurs?

Mancio parks the Tesla in a large lot. *This is where my funicular railway once ran. Gone.* Mancio nags him into squinting hard and there, just barely, he detects the scar on the hillside where it had run.

Walker covers his face with his hands. He wants to weep, but a man does not do such a thing.

"Nothing I built is left," he says, accusing Mancio. "You promised to show me my legacy. I have none. Let me return to my fireplace in 1912. I cannot bear this anymore."

"The amphitheatre got built," says Mancio. "Let's go."

Walker is afraid of what he may see, or not see. He, who fought as a mercenary in China, is afraid, but must face his legacy. Simply must. He pushes away the fear, striding up the stone steps to the amphitheatre. He finds a wooden seat halfway down, row fifty-five. From there he sees the hogback where dinosaurs were discovered and a city grown right up to his park.

Concertgoers tramp past in incongruous outfits of foot racing shoes, miner's work trousers and weirdly decorated undershirts (even the women)!

"Mary Garden predicted twenty thousand people would one day come here to listen to the finest musicians," Walker muses. "I predicted a hundred thousand, although I am not known for understatement."

Mancio nods. "Nowadays well over a million people hear music every summer at Red Rocks."

"A million you say. Well, that's a worthy number."

"Some of the finest musicians of the age perform here," Mancio continues. "There are concerts almost every evening except for in the winter. Absolutely world-renowned."

Walker sniffs. "Is that cannabis?"

"Are you surprised?"

"Why would I be? Hashish is quite a popular thing in New York City. At least it was while I lived there. I am not surprised that in a hundred years the fashion found its way westward."

Person after person traipses past carrying cups of beer, sloshing on him, not apologizing, as if he isn't there, because he isn't. "Mancio, I'm thirsty."

The soothsayer leaves, returning with a yellow can that looks remarkably like the label on the bottles in his picnic basket a century before, or a few months ago, or earlier today, depending on how you look at it.

"That German from Golden left more of a legacy than I did." He takes a swig. *Tastes about the same, same bite on the tongue, same tickle against the palate.*

"Your amphitheatre got built, John," Mancio lectures at him. "This is much bigger than a cup of beer. Adolph Coors left a recipe, but I know the future and can tell you that not a single one of these people is going to go home and wax nostalgic about the Coors he drank here. They are going to rave about the time they heard Big Head Todd and the Monsters at Red Rocks, the world's most revered concert venue. This amphitheatre was your idea. You, you brought the first musicians here to sing. Even if it didn't get built until after you died, this is your legacy.

"You left ideas, Mr. Walker, the best legacy. In the twenty-first century people experience nature hiking up to your home. They marvel at the view from the pinnacle where you planned the Summer White House. They talk about what might have been. They dream. You left dreams, and experiences."

Walker harrumphs.

"A legacy is measured by what it is, not against what a man in the past once imagined it would be."

Colorado Phantasmagorias

Perhaps the prophet speaks truth. Walker loosens his tie and collar. It feels good. His evening whiskers no longer chafe against the starch. He relaxes. Not all has changed. The rocks still sport their red, maroon and pink stripes. Creation Rock and Rock of Coios still jut into the sky, even if Mancio insists on calling the one Ship Rock.

Musicians take the stage. Keyboards, guitars and voices ring out at a volume Walker has never heard nor imagined. *Holy hell!* He covers his ears. Colored lights careen back and forth, illuminating the crowd, flashing against the rocks.

"Oh, my God, Mancio! What's happening?" Walker cries.

Mancio puts a hand on Walker's shoulder. He shouts over the music. "Your legacy is huge, man, huge! Listen. Watch."

The crowd sways as one, singing along. They hold glowing objects in their hands, moving to a heart pounding drumbeat.

Walker's mouth stands agape. He lets his hands slip from his ears. He listens, catches the word 'bittersweet,' like his legacy. His foot starts to tap. He sways just a little bit.

"The Monsters are no Mary Garden, but this is damn big. I do like big."

Epilogue

John Brisben Walker's second wife Ethel died in 1916 and is buried at the bottom of Mt. Falcon. He married a third time, to Iris Calderhead, organizer of the National Woman's Party. He died in 1931 in Brooklyn, New York.

Just the Facts, Ma'am

Sacred Stones by Thomas J. Noel (Denver's Division of Theatres and Arenas, 2004) offers real history and great old photos of Red Rocks. Both the **Denver Post** and the **Rocky Mountain News** published articles about Walker during his lifetime and in later reminiscences. His July 8, 1931 obituary is archived by the **New York Times**.

Just for Fun

Hike to the ruins of Walker's mansion and the cornerstone of the proposed Summer White House at **Mount Falcon Park, a** Jefferson County Open Space park. The west trailhead (21074 Mount Falcon Road, Indian Hills, CO) provides access to the Castle Trail, which follows the road Walker built for his Stanley Steamer. It's a fairly flat and short hike. If you desire

Colorado Phantasmagorias 52

something more strenuous, start at the east trailhead (3852 Vine Street, Morrison, CO).

Concerts and events are held at **Red Rocks Amphitheatre** April through October. Tickets are available at https://www.axs.com/. The park is open for hiking every day. While you're there, visit **Dinosaur Ridge**. Impressive fossils can be seen at The Discovery Center just inside Gate 1 to Red Rocks Park. See real dinosaur bones and tracks *in situ* along a walking trail just across the road. Limited parking is available. For a **guided bus tour** and entrance to the Exhibit Hall, visit the Dinosaur Ridge Main Visitor Center at 16831 W. Alameda Parkway, Morrison. Outside you'll see replicas of a Stegosaurus and Iguanodon, similar to the dinosaur sculptures Walker envisioned for Red Rocks Park.

Golda Meir
1898 – 1978
Nation Builder

GOLDIE FEELS WOOZY, just a bit, straightening the heavy chinchilla coat on its hanger. So beautiful, the fur so soft. The first thing Golda Mabovitch ever bought with her own money was a coat. She'd saved her pennies for many months to afford a black woolen coat, plain but warm. It would take a hundred years of her small wages to afford something as wonderful as this.

Along with the wooziness, she feels a light, scratchy sensation run down her arms, as if she is wearing sleeves of tulle, which of course she has never worn, only touched while handling the gowns of society ladies. Goldie owns one blouse, white cotton, which she hand-washes and presses every morning. She's wearing it now as she helps Shamai at the cleaners after school.

What's making me feel so peculiar? She stops working to collect her wits.

"Mr. Korngold," she overhears her brother-in-law's dry-cleaning customer say, "it would be my privilege to welcome your community's help."

"Mrs. Brown," says Shamai, Sam that is. "I'm just a poor cleaner and presser, but I will put in a good word for your charity among my friends, who are almost all Jewish."

"Jews, Catholics, whatever," the customer responds. "Protecting young children from being jailed with horse thieves and safecrackers is everyone's concern. Back when I was in Leadville, and here in Denver, too, I found your community very willing to team up with me for a good cause, like juvenile justice reform. Your children are as likely to be mistreated as ours."

A few more words filter from the front counter to the back room, then the gentle click of the front door latching shut. Goldie turns her attention back to Mrs. J.J. Brown's fur coat. No matter what she does, the coat keeps listing to one side. Must be something in the pocket. Goldie reaches in.

There's a rough rock in there. Why would a rich lady keep a rock in her pocket?

She pulls it out. The rock falls apart. One rock in two pieces, a geode. She knows this because her science teacher split one apart with a hammer in class. This one has purple crystals inside. She runs out the door. Mrs. Brown has already disappeared.

The world spins. Sand swirls like a storm, but Denver's city streets are cobblestoned, so that makes no sense. She feels the bite of sand grains against her cheeks. Lights glitter, like the chandelier in the Brown Palace next door, but she's still on the street. She smells lemon. Tastes almonds. Lights burst, like flashes from news men's cameras. It's confusing and weird. Goldie isn't superstitious; there must be a sensible explanation.

She stumbles back into the shop, puts the rock on a shelf, tags it with Mrs. Brown's name so it can be returned with the coat. The world settles down.

What just happened? No time to worry. She has work to do, and then get tidied up for this evening.

Morris Meyerson might show up.

ي

Denver
May, 1913

GOLDIE SLICED LEMONS in her sister Sheyna's small kitchen, thinly, to make the most of this small extravagance. She arranged them on a plate. Tonight there would be people here, sharing dreams, arguing ideas, drinking tea. Cup after cup, flavored with lemons. She couldn't wait.

Her mother's annoying voice invaded her thoughts: 'American fruit. No good. Better in Pinsk.' Like they ever ate fruit in Pinsk! Certainly not lemons. Not even in Kiev. Unless you consider potatoes a fruit, because that was about all they ever had back in Russia, and not enough of it. She remembered the pangs in her stomach when there wasn't enough to go around. Was it hunger that had made her delirious this afternoon? No, Shamai and Sheyna had plenty of healthy food here.

She sliced a second lemon. The juice spurted, freshening the air with a sharp tang. These lemons, brought to Denver on a railcar from who knows where, fed her dream—to live where lemons grow on lemon trees. She dreamed of a kibbutz, working the lemon grove. Picking the yellow fruits, hearing the soft plunk as they fall into a basket. Or when lemons are out of season, almonds. She imagined picking almonds in Palestine, side by side with Morris, a toddler underfoot and a baby at her hip. Just a dream, but it could happen. Palestine seemed as familiar as any place Goldie had ever lived, thanks to everything Sheyna's friends had told her about it.

If Sheyna had not taken ill with tuberculosis, she would never have met these friends, and Goldie would still be in Wisconsin. Was it wrong to feel grateful? Goldie was not religious, so she did not think in terms of sin, but it was absolutely essential to know right from wrong. Was it wrong that she, with a constitution strong enough to fend off germs, was benefitting from poor Sheyna's illness? She remembered when her sister had started coughing, back home in Milwaukee, after they'd fled Russia. First they'd try to ignore it. Just a cold. She'll get better. But she didn't. Sheyna had kept the whole family awake every night with the hacking. Then came the blood, soiling the rags she'd held to her mouth. Of course it had been tuberculosis. Half their neighborhood, probably half of Wisconsin, was infected. And there was no cure.

Nothing for it but high altitude, fresh air and bed rest. Sheyna left the family, left Shamai, came west for rejuvenation, dry air and good food, paid for through the benevolence of better-off Jews. That was four years ago. When the doctors at the Jewish Consumptive Relief Society sanitarium finally deemed her well enough for discharge, and Shamai had saved a bit of money, he came to Colorado to propose. Sheyna's doctors advised against it, because she could relapse, maybe die, but they married anyway, and had a baby. Better a short life of love then a long life without, he said. Shamai, Sam he started calling himself, started a dry cleaning shop and rented half of this little red brick duplex in between the city and the sanitarium, JCRS.

Meanwhile, back in Milwaukee, Mother had found a thirty-year-old real estate salesman for Goldie to marry. *An old man! Twice my age! And the end of my studies!* Goldie refused. She would not let that happen. Absolutely not. She and her best friend Regina plotted her escape.

First, she had needed funds. English skills were her most valuable asset. The immigrants in the neighborhood eagerly shelled out ten cents an hour for her lessons, but it soon became apparent that she'd be standing under the *chuppa* with the real estate agent before she could save enough that way. So Sheyna sent her the rest of the train fare, in secret.

With that taken care of, Goldie and Regina finalized the plan. One evening she smuggled out a small bundle of clothes for Regina to hide. Then she scribbled a goodbye note to her parents, which she put in a place they would notice eventually, but not too soon. Then she sneaked to the train station after school, taking Sheyna's wise advice to act calm and cool no matter how much her heart raced, to always show a brave face. She boarded a train, alone, fourteen years old, heading west to live with the Korngolds at the edge of the Rocky Mountains.

When she got to Denver's Union Station, Sheyna extracted her from the hustle and bustle and led her underneath the wrought iron arch outside the train station. 'Welcome' it proclaimed on one side, the Hebrew '*Mizpah*' on the other. A yellow trolley took them west to Sheyna's house on Julian Street. Such a nice little place, brand new, almost, with running water and a flush toilet.

And now here she was, earning A's at North High School, making her own money, slicing lemons, eager to serve tea to Sheyna's friends, hoping to see Morris. His beautiful soul, those gentle eyes behind his smart spectacles. Sometimes, even when Sheyna's kitchen was crammed full of people shouting, laughing and slurping tea, she could look at Morris and it would be like they were alone, just the two of them, and it made her insides melt.

Her thoughts were interrupted by the stomp of shoes on the porch. The sound reverberated from the front door, through the first little room, then the second little room and into the kitchen. She heard Shamai greet their guests. Sheyna bounced the baby on her hip as she spooned tea leaves into cups. Goldie wiped lemon juice on her apron, then unknotted it and hung it on a hook.

How many steps was it from the front door? Ten? Yet the two men were already locked in debate before they reached the kitchen. Goldie looked past them to the door. No Morris yet. She poured hot water from the kettle into two cups. The men reached for the tea without skipping a word. Exploitation of workers. Cough. Inherent dignity of labor. Evils of capitalism. Cough. Always the coughs.

More noises sounded on the porch, fresh voices, women's voices. Only four chairs fit around the kitchen table, but nobody minded crowding into the room, debating each other standing up, nose to nose. Trade union organizing, unsafe mines, the plight of the abandoned synagogue in Leadville. Cough. Anti-Semitism. Cough. Anarchy, pacifism. These kitchen conversations were like sandstorms in the desert, each concept a gust of wind, each word a grain of sand. Gritty and real. Passionate. Goldie couldn't get enough of it. They were going to change the world!

But where was Morris?

Next subject: the role of women in politics and leadership. Goldie looked over at her sister, who only let her participate because she disinfected the cups afterwards. *Will she kick me out if I speak up?* Sheyna was tending the baby.

"Why shouldn't women share equally in politics?" said Goldie. "It's our world, too. If there's a job that needs to be done, and a woman can do it, why should she not? We can't change the world with half of us sitting on our hands."

Light clapping. *There he is!*

Morris was squeezing himself into the back of the small crowd in the even smaller kitchen, listening in his quiet way, smiling at her, applauding gingerly and not coughing. He, Shamai, and the baby were the only ones besides Goldie not lung-sick. Morris had come to Denver to be with his ill sister, as she had. The rest of the *catootnicks,* as Mother would call them, were on the mend, some better recovered than others.

Goldie smoothed her auburn hair. Her father claimed men didn't like smart women, but that couldn't be true for Morris. He seemed to like her quite a lot, and it couldn't possibly be on account of her looks. No matter how often he praised her hair and her eyes, she didn't believe him. *Why can't I have black hair and big, lustrous eyes?* Still, it didn't hurt to look as best as one could manage. She stood a bit straighter, licked her lips to make them shine, and maneuvered her way to Morris's side, careful not to spill the tea, which was almost impossible since her hands were so sweaty. She handed him a teacup. His fingers brushed against hers. Her heart about stopped.

Shamai mentioned Mrs. J.J. Brown's request for help with juvenile justice reform. Heated discussion ensued.

"She's a social parasite!" said Sheyna. "A mine owner!" Such a pill Sheyna was, even when she made a good point.

"Her husband's the capitalist. She's a Socialist," a friend countered in Mrs. Brown's defense.

"More philanthropist than Socialist, and I hear her husband is none too fond of the way she doles out his money," said another.

After much shouting, it was decided that those who wanted to help should and those who didn't shouldn't. And then the talk turned to

Palestine, the subject dearest to Goldie's heart. None of them had been there, but all were experts. It was a land of milk and honey, pomegranates, cucumbers, onions and leeks. They knew this from the Torah. Goldie could taste it. Yearned for it. She remembered the fear of pogroms they'd felt back in Russia, the midnight raids, screams, blood in the streets, the terror in mother's eyes. *Never again.*

Morris did not join in. There was a time when she wondered why he even came to Sheyna's kitchen. He rarely spoke and when he did, made it clear he thought they were all idealistic dreamers. Odd, that accusation coming from a poet, a man who picked flowers for her.

"We can suffer as well anywhere," he sometimes said, in his gentle way. "I have no interest in picking almonds."

Flowers, but not almonds? Palestine is our future. A country to call our own. Nothing made her heart pump more than this—*Eretz Yisroel.* Not just to dream about, to live there. *Morris will come to see that. In due time. He will, I know he will. He will move there to be with me.*

FLUTES, OBOES, TROMBONES, French horns, violins and cellos. Weekend concerts in Denver's city parks were free, and she and Morris tried never to miss one. The music flowed from the orchestra in the park bandstand. Starting mildly, growing stronger and braver, the notes floated around and above in the thin, mile-high air.

"This is the Overture from Wagner's opera *Tannhauser*," Morris said. He knew everything about music.

"What's it about?" asked Goldie.

Morris looked at his hands. "Love," he said quietly. "It's about love."

"What, specifically, is it about love?"

"Just love. That's all."

SLOAN'S LAKE was just a few blocks from Sheyna and Shamai's house at Sixteenth and Julian. The aromas of popcorn and hot dogs from Luna Park were enticing, and the Ferris Wheel looked like fun, but Goldie knew the cost of admission to the amusement park was too dear for a poetic sign-painter like Morris. But he was strong, willing to pull his own oars, and a small boat rental was within his means.

Slip, splash, slip, splash, went the rhythm of the oars. As she sat in the boat, Goldie's mind was ajumble, as always. She wanted to study, graduate from high school, become a teacher, but she also wanted to marry Morris, and teachers can't be married. She also wanted to move to Palestine, which Morris didn't. She wanted to get out from under Sheyna's thumb. The older sister she had idolized her whole life was a shining example to follow and admirable beyond all measure, but bossy and a pain in the neck to live with. Almost as bad as Mother. Maybe worse.

To the west of the lake rose the JCRS water tower at the hospital where Sheyna had been a patient. Beyond that, snowcapped mountains scraped the Colorado sky, the bluest blue she'd ever seen. The splish splash of oars finally set her heart to calm. She dipped her fingertips in the cool water, watched the trail they left behind. Sunday was drawing to a close. The sun began its descent behind the peaks.

Morris began reciting a poem, one he'd read to her before. By Lord Byron, from *Hebrew Melodies*:

> "It is the hour when from the boughs
>   The nightingale's high note is heard—
> It is the hour—when lovers' vows
>   Seem sweet in every whisper'd word—
> And gentle winds and waters near
> Make music to the lonely ear."

Tomorrow she would be back at school, then working with Shamai at the cleaners in the afternoon, fixing tea in the evening, making plans to save workers and change the world. But for now, just for now, she was with Morris, and the future would take care of itself.

༄

THE ROCK SITS on the shelf, its tag still attached, when Goldie arrives at the Wisconsin Cleaning and Pressing Works after school. But the chinchilla coat is gone. She decides to return the rock to the rich lady herself. The Brown Palace Hotel is a very short walk. Shamai can manage alone for a few minutes.

The woozy feeling returns before she's out the door. Suddenly, in an inexplicable blur, she finds herself outside Sheyna's house. That's impossible, for Julian Street is a trolley ride away. Everything is amiss. The house is facing the wrong direction! A sign says 'Ninth Street,' but except for a row of semi-familiar houses, this looks nothing like Ninth Street. People are milling about where the autos and carriages run. They're wearing strange clothing, chattering, their arms full of books, knapsacks slung over their shoulders. *Where on earth am I?* A woman taps her shoulder.

"Golda, don't be afraid."

Don't be afraid? Like I'm ever afraid?

"I'm Sybylla," the woman continues, "released from the geode you're holding. I'm a prophetess, a soothsayer, sent to show you your legacy."

"Prophetess! I don't believe in prophets!"

"And yet, here I stand, ready to show you your legacy."

"Legacy? I'm fifteen years old!"

Sybylla continues, unheeded. "You're standing now far into the future. I've brought you to the twenty-first century."

This woman is crazy! Maybe I should be afraid. Goldie considers running, but remembers Sheyna's good advice—act calm and cool, be brave.

"Sheyna's house has been moved here to Auraria," the strange woman continues. "It's a college campus now. See, the little plaque? Her house is on the National Register of Historic Places."

Historic? Goldie, reeling from this fantastic turn of events, doesn't know what to think. This is very confusing.

"Shamai needs my help at the shop. I can't waste time here. I need to work. And return this geode."

"When you return to the shop, it will be as if you never left. Don't you want to know your legacy?"

Goldie doesn't understand what legacy this Sybylla is talking about, but she does wonder about the house. "Why would anybody move Sheyna's house all the way to Auraria?"

"Because *you* lived here."

"I'm just a high school girl."

"A high school girl whose dreams, the dreams you conjured here, become real. This house was going to be demolished, but instead it is moved and turned into the Golda Meir Center for Political Leadership."

"Who is Golda Meir?"

"You, dear."

Golda Mabovitch's dream is to become Golda *Meyerson*. The strange woman predicts her dreams come true, so this is confusing. She fights off a tear forming in the corner of her eye. "I don't marry Morris after all?"

"You do indeed! And you have two children together. But he never does get into the swing of picking almonds."

Colorado Phantasmagorias

"Almonds? Do we move to Palestine then? Work in a kibbutz? Like my dream?"

"You do."

"What happened to Morris? Why is my name Meir?"

"You and Morris, always loving, have a complicated relationship, as you must already sense. You two will not always stay young. After many years, when he dies, you change your name to Meir. It's Hebrew for 'one who shines.'"

It feels bad to know Morris dies first, but somebody has to, and that's obviously many years away. "Why does the sign say 'Center for Political Leadership?' That's an awfully la-de-da description of our kitchen debates. None of us could hardly be called leaders."

"On the contrary. You become a mighty leader. You become Prime Minister of Israel."

Goldie's jaw dropped. "You're crazy! You're pulling my leg!"

"No, dear, I'm surely not."

"Do you mean Palestine?"

"No, I said it correctly."

"Israel? Prime Minister?" It's too much to take in.

Sybylla walks up the short flight of steps to the porch. Goldie follows. Sybylla unlocks the front door and swings it open.

Inside, the walls are lined with pictures of an old lady with wiry gray hair. There's a framed telegram Golda Meir sent to a U.S. president named Truman that Goldie has never heard of. There's Sheyna's medical records from JCRS on display, and a beribboned gown with tulle sleeves.

Next to the gown is a framed photograph. It's a flash photo, taken by a newspaper photographer, of an old lady wearing it. An explanation is posted: Golda Meir wore this gown when she dined with President Nixon. *Never heard of him, either.*

"You build a Jewish nation, Golda. A country of sandstorms and lemon groves. You say it has the bluest sky, bluer even than the Colorado sky."

That's hard to believe.

There in the back is the little kitchen, empty of people like she's never seen it.

"Your path to Prime Minister, it begins here."

WITH THAT, GOLDIE finds herself snapped back to the Brown Palace, handing the mysterious rock to the concierge. She returns to work, cleaning and pressing pants and shirts. Then she goes home to slice lemons and brew tea. She's got a future to accomplish.

Epilogue

Whatever your opinion of today's political situation and conflict in Israel and the occupied territories of Palestine, there is no doubt that Golda Meir and her fellow Zionists had an enormous impact on the world. In 1972, Italian journalist Oriana Fallaci wrote: "Even if one is not at all in agreement with her, her politics, her ideology, one cannot help respect her, and admire her, even love her."

Golda Mabovitch lived in Denver only two years. She reconciled with her parents and returned to Milwaukee to finish high school. Morris also moved to Milwaukee. They married, moved to a kibbutz in Palestine (Israel was not founded until 1948), left for Tel Aviv and had two children. Golda's political duties and travel eventually estranged them and they separated, but remained friends until his death.

Golda Meyerson was present at the founding of the state of Israel in 1948. She changed her name to Meir in 1956 when she became Foreign Minister. She held a succession of high-level posts, culminating in Prime Minister from 1969 to 1974.

Sheyna and Shamai Korngold were married 43 years and had three children. The discovery of antibiotics in the 1940s finally provided a cure for tuberculosis (TB). The Jewish Consumptive Relief Society, where Sheyna had been a patient, eventually closed and was repurposed as a cancer research facility and is now an art college. She was also a patient at what is now called National Jewish, a nationally-recognized hospital specializing in all respiratory ailments.

Just the Facts, Ma'am

Golda Meier's 1974 autobiography, ***My Life,*** is said to have been ghost written and is sometimes criticized as self-serving (as autobiographies tend to be), but it is an easy read and the closest to her voice. ***Golda: The Romantic Years*** by Ralph Martin includes details of her time in Denver.

For more on the Jewish influence in Colorado, seek out the **"Jewish Pioneers"** episode of *The Colorado Experience* produced by Rocky Mountain PBS. It can be streamed online at https://www.pbs.org/.

By 1925, more than half of Coloradans had come to the state because of tuberculosis, either as patients or the families of patients. To learn more about how this disease impacted Colorado, watch the **"How Tuberculosis Fueled Colorado's Growth"** episode of *Colorado Matters*, produced by Colorado Public Radio, which can be streamed at https://www.cpr.org and **"The Forgotten Plague"** episode of *American Experience*, produced by PBS, which can be streamed at https://www.pbs.org/

Just for Fun

The Golda Meir Center at Metropolitan State University is just north of the Ninth Street Historic Park on the Auraria Campus in downtown Denver. The museum is not open for regular tours, but if you call 303-556-3291, MSU will be happy to unlock it for you. While you're there, visit the wonderful hidden architectural gem that is **Ninth Street Historic Park**. Lining both sides of the park are Italianate, Second Empire, Vernacular and Cottage style houses from the late nineteenth century. The interiors are not open to the public, but historical markers relate the style of architecture, date of construction, and brief stories of the early occupants. The park is also just a nice shady respite in the middle of the city.

A walk around **Sloan's Lake** is always a pleasure, and you can see the water tower and mountain peaks to the west just as Golda and Morris did. Boats are no longer for rent, but if you have your own you can row or motor around the lake. Sloan's Lake has two playgrounds for children. Most Reform and secular Jews (such as Golda was) left west Denver for east Denver in the latter part of the twentieth century, but the area remains a vibrant center for Orthodox life. You are likely to see Orthodox parents pushing strollers through the park.

The buildings and grounds of the Jewish Consumptive Relief Society (JCRS) are preserved and currently in use by the **Rocky Mountain College of Art and Design** (RMCAD) in what is now Lakewood, Colorado. It's a wonderful place to walk, imagine a life here as a 'consumptive,' and admire student art. Check in at the Texas Building, 1600 Pierce Street, and ask for a copy of their Walking Tour brochure

If that's not enough art for you, follow the green lines on the sidewalk outside campus to take the **40 West Art Walk**. You'll see murals, sculptures and studios with artists at work. You won't be able to miss noticing the big pink tower. That's the quintessential kitschy tourist destination, **Casa Bonita.** Built in 1974, it has nothing whatsoever to do with Golda Meir or tuberculosis. But if you have young kids in tow, or are a South Park fan, it's a very short detour to see the cliff divers and Black Bart's cave. Consider the cost of the enchilada your cover charge and load up on the unlimited sopaipillas with honey.

Margaret Tobin Brown
1867 – 1932
Feminist, Activist, Survivor

DID SOMEONE POISON this coffee? The middle-aged woman sees unreal visions. A crowd of people milling about the green and red mosaic porch of the House of Lions, her former home. A sea of pink hats swirling in front of the golden domed capitol, placards, petitions, shouted exhortations. Yet Mrs. J.J. Brown knows she is in her hotel room, surrounded by wallpaper and framed art, with a view of the Trinity Methodist Episcopal Church. What she sees make no sense. The people are unrecognizable, the hats fuzzy and pink, the golden dome familiar but not something actually visible from this hotel window.

It can't be the coffee. Denver's finest hotel serves only the best. Made with pure artesian water. They would not allow anyone to pollute it. Confident in the integrity of the hotel staff, she lifts the china cup from its saucer and takes another sip. Fragrant, slightly oily, her favorite vice. The visions are probably related to the headaches that come at increasing frequency, even when she's not at this hotel.

Margaret Brown pushes aside the geode she is reminiscing over, a rough rock, split in two and filled with glittery lavender crystals, the color of the dress she is wearing. It brings fond memories of her daughter. Helen gave her the souvenir geode as a gift years ago.

The strange visions clear. No time to fret over them, anyhow. She clips on swingy earrings, adjusts a brimmed hat over what used to be naturally auburn hair, smooths the lavender silk of her flapper-style gown (or as flapper-fashion as a sixty-year-old dares), untangles several long strings of beads, tassels and pearls. *Ready.*

She exits her private room, striding with a purposeful gait along the interior balcony of the Brown Palace Hotel, beneath the blue and gold stained-glass skylight, past the lacy wrought iron railings with the griffin heads, touching the upside down one for luck. She sweeps past the onyx pillars, descending the grand stairway, her walking stick tap tapping against the lobby floor. The weird visions are gone now. Good.

No time to waste. There are funds to raise.

༄

Denver
November 1, 1927

MARGARET TOBIN BROWN, more properly known as Mrs. J.J. Brown, sat in the place of honor in the front row at the dedication for the home of Eugene Field, her favorite poet. It was a modest place, white clapboard with a little porch, worth every effort and the goodly sum of money she'd expended to save it from demolition.

When her children were small, she'd read to them Mr. Field's most famous poem. Those were the days, Helen and Lawrence snuggled into their beds, eyes drooping after a long day in mountain air. The Brown family's little house in Leadville had been not that much different from this one. Days long past.

Bright voices of school children recited perfectly:

> "The old moon laughed and sang a song,
>   As they rocked in the wooden shoe;
> And the wind that sped them all night long
>   Ruffled the waves of dew;
> The little stars were the herring-fish
>   That lived in the beautiful sea.
> "Now cast your nets wherever you wish,—
>   Never afraid are we!"
>   So cried the stars to the fishermen three,
>   Wynken,
>   Blynken,
>   And Nod."

Mr. Field's words, "Never afraid are we!" sustained her often, never more so than that awful night in 1912 on Lifeboat Six as she watched the Titanic sink into the ocean depths right in front of her.

"All night long their nets they threw,
    To the stars in the twinkling foam,—
Then down from the skies came the wooden shoe,
    Bringing the fishermen home:
'Twas all so pretty a sail, it seemed
    As if it could not be;
And some folk thought 'twas a dream they'd dreamed
    Of sailing that beautiful sea;
But I shall name you the fishermen three:
    Wynken,
    Blynken,
    And Nod."

So long ago the Titanic disaster had happened that even Margaret sometimes thought 'twas a dream she'd dreamed, rescued not by a wooden shoe, but by the wonderful British ship RMS Carpathia.

Applause for the pupils of Woolston School interrupted that shivering memory. Margaret stood to plead for funds to keep the poet's house maintained. The program concluded with an invitation to cookies and tea, cocoa for the little ones.

Margaret swished her lavender gown through the other smartly-gowned matrons to the clutch of children. "Bravo!" she exclaimed. "You're the cat's pajamas!"

"Thank you, Mrs. Brown, for inviting us," said a girl, twelve years old, perhaps, extending her hand. "My name is Lucy. It is an honor to meet you. You are the lady who survived the Titanic."

"Brined, salted and pickled I was!" she said. "But the pleasure is all mine, I assure you. I'm an old lady preserving the past. You are the future!" The other children smiled politely and concentrated on their cocoa.

Except Lucy, who followed at her heels as she shook hands and extracted donations. When she'd done all the squeezing it was prudent to do, Margaret turned her attention to her acolyte.

"What are your goals in life, Miss Lucy?"

"I would like to marry a miner, and get rich, like you did, Mrs. Brown."

"Oh, for crying out loud, Lucy! You can do better than that!"

"Ma'am?"

"Mining is a terribly dangerous occupation. Nothing to wish on a man you love. My J.J. was smart, but he was also lucky. Could just as easily have had a timber fall on his head and crush him. Or had his lungs rot out before he made thirty. Then where would I have been? Not chatting with you here today, that's for sure."

Lucy's face slumped, her lip quivered a bit.

"My dear Lucy, what do *you* want to do with *your* life? There's a great big world out there! So much to see! To do! So much to make better!"

Lucy's look changed from crestfallen to confused.

"Listen, Miss Lucy, women are the future. We won the vote nationwide seven years ago, after much marching and hard work, I tell you, and now we're working toward equal rights. You can do anything! Anything! I ran for Congress myself. Would have won, too, if not for family complications. You could be president! Education is key, especially for women. What interests you?"

"I would like to learn foreign languages, like you," she said.

"French is my favorite! My husband used to say it sounded like somebody choking on his potatoes, but what did he know? He also wanted me to stay home and keep my mouth shut, fat chance of that. German is a useful language, and I know some Italian, too. Study hard and you could become a translator for the League of Nations. You could be part of protecting workers, ending child labor, advancing the cause of women through the world. You could be a peacemaker."

Finally Lucy smiled. "Why, yes, that sounds fine."

"Sure thing, you would. Now, no more of that *caqueterie,*" she winked, "that's French for nonsense—about marrying a miner." With that said, she twirled her long strand of beads and took her leave.

Exit, stage left. Leave with a flourish, because life is drama. Or is drama life?

MARGARET CLIMBED into her Fritchle electric car and motored more or less in the direction of the Brown Palace. No relation, the Mr. Brown who built it, but a fine hotel and pleasant place to live when she wasn't in Newport or Paris or the Barbizon in New York City. The weird vision from the morning was bothersome enough that she detoured along Pennsylvania Street to see the House of Lions, where she used to live, and still owned. Mrs. Grable, the house minder, assured her the boarders were upstanding people and they paid their rents on time. Still, it wouldn't hurt to check. Driving past she waved at the two lion statues guarding the empty porch. All fine and good. She drove on toward downtown.

The day was dimming as she pulled up to the red granite and sandstone hotel. It was a dowager of a place, grand and sturdy, like herself. Inside, the concierge welcomed her home. Lighted archways guided her to her room. That old geode still sat where she had left it, although the maid had tidied up and carried away the soiled china.

Marry a miner and get rich. She grunted to herself. Margaret had been born under a lucky star, that's for sure. J.J. had been a mere superintendent of mines at the Little Jonny silver mine in Leadville when she fell in love with him. He made a good enough living until the idiots in Washington repealed the Sherman Silver Purchase Act and put nine out of ten silver miners out of work just like that. But J.J. hadn't let Washington's stupidity ruin him.

Everybody called him a fool for suggesting they try again for gold, which still had value. "Petered out long ago," they sniffed. He dug deeper and they laughed. Then he struck it and they changed their tune. Called him a genius. It was part genius, part twenty years hard labor, and a whole lot of luck that brought up one hundred thirty-five tons of gold ore per day.

That gold bought them the House of Lions in Denver, her Avoca Lodge summer escape along Bear Creek, world travel and a lot of parties. Too bad J.J. had been such a fuddy-duddy about it all, not to mention a skirt chaser. So they'd separated and she set to doing good. The Cathedral of the Immaculate Heart would have stayed a hole in the ground if not rescued by their money and her pluck and energy. Poet Field's house would have been flattened.

Of course she couldn't afford to save the world all by herself. What she understood was that money begets money and separating rich people from it had been the joy of her life—still was.

Her Denver Woman's Club funded libraries and art for schools, established vegetable gardens for poor families, and public health clinics. They built a playground at what used to be John Brisben Walker's old River Front Amusement Park. They lobbied successfully for child labor laws and set up day care programs for working mothers. She worked to smash the system that put little children in cells with hardened horse thieves and safecrackers.

Money did so much good, and so much bad, too. Squabbles over it poisoned her relationships with her children, the little ones who'd fallen asleep to 'Wynken, Blynken and Nod.' J.J.'s legacy had been dying without a will, which had muddled everything. She hadn't actually seen him in years, but as his legal wife, she was entitled and still had a lot of good still left to do. Lawrence and Helen disagreed quite vehemently, fought her for years, but now that the estate was settled, things with them were on the mend a bit. Someday she would die, too, not soon she hoped. *Will I leave such a mess? And what will my legacy be?* She fell asleep wondering.

When the morning sun came through the window, she called down to room service for breakfast. In a never-ending effort to slim down, she ordered mere cornflakes and coffee, so it arrived quickly. With that finished, she dressed and tidied up her personal effects, the things the maid would not want to touch, such as Helen's gift, the old geode. A pain struck her head as she reached to put the rock back on the shelf. She dropped it. The geode fell open, purple crystals exposed.

She heard a woman's voice: "The world will always be a mess, my dear, and we women can never stop cleaning it all up."

༄

MAID SERVICE? Already?

Before her stands a woman not wearing a maid's uniform. How had she gotten in?

"My name is Sybylla. I'm a prophetess, let loose from your geode. Rather like the genie in the story of Aladdin you used to read to your children."

Margaret's familiar furnishings dissolve and reappear differently. The carpet and draperies transform into unfamiliar colors and fabrics. The bed and the chairs and her desk, all transmogrified. The Methodist Church outside her window looks pink, scrubbed free of gray soot like she's never seen it before.

Never afraid are we! This all must have something to do with the hallucinations. Caused by the geode and not the coffee?

"Have I finally fallen over the brink? Am I ready for the loony bin?"

"Not a mite," says Sybylla. "Put on your warm coat, warm gloves and sturdy footwear. We're going to see the future, in January."

"January is not much into the future."

"Twenty-first century January."

Twenty-first century? Preposterous! But an adventure! Still, she preferred Palm Beach, Florida, in the winter. "If we're going into the future, why not choose a warmer month?" she says, pulling a full-length chinchilla coat out of the hotel armoire.

"January is when the women march. Now, for the first time in your life, do as you're told."

Margaret laughs. This prophetess tells it like it is.

THERE IT IS, her morning hallucination in real life, a sea of women milling about the Colorado State Capital, many sporting those funny pink hats, and all in all very slovenly dressed, wearing what look like men's coats and miners' Levis. Her chinchilla must appear outrageously high fashion in this crowd. Most are toting placards, similar to the ones she used to carry at women's suffrage rallies in Newport, Rhode Island, before the Nineteenth Amendment passed. There had been little point protesting in Colorado where women got the right to vote in 1893, when she'd been a mere twenty-six.

Some of today's signs are befuddling; she doesn't understand what they mean. Others use decidedly unladylike words and images. Some she approves of:

Be the Change You Wish to See in the World. That could be her life's motto.

Nasty Women Keep Fighting. Boxing is good, fun exercise for women, although fighting for rights is more fun. She tries not to get too nasty, though.

Girl Power. The very thing she tried to stress to Lucy yesterday, but in fewer words.

A Woman's Place is in the House – and the Senate. If her sister's German husband hadn't been such an obstacle, she could have proven that true!

"Sybylla, what are we looking at?"

"A march for women's rights."

"Surely we've won equal rights by the twenty-first century!"

"No, my dear," says Sybylla. "Not quite."

"Has a woman won the presidency yet?"

"No, my dear," says Sybylla. "Not quite."

Margaret stamps her feet, partly to warm them up, partly in protest. "I should have run for president! I would have straightened out this country! I considered it, seriously I did. I would have won, too."

Margaret touches the shoulder of a woman walking past with a *Women's Rights are Human Rights* sign. "Why have we not had a woman president yet?" she asks. The marcher doesn't miss a step, doesn't even turn her head.

"You're not really here, my dear," says Sybylla. "No one can hear you or see you or feel your touch."

Well, that's a first.

"The struggle is not won! They need me here in the future. How do I join the march, Sybylla?"

"Your legacy lives," says Sybylla. "Your voice for women, and for workers and children, does live here in the future. Almost a hundred years into the future and you still get lots of attention. At your home. The House of Lions, that is. It's not such a long walk. Let's go."

Margaret huffs, curiosity compelling her to follow. Plus, she needs the exercise.

THE TWO LIONS sit proudly on either side of the porch steps, claws out, manes curled, just as always. The exterior looks the same, stout tan and red stone blocks with Queen Anne details and Romanesque arches. Margaret misses her home, even though it makes good financial sense to rent it out, seeing as how her travels take her away so much. *Took* her away so much. They are in the future now. It shouldn't be so hard to remember that, with so much changed, like that gawdawful hunk of cement across the street from her house. *What incompetent architect designed that building? What is it? Besides tasteless?*

A horde of scruffily-dressed people mill about her mosaic-floored porch. She disapproves of their casual demeanor, but they seem behaved well enough not to destroy anything. She hopes. A man comes out the front door, dressed somewhat like a butler, and ushers them all through her front door.

Inside looks a lot like she remembers, before the boarders took over, which is comforting, but her feet ache, so she heads straight to a chair. Just as she starts to lower herself, the butler says, in a tone of authority, "Please don't sit on the furniture."

Who does he think he is?

"He's not speaking to you, Mrs. Brown," says Sybylla. "Your home was purchased for preservation, just as you purchased Mr. Field's home. This man is a docent, leading a tour. You're not actually here."

Margaret lowers herself into the chair. The butler docent seems not to notice. *Ahhh.*

From her seat she sees her beautiful stained glass windows at the landing of the stairs. Like looking through a floral arbor at the sky. There's the elegant green embossed wallpaper, and the hall telephone where Mrs.

Grable bellered out her goings on, no matter how often she was chastised to be discreet. *Preserved pretty well, all things considered.*

The docent introduces a "special guest," Denver's Congresswoman. The woman waves in a friendly manner from the back of the tour group. *Congress*woman, *I like that.*

He starts Margaret's life story with her birth, of course, to progressive, abolitionist parents in Missouri. Her father had joined up with John Brown in his famous Christmastime raid, liberating eleven slaves, but that was before she was born. He sums up her childhood quickly and moves on to Leadville, where she married J.J. and struck it rich—eventually.

It doesn't take too long for him to get to the sinking of the Titanic, which is what everybody fixates on. His description brings to mind the all too real feel of the wet velvet sopping against her skin, the deep darkness after the ship's electric lights disappeared, only twinkling stars overhead, the stinging of ice shards in her lungs, the dank mineral smell of the iceberg, not exactly like the odor of a mine, but somehow bringing it to mind anyhow.

He describes how she and the other women on Lifeboat Six rowed to beat the band while the doom and gloom quartermaster sat shivering like an aspen, refusing to take an oar. "There's no use, the suction of the sinking ship will soon pull us under," the creature had whined. *I cannot think of him as a man, so craven he was. Almost wish I'd bumped him overboard.*

"We have a fighting chance!" she had countered, so the women fought hard and survived. *The docent tells the story pretty well, as accurate as need be.*

Even better is his account of the rescue. "Sprinkled among the affluent were our sisters of the second class," he quotes her. "And for a time there was that social leveling caused only by the close proximity of death." *Yes! I did say that. Ye, gods, we had some fun on the Carpathia, all together like that.*

The docent continues, telling of the funds she raised for the immigrants on board, who would be friendless and cashless upon docking. How she posted a list of which First Class survivors had and hadn't pledged. *Nothing like shame to separate rich people from their money!* The fund for the foreigners grew to over $10,000 by the time they docked.

"This is fun," she says to Sybylla. "But how is just a house a legacy?"

"Sixty-thousand people a year go through your house," Sybylla whispers. "Your stories are still relevant. Immigrants today struggle, too. Many still think of them as un-American, just as they did in your day. Your story of generosity is instructional. Some of these folks will think more kindly of today's immigrants, maybe even donate money."

The docent is moving on. Margaret rises from her chair to follow the scruffy horde to the library. *Our family encyclopedia! Still here!* Docent is talking about how much she loved reading, learning new languages, discovering foreign customs. Don't forget Carnegie college, she wants to say, and the Denver Woman's Club: "to study and to encourage the study, by women, of matters relating to the home, domestic relations, education, art, literature, music, science, philosophy, philanthropy, sociology and reform." *Ye gods it's frustrating to be here, mute while aware.* Still, it's not a bad tour.

A young woman raises her hand and the docent acknowledges her. "My great-grandmother met Margaret Brown. She liked to tell the story about how the 'Unsinkable' urged her to become somebody in her own right, not just a wife. She became a judge!"

"That's Lucy's great-granddaughter," says Sybylla.

Not a translator as I advised, but a worthwhile profession, when done with compassion.

The docent takes the opportunity to describe how Margaret teamed up with Judge Ben Lindsey and raised money for a separate juvenile justice system in Denver. *You have to be awfully hardboiled to put little children in cells with gangsters! Had to put a stop to that!*

How her Carnival of Nations Fundraiser, a celebration of the diversity of race, culture and language in the United States and throughout the world, raised more than $11,000 to get the Catholic cathedral off the ground. *People said the Carnival was to Denver what the World's Fair was to St. Louis!*

How she stood up to the Rockefellers after the Ludlow Massacre. *Heartless, they were, heartless!*

How she addressed an overflowing audience at Alva Vanderbilt's international conference on votes for women and even ran for Congress herself. *Too bad that last thing didn't pan out.*

My, my, what a wonderful hodge-podge my life has been! I found many opportunities to be useful and was glad to be. The less you think of yourself, the better off you are. Disturbing, though, how he never mentions anything after 1927. *Is it all soon to be over?*

The tour is like looking at one's life through a stereopticon, a few fascinating pictures, only the highlights, frozen in time.

When the docent finishes up, Margaret tells Sybylla she's not up for a walk back to the Brown.

Colorado Phantasmagorias

Sybylla offers to call for a Lyft. "It's like a taxi," she says.

"Feel free to use my telephone," Margaret offers, "It's still there on the wall inside the front door." But Sybylla is already tapping on a shiny wafer from her pocket. She shows Margaret a picture of a motor car and a driver. A minute later they climb into a small car, five minutes later they arrive back at the Brown Palace.

From her room telephone Margaret orders room service delivery of a corned beef Reuben. "It's my favorite." She offers the same to Sybylla, who declines to dine.

Margaret's shoes come off. She sets her feet on an ottoman, wiggles her toes in her stockings.

"Prophetess, how does it end?"

"End? Whatever do you mean? The cathedral was built, you know, and the pope even visited."

"The Pope! In Denver! I wish to live to see that!"

"You would be one hundred twenty-six years old before that happens. Even you, dear, aren't stubborn enough to live that long."

"How much longer do I have?"

"Ask rather about your legacy."

"Aren't you the wet blanket. The cathedral is a fine legacy, but go on, then, tell me more."

"The juvenile justice system continues to be separate from the adult criminal process, but there are still problems with the juvenile system.

"Ships are safer, thanks to the lobbying by you and the Survivor's Committee. Although most people travel by airplane. Passenger ships are nowadays floating resorts more than a means of travel.

"But there's always the danger of moving backwards. That's why the house tours are important, because people hear the stories of the Progressive Era. The reforms you fought for and the tragedies that led you to do them. Like the Ludlow Massacre."

"An unnecessary tragedy if there ever was one," says Margaret, frowning. "All those men from the depths wanted was to send their children to school, paychecks they could spend wherever they wanted, not just at the company store in the company town. Our Leadville was a mining town, too, but we had schools, newspapers, department stores, an opera house. Our miners got paid in real money! Such simple requests the coal miners in Ludlow made."

She shakes her head at the memory. "I was so peeved! At first I assumed those Rockefellers were like J.J., doing their best in a dangerous industry.

"J.J. was at least human. But that Rockefeller! He let his minions torch the tents where his miners lived—with their families! Two women, eleven children and an unborn baby, burned to death! I was in a fire, you know, a hotel fire in Florida. Led my fellow guests down the stairwell so we wouldn't get cooked. Fire is hell!

"I had never heard of such inhumanity to man. Went down to the Ludlow camp to see it myself. Organized nurses, raised money." She jabs an angry tear from her face, gets up from her chair, takes out a yellowed newspaper clipping from her desk and slaps on a pair of reading glasses.

"Here's what I told the press." She reads the clipping: "The solution is for the people of Colorado to rise in a body and demand Rockefeller put into practice that which he has been teaching his Sunday School class. For years, this man has stood before his class and told them the answer to an ancient biblical question. The question is, 'Am I my brother's keeper?' Now is the time that the entire state demand that he settle the strike."

She slams the clipping down. "Hypocrisy. I hate it."

Sybylla nods. "Mines are still dangerous, but less so, thanks to you and your progressive sisters. There are safety regulations, and union protections, and companies can no longer pay workers in scrip and evict them from their homes."

"Thank God," says Margaret, crossing herself. There's a knock on the door. A waiter slides in a tray with her sandwich. She peels off the top layer of bread. "Starch puts on unwanted pounds," she tells Sybylla. After a bite from her fork, she asks, "But no woman president yet?"

"Not yet."

"I could have won the presidency, I think, if circumstances had been different. 'The iron hand beneath the glove of glistening silk,' they called me. That's a winning slogan, I say." She licks a bit of dressing from her lips.

"Catchy," says Sybylla.

"Please tell me we at least managed a Negro president."

"African-American we say now, but yes, President Obama. Two terms."

"What *have* women achieved in politics?"

"About a quarter of the members of Congress and state legislatures are women."

Colorado Phantasmagorias

"Not enough. My friend Alva Vanderbilt says true change will only happen when women hold political office. And stand side by side with men on the battlefield, I say."

"There's progress there, too, women in combat today."

"The way it should be." Margaret sighs, pushing away her tray and folding her napkin. "Women are not the weaker sex. Miss Martin and I proved that on Lifeboat Six, rowing all night while that poltroon quartermaster just sat there. I served in the Ambulance Corps in France in 1914, too. But I was younger then, and I do tire these days." She rubs her eyes. "I've heard enough of the future. Allow me to prepare for bed. This day has been tiring, interesting, but very tiring. And my head hurts terribly."

"When you awake, I will be gone," says Sybylla. "You will be back in your own time."

Margaret retreats to her dressing station, returning in a white nightgown. She climbs into her bed.

Sybylla opens a book of Mr. Field's poems.

". . . So shut your eyes while Mother sings
    Of wonderful sights that be,
And you shall see the beautiful things
    As you rock in the misty sea
    Where the old shoe rocked the fishermen three:
        Wynken,
        Blynken,
        And Nod."

Epilogue

Margaret Brown summed up her own life this way: "I am a daughter of adventure. This means I never experience a dull moment and must be prepared for my eventuality. I never know when I may go up in an airplane and come down with a crash, or go motoring and climb a pole, or go off on a walk in the twilight and return all mussed up in an ambulance. That's my arc, as the astrologers say. It's a good one, too, for a person who had rather make a snap-out than a fade-out of life."

Margaret Tobin Brown died on August 26, 1932 at the Barbizon Hotel in New York City. She was sixty-five. Upon her death it was discovered she had been suffering from a brain tumor for some time. Although she had been legally separated from her husband since 1909, they never divorced and she is buried next to him at the Cemetery of the Holy Rood in New York.

Just the Facts, Ma'am

The quintessential biography of the real Margaret is *Molly Brown: Unraveling the Myth* by Kristen Iversen, updated 2010. This story relies heavily upon it, as does The Molly Brown House Museum. Margaret Brown's colorful personality and eventful life have inspired much mythology. The *Unsinkable Molly Brown* stage play and movie are fine entertainment, but even less historically accurate than this! For starters, they changed her name to Molly because it was easier to sing. In real life she was known only as Margaret or Mrs. J.J. Brown. I also recommend *Ladies of the Brown: A Women's History of Denver's Most Elegant Hotel* by Debra Faulkner; it's a fun read.

Just for Fun

The Molly Brown House, aka The House of Lions, at 1340 Pennsylvania Street in Denver has been accurately restored and furnished by Historic Denver based on photographs commissioned by Margaret herself. Many Margaret-owned artifacts from her life and travels are on display. A tour is well worth the admission price, and there's a wonderful gift shop. Open Tuesday through Sunday. Visit https://mollybrown.org/ for more information.

The beautiful and historic **Brown Palace Hotel,** 1730 Tremont Place, where Margaret lived when she was in Denver after renting out The House of Lions, offers tours two days each week. Overnight guests tour for free; the public is welcome for a fee. Reservations can be made online. Visit https://www.brownpalace.com. Margaret's favorite sandwich (Reuben) is on the menu of the Ship Tavern.

The **Eugene Field House** was moved to Washington Park (called Wash Park by the locals) in 1930 as stipulated by Margaret. The house was a public library for many years. Although the interior is no longer open to the public, you can still see it at 715 South Franklin Street. It's worth the visit just to see the adorable marble statue interpretation of Field's poem 'Wynken, Blynken, and Nod' on the lawn just north of the house. While you're there, walk the trails and enjoy the ducks on the ponds. If it's summer, you can rent bicycles or paddle boats, or just grab an ice cream. Wash Park was designated one of the Great Public Spaces in America in 2012 by the American Planning Commission.

Cathedral of the Immaculate Conception holds several masses every day, as well as concerts and events, including Friday Night at the Movies. It is located at the corner of Colfax and Logan in Denver.

Leadville is the highest city in the United States. Although much smaller than when Margaret and J.J. lived there, it's a fun day trip. The sprawling **National Mining Hall of Fame & Museum** at 120 W. 9th St., is a must-see where you'll learn about gold and silver mining (which made J.J. and Margaret rich) as well as coal, molybdenum and marble. The museum has an astonishing collection of really cool rocks and minerals. Since you're reading this book, be sure to see the giant amethyst geode. Then hike, bike, or ski the **Mineral Belt Trail.** Interpretive signs tell the stories of the ghost mines along the route. Stay at the historic **Delaware Hotel**, built in 1886 when Margaret and J.J. were still living in Leadville.

This final suggestion is meaningful, but probably not so 'fun.' The site of the **Ludlow Massacre**, on County Road 44 northwest of Trinidad, is a National Historic Landmark, one of only two such sites in the country commemorating labor history. The United Mine Workers of America, Local 9856, holds a memorial service in late June every year. While in the area, check out the **Trinidad History Museum**, 312 East Main Trinidad, CO, 81082.

Ralph Carr
1887 – 1950
Governor with Guts

THE HATE MAIL is piled so high Governor Carr worries it will avalanche to the floor. And that's just the afternoon delivery. More will arrive in the morning, and even more the next day, like it has for days.

Some of the invectives are practically chiseled into the paper, angry splats of all capital letters yelling, 'JAP LOVER!' More disturbing are the letters carefully penned in schoolmarm cursive, 'Someone will dig a lot of graves if the Japs come to Colorado.' Pearl Harbor has turned Coloradans jittery and a little hysterical.

What would Lincoln do?

Whenever he's in a quandary, Governor Carr thinks on what Honest Abe would do. He's working late. Staff offices are dark. The marble rotunda outside the Executive Chambers is empty. He puts his head in his hands. The governor straightens up in his chair, grabs a pen, puts it down again, picks it up, sets it down. He leans back, stares at the ceiling. Lincoln would counsel 'malice toward none.' Clearly, Coloradans aren't in the mood for that these days.

Carr fiddles with a rock on his desk. The geode's rough and ugly exterior, disguising the beautiful crystals inside, reminds him of old Scar-Faced Mag from his days in Cripple Creek. That poor woman was mocked on account of her fire-scarred skin. She should have been judged on her heart. He regrets not standing up for her back then, but he'd been just a curly-haired little boy the other kids called 'Sissy.'

Today thousands of Americans are being judged on their skin and their hair and their eyes, instead of their hearts. Race hatred hurts everyone.

What would Lincoln do?

Broken apart, the halves of the geode make two beautiful paperweights. He sets one on the pile of mail to keep it from crashing to the floor. He touches the crystals inside the other. Suddenly, inexplicably, he hears voices. Men talking. *Who's there?* The staff have all gone home.

He gets up from his desk and walks into the rotunda. No one's there, either. He returns to his office. *Is this controversy over the Japanese driving me crazy? Will I go straight from the governor's office to the state asylum in Pueblo?* The voices return. *Somebody must be outside. Perhaps a cleaning crew.*

He leaves his office again. The familiar brass rail and marble pillars are all as they should be, but there's a plaque between two arches. *How'd that get there?* He hadn't heard any workmen. A face on the plaque looks rather like himself, but when he inspects more closely, the thing turns blurry. He feels woozy.

Now men in suits appear, as if by magic, the men whose voices he's hearing. Two are heavy-set, bespectacled, fluffy-haired fellows like himself. Then there's a younger man with peaked eyebrows, another with friendly wrinkles about his eyes, a lanky man with scraggly hair, and one with pudgy cheeks. He walks over, but they pay him no mind, keep on jabbering, as if he's not even there.

Is this a diabetic hallucination? That would be disappointing. He's been avoiding sweets, and, in spite of his Christian Science practice, taking his insulin shots religiously.

A sense of camaraderie comes over him, a feeling that these imaginary men also are governors. He hears their voices again. They're all asking the same question:

What would Ralph Carr do?

He must telephone his doctor.

Back at his desk, he reassembles the two halves of the geode and stuffs the hate mail into a drawer. The voices dissipate. He leaves again to inspect the rotunda. Empty. He feels sensible again. Health crisis averted, no need to bother the doctor.

Then he asks himself:

What *would* Ralph Carr do?

Ralph Carr would rise above bigotry.

He puts pen to paper. He has minds to change and hearts to soften.

༄

**Colorado State Capitol
February, 1942**

HIS RADIO MESSAGE last December, less than a day after the attack on Pearl Harbor, was not the most politically-astute thing Governor Ralph Carr had ever done.

"We have among us many of a new generation of Japanese people, born in the United States, sincere, earnest, and loyal people. I want to caution the defense council against taking the attitude that because a man may be brown-skinned, he is our enemy. We must be sensible about these things," he had said over the airwaves. The attack in Hawaii had been too hot on every Coloradan's mind, burning through their hearts, at least in the short run. He realized that now. Still, he didn't regret saying it.

The letter he wrote to the *Pacific Citizen* newspaper had been even worse political folly. "To the American citizens of Japanese parentage, we look for example and guidance. To those who have not been so fortunate as to have been born in this country, we offer the hand of friendship, secure in the knowledge that they will be as truly American as the rest of us," Carr told the readers of the Japanese-American newspaper. Never mind the consequences, he didn't regret that, either.

Nevertheless, now was the time to do damage control. In the past couple months it had become clear that his fellow Coloradans misunderstood him. The *Denver Post's* editors hadn't helped clarify. Instead of explaining the constitutional implications to their readers, they just called him 'Mr. Softy' and a 'sappy sentimentalist.'

Soft but stubborn. He would make a speech better explaining his position. But he would not back down, no matter how high the mountain of hate mail, no matter how raging the river of ink the *Denver Post* poured out against him. He hadn't wanted this governor job in the first place, but since he had it, he would do what was right. He would lead.

RALPH CARR had come a long way from his birth in little Rosita, Colorado, and a childhood moving from one mining town to another. Fresh out of college he'd been a journalist, then a small-town lawyer in Antonito. He'd devoted eleven years to settling farmer disputes, writing wills, reading law books, and fishing for trout on the Conejos River. As lovely as the San Luis Valley was, he'd been happy for the higher salary that came with moving to

Colorado Phantasmagorias

the big city of Denver. He and Gretchen had two kids, Bob and Cynthia, and they were going to need college tuition.

Working for the state's Attorney General, his focus had been water law. Then he was named U.S. Attorney for Colorado and had some fun capturing bootleggers and gangsters. When Gretchen died, he found himself raising teenagers alone. Being governor had not been on his agenda. Not. At. All.

Who would have expected his Grand Old Party to descend into complete chaos, just when the Democratic governor Teller Ammons was ripe for defeat? Well, frankly, anybody who knows politics. Even so, when he took Bob to Colorado Springs for the 1938 State Republican Convention, it was just supposed to be a father-son trip, a vacation at the fancy Antlers Hotel, a chance for Bob to see the hurly-burly of democracy up close. Vote after vote after vote yielded no viable candidate. When Carr overheard his own name bandied about on the floor, he grabbed Bob by the collar and they high-tailed it back to Denver.

But he could not escape the telephone. It rang off the proverbial hook. Party big-wigs harassed him mercilessly until he drove back down to the Springs.

"I'll do it under two conditions," Carr told them.

"Name your conditions," said the men.

"One, I'm not going to raise money. The party has to do that for me. And two, I'm going to call my own shots. I won't be beholden to anybody. If I'm elected, I'll always do what I think is right."

"You got it," said the men.

His name was submitted from the floor. The enthusiasm was ear-splitting, the vote lopsided in his favor. The *Denver Post* wrote, 'Nobody has any strings on Ralph Carr.' The editors really liked him back then. He campaigned on fiscal responsibility and ethical leadership. He was elected and reelected with bipartisan support. Now the people of Colorado got exactly what they'd asked for.

He was doing what he thought was right.

JAPANESE-AMERICANS would remember his radio message and his interview with the *Pacific American*.

Two months after the attack on Pearl Harbor, President Roosevelt issued Executive Order 9066, ordering the evacuation of one hundred twenty thousand Japanese-Americans from the west coast. Two-thirds were

American citizens. The idea was for the Japanese-Americans to move voluntarily to interior states. But how does a family pull up stakes and move to some totally foreign place with no job, no home, no farm?

Carr figured Colorado would be a fine destination. He knew of Japanese farmers already scattered about on the eastern plains and San Luis Valley. The Japanese in the tiny town of La Jara had even built themselves a Buddhist temple, helped by donations from their Christian neighbors. They'd been farming potatoes and cauliflower in the valley for almost twenty years. La Jara was just fourteen miles up the road from Antonito. He'd still been the Conejos County Attorney when the first Japanese families arrived in the Twenties. They had impressed him. Hardworking, law abiding.

Until Pearl Harbor, his friends in Conejos County used to tease him: "We know how you taught yourself Spanish when you lived down here, *Rafaelito*. If you'd stayed any longer, you would've learned Japanese, too!"

Nobody was cracking jokes anymore. Thousands of Japanese-Americans were moving voluntarily, as the government expected them to do, hundreds to Colorado. People talked like it was millions. 'Yellow horde' they said. That kind of talk made him sick.

A hundred Japanese people in Pueblo signed a loyalty pledge. The Japanese American Citizens League of rural Blanca collected several tons of scrap metal for the war effort. Good citizens and patriots deserved to be treated as such, but they weren't.

And not enough were leaving the west coast voluntarily. The feds were getting antsy. Now came the distinct probability that involuntary evacuation would be the next step. The War Relocation Authority was considering evacuation centers, concentration camps, for Japanese-Americans. Carr balked. Locking up innocent citizens was against everything the U.S. Constitution stood for.

"The suggestion that an American citizen would be seized, deprived of his liberty, or otherwise placed under restraint without charge of misconduct and a hearing is unthinkable," Carr had said.

Apparently, not only was it thinkable, there seemed to be no stopping it. The country was going to force innocent citizens into camps. Carr thought on it some more. The scheme was unconstitutional, reprehensible, but in Colorado he could make sure they were treated as civilly as possible.

The WRA called a meeting of the western states governors. Milton Eisenhower explained the scheme. All ten of Carr's fellow governors responded: Hell No. Not because they disagreed with concentration camps, which Carr did. They were gung-ho for locking up innocent people. Just not in their states. Because they hated Japanese.

Carr said yes.

CONFIDENT AND OPTIMISTIC by nature, Carr was convinced that, in time, the good people of Colorado would recognize the loyalty of their Japanese-American neighbors, old and new. In the meantime, he would appeal to their patriotism and sense of duty. He would go on the radio again, this time with more aforethought. He'd spent a long night at the capitol writing out a fine speech. Damage control with integrity. He was ready.

The radio sound booth had the aura of a cloister. He cleared his voice to break the silence. The station technician adjusted the microphone in front of him. Behind glass a producer raised one finger, two, then three fingers . . .

"People of Colorado," he began, imagining thousands of good Coloradans gathered around their radio sets.

He started with patriotism: "Our people have sent their dearest possessions to the ten or a dozen battlefronts where the Stars and Stripes are leading the fight on savagery, paganism, and the worldwide imposition of servitude upon free men . . . Colorado must never be charged with a failure to cooperate in the gravest moment of our nation's history." He reminded them of their responsibility to the war effort: "If any enemy aliens must be transferred as a war measure, then we of Colorado are big enough and patriotic enough to do our duty. We announce to the world that one million one hundred eighteen thousand red-blooded citizens of this state are able to take care of three thousand five hundred or any number of enemies, if that be the task which is allotted to us."

If he had stopped there, maybe the hate mail would have stopped, too. Maybe. But Ralph Carr would not allow bigotry to remain unchallenged. He kept going.

"In justice and fairness, let us pause here to speak a word on behalf of loyal German, Italian, and Japanese citizens who must not suffer for the activities and animosities of others. In Colorado there are thousands of men and women and children—in the nation there are millions of them—who by reason of blood only, are regarded by some people as unfriendly. They are as loyal to American institutions as you and I. Many of them have been here—are American citizens, with no connection with or feeling of loyalty toward the customs and philosophies of Italy, Japan or Germany. The world's great melting pot is peopled by the descendants of every nation on the globe. It is not fair for the rest of us to segregate the people from one or two or three nations and to brand them as unpatriotic or disloyal regardless. The coming of these evacuees will, of necessity, give rise to social problems, to business and labor questions, and similar vexing issues. But surely we possess the brains, the resources, the solid American character which will enable us to solve these problems properly and intelligently. . . People of Colorado, let us all be good soldiers. . . . "

GOOD SOLDIERS were not what Coloradans were in the mood to be, or so it seemed from the mail that continued spewing into his office, like this: 'Over thousands of protests, he, claiming his was his Patroitic Duty, stated Colorado would be able to take thousands of Japanese (and since they multiply like rats think what it will be like in 20 years from now). . .'

He could excuse the typographical spelling error, but not the race hatred.

Surely these writers did not speak for the majority of Coloradans. Fair-minded, patriotic, church-going citizens understood their duty. The Council of Churches and a few pastors praised his views. So did his head of Agriculture, and the Colorado Federation of Labor. The majority just weren't bothering to write letters. He believed that. He had to. There was a war to win.

Armies march on their stomachs, and Colorado had acres of sugar beets, and a God-given duty to supply the boys overseas. A bit of sweetener for their coffee, a chocolate bar, soldiers and sailors deserved at least that. But the farm boys were getting drafted. Beet seedlings had to be thinned by hand, then weeded with hoes. The work was hot and dirty and if Japanese families from the west coast would come to Colorado to do it, the country should be grateful. Better than letting valuable cropland lay idle, or, as the *Rocky Ford Gazette* suggested, exempt all farm boys from the draft. Keep the strongest young men out of uniform? The U.S. may as well surrender straight away.

Most troubling of all were the leaders of his own party. At a meeting in the Brown Palace Hotel, they gave him an angry earful. He reminded them of what he'd said when they recruited him to run four years before. He would always do what he thought was right.

Colorado Phantasmagorias

"I've stuck my neck out on matters of policy," he said, "but I'm making no apologies because I believe I am right. Colorado leads the western states on this."

He walked back to his office from the Brown, sick to death of hearing innocent people accused of being murderers, rapists, robbers and spies—only on account of the shape of their eyes and the tint of their skin. He could not stand to hear 'yellow peril' one more time. He picked up the geode paperweight.

What will it take to convince Coloradans that I am right?

❧

"TIME, GOVERNOR CARR. It takes time. As you yourself say, it takes years, sometimes generations, to wipe out prejudices and ill-feeling."

A strange man seems to have magically appeared in his doorway. *How did he get past my receptionist?* Mr. Robinson escorts all guests into the governor's office. Nobody just walks in unannounced.

Carr stands up. "Mr. Robinson!" he shouts. "George!" No answer.

Carr's knees buckle, his vision blurs, the carpet changes color. *Another hallucination.* He really must have his blood sugar checked. Cynthia and Bob already lost their mother. It would not do to let diabetes take their father as well.

"It's not your health, Governor Carr," says the stranger. "Please allow me to introduce myself, sir. My name is Mancio. I'm a seer released from your geode to show you the future."

Carr sits, reaches for the telephone.

Mancio puts his hand over the governor's. "Look outside," he says.

It seems the intruder won't take no for an answer. Carr swivels his chair. Looks past the drapes. His vision is sharp again. On the other side of Civic Center Park is the familiar curve of the Denver City and County Building. The trees in the park are barren, too early to be budded out. Patches of snow litter the brown grass. Hardy pigeons strut about. It seems familiar and unfamiliar at the same time. He squints through his spectacles. There's a red obelisk he does not recognize, and far too many motor vehicles on Colfax and Broadway, vehicles of peculiar design. Most astonishing is what's to the south across Fourteenth Street. An entire building that shouldn't be there, a glass-domed gray edifice, more imposing even than the Capitol itself. *What in heaven's name is that building?*

Inscribed above sturdy pillars, chiseled in gold script, are the words: 'Liberty and Justice for All.'

Not true. For the Japanese Americans, there will be neither liberty nor justice. He hopes, though, to preserve a few of their rights and a bit of compassion.

"That's the Ralph Carr Judicial Center," says Mancio, pointing toward the gray edifice. "Home of the Colorado Supreme Court and Court of Appeals."

"You're full of it. Who do you claim to be? Who are you, Mancio?"

"Think of me as a metaphysical being. As a Christian Scientist, you are familiar with the primacy of the mental world over the physical. I'm letting your mind of today experience the matter of the future."

"You do not understand the theology taught by the founder of Christian Science, Mary Baker Eddy."

"Probably not. But I do see the future. I know your legacy."

Carr fights the hallucination. He does not want to burden his children with a lunatic father. It's no use. He needs to know. "And what is that? What is my legacy?"

"Integrity. Just as you always ask yourself, 'What would Lincoln do?' Colorado governors ask themselves, 'What would Ralph Carr do?'"

The voices from his late-night hallucination. That is what he thought he'd heard them saying. "What would Ralph Carr do?"

"In the future, Colorado governors look out their window, see the gold script, and are reminded of what you stood for. Liberty and justice for all."

"You talk like I'm a saint. I'm no saint. Talk to Bob and Cynthia. They'll tell you my faults."

"Not a saint, but a civic inspiration. And if your memory inspires politicians to behave with a little more integrity than they'd otherwise be inclined to do, aren't you glad to have left such a legacy?"

Carr folds his arms across his chest. "It seems dishonest."

"You think Lincoln was perfect? He wasn't, but you look to his legacy for wisdom."

Carr knows it must be true. Nobody's perfect. "Where did that plaque come from? The one with my face on it? By the flags outside my office? Where all the ghosts huddled the other night?"

"Ghosts? Oh, I suppose the gaggle of governors could be called ghosts," Mancio answers. "The plaque is placed in 1974 by the Japanese Community of Colorado. The men you saw and heard, they are the governors who have served since that sign went up."

The Japanese community would not honor a man who let their people be incarcerated in his state. "The concentration camp, relocation center I mean, does that not get built in Colorado?"

"Yes, it gets built, Mr. Carr, near Granada. Over ten thousand Japanese Americans live at Camp Amache over the course of the war."

"Ten thousand!?! I was told thirty-five hundred!"

"Put on your overcoat and hat. We're going to the eastern plains."

This strange man, Mancio, seems not to respect a governor's time or inclinations. Carr has barely got his arms in the sleeves of his overcoat before he finds himself magically transported to the flat, sage-studded, wind-whipped Colorado prairie. He puts his hand on his head to keep his fedora from blowing into Kansas.

There's nothing here, not counting ragged rangeland and endless sky. How'd they get here? What is this place?

Mancio reads his mind. "This is the site of the Granada Relocation Center, which the Postal Service calls Camp Amache to keep the mail separate from the town of Granada. Ten thousand Japanese Americans, two-thirds of them citizens, live and work here during the war. No more than seven thousand at one time, but more than that come and go. Amache becomes one of Colorado's biggest cities, while it lasts. It has a farm, livestock, a poster-making shop. Even a high school. In fact, one of the governors you saw in your late-night vision, one who looks rather like yourself, plays football for Holly High School against the Amache team. Governor Roy Romer."

Carr knows this is craziness, but as a sports fan, he has to ask. "Who wins?"

"Amache. Seven to nothing."

"Well, well, isn't that something?"

"Never mind the high school sports, Amache is still a concentration camp. Accommodations are meager, sand blows through every crack, mess hall food is awful. But you do your best to give the residents as much freedom as you can, considering that the federal government puts up barbed wire and points guns into the camp. The Japanese leave with permission, to shop or for work. One resident even sets up a sashimi shop in Granada."

"What's sashimi?"

"Raw fish."

"The Japanese prefer raw fish to what's served in the camp mess?"

"It's traditional. Delicious."

Trout fishing is the governor's favorite pastime. But he always grills his catch.

Setting aside the fish issue, he has more important questions. "I have to know. Do we win the war? And then what?"

"Not to worry on that score, Governor Carr! The allies win the war. Both theaters. European theater against Italy and Germany, Pacific theater against the Empire of Japan. The allies win both."

"What happens to our Japanese when the war is over?"

"Amache internees are released. Camp buildings are sold off or torn down. We try to forget that we took away the constitutional rights of our own citizens. We're ashamed. We want it all to blow over."

"Literally," says Carr, pulling his coat close against the wind. He raises his voice over the howl. "We're right to be ashamed. So I can't help wondering, why do the Japanese Americans honor me, when they are incarcerated here on my watch? And why name the Judicial Center after me, when liberty is taken away and justice ill-served within the borders of my state?"

"Because when anyone asks, 'What would Ralph Carr do?' the answer is always, Ralph Carr would rise above bigotry."

Epilogue

Ralph Carr did not run for a third term (governorships were just two years back then). In the summer of 1942, when Camp Amache was opening its gates for its first residents, he began his campaign for U.S. Senate instead. He lost. In a year when just about every other Republican candidate in Colorado won, Carr's support for the rights of Japanese Americans cost him too many votes.

One of Carr's last acts as he was leaving the Governor's Mansion was to call Amache Camp and ask them to release a Japanese American to keep house for him at his personal home at 747 Downing Street in Denver. He met 27-year-old Wakako Domoto's bus personally and told her he was a tidy man with few housekeeping needs, so she should enroll in Emily Griffith Opportunity School, which she did. "She is fitted into the picture

Colorado Phantasmagorias

admirably, and is meeting every situation in a manner which calls for intelligence, tact and ability," Carr wrote to the WRA.

He was appointed Regent to the University of Colorado, the *alma mater* of himself and his two children. He described CU as 'the most beautiful campus in the world.' He ran again for governor in 1950, but died from complications of diabetes before the election. He is buried at Fairmount Cemetery.

It took a generation for Coloradans to recognize Governor Carr appropriately for his integrity at a time of hysteria. Coloradans of Japanese heritage led the way, installing the plaque in the State Capitol in 1974. A bronze bust and epitaph on a large plinth was also placed in Sakura Square at Nineteenth and Larimer in downtown Denver, next to a similar monument to Carr's friend, Minoru Yasui, a Japanese-American who fought laws that directly targeted Japanese-Americans after Pearl Harbor. There's also a monument to Governor Carr on Kenosha Pass.

The stated rationale for depriving Japanese Americans of their constitutional rights was to prevent sabotage and espionage. That fear proved unfounded as no such acts by Japanese Americans were ever discovered. The head of the relocation project, Milton Eisenhower (Ike's brother), later called it "an inhuman mistake." In 1983, the U.S. Commission on Wartime Relocation and Internment of Civilians condemned the internment of innocent Americans of Japanese origin or ancestry as unjust and motivated by racism. Reparation payments to surviving internees were authorized in 1988 and 1992.

Just the Facts, Ma'am

Adam Schrager's ***The Principled Politician: The Ralph Carr Story*** is a deeply researched and easy to read biography. A shorter biography is included in ***Pioneers & Politicians: 10 Colorado Governors in Profile*** by former Governor Richard D. Lamm and Duane A. Smith. ***Amache: The Story of Japanese Internment in Colorado During World War II*** by Robert Harvey and ***Colorado's Japanese Americans from 1886 to the Present*** by Bill Hosokawa are also recommended. For younger readers, ***Ralph Carr: Defender of Japanese Americans*** by Jamie Trumbull is part of the Great Lives of Colorado History Series. ***Amache***, a Rocky Mountain

PBS documentary, is excellent and can be streamed at https://video.rmpbs.org/video/colorado-experience-amache-1-hour-special/.

Amache was the smallest of the ten internment camps set up by the WRA during World War II. Ironically, the other western governors who told the WRA "hell no," got bigger camps. Amache was also the least restrictive. Passes for work and shopping were granted more freely than at other camps and the small town of Granada (population 350 at the time) was within walking distance. Although not everyone was open-minded, smart businesses in Granada and Lamar welcomed this influx of new customers, especially after the hard years of the Great Depression. The drugstore in Granada built a soda fountain and ordered a shipment of sake from California. Ed Newman, proprietor of the Newman Drug Store in Granada, donated basketball uniforms to the Amache team.

But as the camp quickly grew to become the tenth largest city in Colorado, the small-town businesses could not keep up. Amache residents opened a co-op store at the camp, and Granadans went there to buy shoes and other items not available for sale in their tiny town.

A large, but not lavish, high school was built for Amache students. This expenditure was wildly controversial, both because the students were Japanese Americans ("enemies" some said) and because the school would be temporary. It had 24 classrooms, an auditorium, library, vocational shops, and staff offices for 850 students in grades 7-12. The 1,000 children in grades 1-6 made do in makeshift barracks classrooms.

Amache had a print shop that churned out patriotic posters for the Navy, and its own 5,000-acre vegetable farm, plus chickens, hogs, cows and a dairy. A large number of residents worked for local farmers or took other odd jobs outside the barbed wire.

A thousand Amache residents volunteered for service in World War II, in spite of the fact that their own country had deprived them of their constitutional rights. Japanese Americans fought in Italy, France and Germany or, if they could speak Japanese, served in Military Intelligence. The 442nd Regimental Combat Team was the most decorated unit in the Army for its size. Its motto was 'Go for Broke.'

Colorado Phantasmagorias 93

Governor Carr was also unique among governors in offering the University of Colorado at Boulder as a site for the Navy Officer Japanese Language School. Japanese American instructors taught their language to 685 Navy and Marine officers and WAVES (Women Accepted for Voluntary Emergency Service).

In addition to Camp Amache, which housed innocent civilians, Colorado had forty-three POW camps for captured German and Italian soldiers. The largest were at Greeley, Trinidad, and Colorado Springs. The others were satellite camps.

Just for Fun

It's a long drive to Granada from most places, but totally worth it if you love history. The **Amache Museum** has a mouth-dropping treasure trove of artifacts, including a stack of actual suitcases brought by evacuees from California to Granada, paintings and carvings created at the camp by evacuees, a uniform donated by an Amache veteran, a cask that once contained soy sauce (you can still smell it!), and much more. The museum is usually open five days a week in the summer, and on demand during the school year. The University of Denver operates a field school during July of even-numbered years which may affect operation days of the museum. The docents at the museum can advise you on the best way to experience the actual Amache site. There you'll see the remains of foundations, a reconstructed barracks, guard tower and water tower. The little cemetery is a heartbreaking collection of children's graves and a monument to the 31 Amache patriots killed in action during World War II fighting with the 442nd Army Infantry Regiment. Drive west from Granada and turn south on County Road 23 5/10. The entrance is just past W. Amache Road. Check out www.amache.org. If a trip to Granada isn't possible, **History Colorado** at 1200 Broadway in Denver has a permanent Amache exhibit with artifacts, displays, video and a replica of the living quarters. Be forewarned, the replica is inaccurately roomy, in order to make it accessible for wheelchairs, an ahistorical accommodation for which you can blame Coloradan Wade Blank, also profiled in this volume.

A block away is the magnificent **Ralph Carr Colorado Judicial Center** with its interactive Learning Center on the Rule of Law. Want to know what it's like to be a judge? Here you'll be given facts and law and asked "What would you decide?" Across the street is the State Capitol, where the plaque to Governor Carr hangs outside the Executive Chambers. The **Colorado State Capitol** building is open to the public from 7:30 a.m. - 5:00 p.m. Monday through Friday, except legal holidays. Fiction readers will enjoy *Tallgrass,* a novel by Colorado author Sandra Dallas, that illuminates the complexities of smalltown Granada during the Amache years.

Most evacuees returned to California after the war, but a few stuck around and established businesses where you can still **shop** and **eat** today. Down by Centennial Airport and the Broncos Dove Valley Training Center is the massive and impressive **Tagawa Gardens** retail garden center and flower shop at 7711 S. Parker Road in Centennial. Way north on the other side of the Denver metro area is **Lafayette Florist Gift Shop and Garden Center** founded by the Yoshihara family, in Old Towne Lafayette (600 S. Public Road). The two-story floral and gift shop is the highlight, but they also offer shrubs, bedding plants and garden supplies. Times being what they are, some of their greenhouses have been converted to growing hemp for CBD.

To experience the food that your parents and great-grandparents enjoyed, sit down at the comfy and retro **Twentieth Street Café** at 1123 20th Street in downtown Denver. A Maneki Neko (ceramic beckoning cat) in the window and a noodle bowl at the bottom of the menu are the only clues that a family named Okuno bought this restaurant after release from Amache. Japanese cuisine would have been a hard sell in the 1940s, so they stuck with American comfort food, a tradition that continues today. The open-faced sliced beef sandwich on white bread with brown gravy and mashed potatoes is an absolute blast from the past.

Catty-corner from the cafe is **Sakura Square**, home of the **Tri-State Denver Buddhist Temple**, 1947 Lawrence Street, offering religious services (in English and Japanese), education and a book shop. Www.tsdbt.org has all the info you need.

Next door, the amazing **Pacific Mercantile Company**, 1925 Lawrence Street, is Denver's premier Asian market. The founding Inai family were interned at various concentration camps in California before moving to Denver in 1944.

Colorado Phantasmagorias

The **Cherry Blossom Festival** is celebrated every June at Sakura Square in downtown Denver. Free dancing, music, and martial arts demonstrations are presented live on stage. Enjoy Japanese food, sake, and craft beer. Clothes, toys, traditional crafts and modern kitsch and anime are for sale. The Buddhist Temple is open during the festival. The Bonsai are really worth seeing. Visit https://cherryblossomdenver.org for information.

Every August brings the most delicious **Rocky Ford cantaloupe** to stores. Governor Carr probably enjoyed some grown by **Hirakata Farms**, as you still can. Japanese immigrant Tatsunosuke Hirakata started growing melons just west of Granada in 1915 and the farm is still owned and operated by the family.

The grand and historic **Antlers Hotel** at 4 Cascade Ave. in Colorado Springs, where Ralph Carr was drafted to run for governor in 1938, is still beautiful, open for guests, and within walking distance of shops and restaurants in downtown Colorado Springs.

There are fun ways to honor Ralph Carr's life in the mountains, too. Take a scenic drive along Highway 285 over **Kenosha Pass** and stop at the monument dedicated in 2010 by Resolution of the Colorado General Assembly (legislature) with funds from the Colorado Asian Pacific Bar Foundation and private donors. It's located just over the crest if you're coming from Denver, or just before the crest coming from Fairplay. The Colorado Trail goes over Kenosha Pass, and there are day hikes for all experience levels. It's a bit beyond the monument, and there's parking for hikers on both sides of the highway. Columbines and Indian Paintbrush are easy to spot in the spring and early summer. Bright yellow Aspen groves make the hikes especially pretty in the fall.

Like **trout fishing**? Governor Carr enjoyed fishing the Conejos River by Antonito, and there are many fishing spots throughout the state. If you own your own waders, rod, tackle box and creel, all you need is to find a map online. Not outfitted? A professional fishing guide will get you all set up. Once you've landed and cleaned your catch, pan-fry it like Ralph Carr would have done: *Beat a couple eggs with milk, dip your fish through it; Dredge the fish in a mixture of equal parts saltine crumbs, corn meal and parmesan cheese; Sprinkle with pepper, and garlic powder if you like that; Fry in hot oil for 2-3 minutes.*

Wade Blank
1940–1993
Disability Rights Radical

With Michael Patrick Smith, the Gang of Nineteen, and Jennifer Keelan

DOWN WITH the establishment! The hippies got that right. The Rev. Wade Blank is angry. Years of letters, petitions, meetings and courtrooms have got his people zero justice.

The revolution starts today.

Wade sets down his morning coffee, picks up his good luck charm, the geode his friend Mike Smith gave him. "This reminds me of you, Wade," he said. "Rough on the outside, beautiful inside."

It all started with those damn poems of Mike's.

"The future stood before him but was out of his reach," the brilliant, disabled poet wrote while imprisoned in a nursing home. And then the muscular dystrophy took him away.

Well, today is for Mike, may he rest in peace, and for all the disabled people still alive and yet to be born. Today they reach for the future. Power to the people!

The reverend lets the broken halves of the souvenir rock fall open. Jagged crystals sparkle in the morning sun. They're purple like the stole he once wore on his shoulders, the liturgical color of repentance, a spiritual practice on which he spends little time. If fighting for justice pisses people off, well, tough shit. Jesus was a table flipper. That attitude cost Wade his church job. As if he cares. He's still ordained. And today he's answering a call from God. To free God's disabled children, God's disabled adults.

Wade flicks his wrist and checks the time. A few minutes to spare. He tucks his t-shirt into his jeans, combs his fingers through his long, lanky blond hair, touches the purple crystals.

All at once, weird perceptions prickle his senses. Humidity envelops the room. He smells sweat, hears a child's voice yelling. *Something about steps?*

Strange images swirl before his eyes, like he's on sacramental peyote. Video cameras, flashbulbs, people chained together. He hears singing.

What the hell? Is this a divine vision? Unlikely. God doesn't send visions to Presbyterians.

Then a row of suits. *Gawd, I really can't stand those kind of guys.* He feels spray as if from a fountain. Smells roses. Hears applause. Silver pens flash in the sunshine.

He shakes his head to clear it, takes a deep breath, grabs the bag hanging from the back of his chair and stuffs the rock into it. The hallucinations disappear. He'd better get going. The gang is assembling.

They have buses to block.

ဢ

Denver
July 5, 1978

ONE BY ONE, the Atlantis Community residents wheeled onto the sidewalk at the corner of Colfax and Broadway, the busiest intersection in Denver. Not long ago, most of them rarely saw the out of doors, cooped up inside, strapped down sometimes. Today they were laughing, smiling, high-fiving, spinning circles, those who could. Wade walked through the group, greeting each by name.

"Linda, good to see you.

"Terri, glad you could make it.

"George, I knew you'd be up for this.

"Willy, ready for a long day?"

And so on, down the line, Carolyn, Mel, Debbie, Kerry, Lori, Bob, Cindy, Renate, Mary Ann, Bobby, Jeannie, Jim, Glenn, Larry, and Paul.

Some of the gang sat up straight in the way society considered dignified. Others flopped sideways over the armrests in the way God created them to do. Some of the women wore lipstick. A few of the men looked like they had never made acquaintance with a comb. The Gang of Nineteen was a motley crew. And destined to get motlier. The day was heating up fast, road dust churned in the air.

Wade watched the cars roll along Colfax and Broadway, looked through the windshields at the drivers, imagined what they were thinking: *What are all the gimps doing on the street? What's up with the cripples?*

People with muscular dystrophy, spinal cord injuries and the like didn't normally wheel around city streets. They stayed home, or, God help them, in a nursing facility. Not that the drivers had a clue what disability any of the gang had, but able-bodied people 'just knew' the last thing a 'wheelchair bound' person wanted to do was parade around in public. Everybody knew that.

Everybody but the gang in the chairs. And Wade.

He watched the drivers scratching their heads, craning their necks out the side windows.

They have no idea. Just wait.

The revolution was starting.

IT ACTUALLY BEGAN seven years ago. A few young people wanted to watch TV, listen to rock 'n' roll, and eat food that required chewing. A poet wanted his poems written down.

Wade had needed a fresh start. His church congregation in Ohio insisted on more pomp, less protest. So he headed west. Heritage House Nursing Home in Lakewood, Colorado, offered him a job where he could do some good. The big, old state institutions were shutting down. Disabled people were let out to live in their home communities. Seemed like a progressive move. Family could more easily visit if their relatives lived in the hometown. Heritage saw a need to fill. The nursing home would open a Youth Wing. Administration hired Wade to recruit and manage the young residents. He was perfect for the job. Young, hip, long hair and all. But ordained, steady, levelheaded and all that.

Or so they thought.

Wade recalled those Heritage smells. Urine and antiseptic. And then that first meal. Baked potatoes, applesauce and scrambled eggs. Cold. The old folk, with teeth worn out from a lifetime of steak and corn on the cob, may have been grateful, or maybe not. But the young people, for all their other maladies, had strong enough teeth. He could make a difference here.

He started by asking them a question they'd never been asked before: What do *you* want?

Pizza, for starters.

And to choose their own clothes, and their own radio stations.

Then he hit the road. *Seek and ye shall find.* And find he did, young people with cerebral palsy and spina bifida still trapped in institutions. Amputees and accident survivors with brain injuries unable to leave rehab centers. He

Colorado Phantasmagorias

gave them the good news of Heritage Youth Wing. Twenty, forty, sixty residents, then a waiting list.

After cranking up the rock 'n' roll radio and replacing the squishy food, Wade fought the 8:00 drug-induced bedtime. He brought in a TV and tuned it to *Laugh-In* instead of *Lawrence Welk*. The place rocked like a college dorm.

He got a van to haul them and their chairs. They headed to the mountains, wheeled around in the dirt, smelled the pine, felt the spray from waterfalls, heard the crackle of campfire, ate s'mores. They cheered at baseball games. Hooted at professional wrestling matches. Went out for ice cream.

The effort involved in getting them into concert venues would have challenged the biblical Samson, but was totally worth it. They rocked with the Grateful Dead at the Denver Coliseum, sang 'Rocky Mountain High' along with John Denver at Red Rocks. Some with gusto, others croaked it out.

It wasn't enough. Nothing could ever be enough. No amount of ice cream and music can fix a prison. A prison for the innocent. How can you make a nursing home acceptable? You just can't. What they needed was freedom. So he moved them out. Eighteen to start.

Like the Presbyterian Church before them, Heritage House thought they'd hired a progressive and got a radical instead. A crazy. He got fired. And fired up.

Severely disabled people, living on their own. Making their own decisions. Wade helped them with dressing, toileting, whatever they needed. More people got set free. Apartment doors were widened, counters lowered. Attendants were hired to help. Whatever assistance a person needed, they figured out a way. They pooled their Medicaid and SSI, shared. Atlantis Community they called themselves. Like the lost continent, or the Donovan song.

But the freedom was incomplete. None of the Atlantis residents could drive. A bus drove past their apartments countless times a day, but there was no way to get a wheelchair on board. RTD's Handi-Ride pretended to be an option. Twelve little buses for five thousand subscribers. What a joke.

Dialing . . .
    Hello, Handi-Ride here.
        I need a ride to the grocery store.
            I'll put you down for a week from today.

I'm out of food!
> Shoulda thought of that sooner.

Dialing . . .
> Hello, Handi-Ride here.
>> *Can I get a ride to the Lakewood Grill?*
> That's a tavern. You shouldn't be drinking.

Dialing . . .
> Hello, Handi-Ride.
>> *Can I get a ride to church?*
> Got an opening in two weeks at nine.
>> *Service is every Sunday. At eight o'clock.*
> There are TV evangelists for shut-ins, ya know.

So Atlantis went political. Americans Disabled for Accessible Public Transit, ADAPT, they called themselves, and they wheeled over to the Regional Transportation District Board to talk and talk and talk.

"The wheelchair ban on regularly-scheduled buses is for your own good," RTD insisted, "plus, you understand we can't inconvenience able-bodied riders."

ADAPT wrote letters. To City Council, the Legislature, Congress. Petitioned. Made a nuisance of themselves. And sued. The judge expressed concern for their safety. Somebody might get hurt, he fretted. *Total bullshit.* Sitting on his pedestal, flapping his black robe, the guy was a freaking ignoramus. They lost.

That was last week.

This is today.

Today they win.

"Let's roll!" Wade lifted his arm and waved.

A man in his chair, hands on the wheels, pushed forward toward the bus stop.

"Kick some ass!" Wade said as the man rolled past to the edge of the curb. A bus pulled up. The man waited.

The door swung open. "Waddaya want?" said the driver.

"I want to ride."

"What are you? Crazy?"

Of course this was crazy, but none of the gang would admit it.

"No, I just want to ride." Calm but firm.

"No way," said the driver, irritation coloring his inflection.

The man wheeled himself right in front of the bus. Thirty protesters witnessed it. Eighteen in wheelchairs, plus friends and family.

"Get out of here!" the driver yelled, flailing his arms, panic raising his voice. "What the hell are you doing? There's another bus behind me and you're blocking the way."

Exactly.

Wade lifted his arm again, motioning toward the bus at the curb. Eighteen more wheelchairs moved forward. Some people rolled in front of the bus. Others to each side. A few in back of the second bus. There they stopped. Two buses surrounded, immobilized.

"We will ride!" they shouted. "WE WILL RIDE!!"

Cars started stacking up down Colfax and Broadway. The intersection came to a standstill. Diesel fumes got thick. Passengers exited the trapped buses. Most looked bewildered. Their faces revealed their thoughts: *What in holy hell is going on?*

Disabled people weren't supposed to go crazy, carry signs, and block buses. They're supposed to stay indoors, have their food brought on a tray, watch soap operas or something. But what about freedom? Rosa Parks got famous by refusing to go to the back of the bus. Disabled people couldn't even get on the bus.

Wade searched the bus passengers' faces for pity, saw little. Some looked red-faced and angry. That was a victory, right there. Inconveniencing the able-bodied would take his people where pity never could.

"Free our people!" the Gang of Nineteen shouted from all sides of the buses. "FREE OUR PEOPLE!!"

Organizing this had been hard, damn hard. And yet, here they are, crushing it.

Police cruisers pulled up, lights flashing red and blue. *Ah, now it gets really interesting.*

Officers meandered through the wheelchairs, consulted with each other, muttered into their radios. Handcuffs swung from their belts, but none reached for them. Wade stood on the sidewalk.

The protesters started singing, "We shall overcome . . ."

Eventually an officer approached the friends and family. One pointed at Wade. That was fine. He'd told them to.

The officer sauntered over. "What's going on?" he asked Wade.

"They want accessible buses."

"RTD has Handi-Ride. They can use that. Tell them."

"They want all buses accessible, so they can go where they want to go, when they want to go. All buses."

"They're blocking traffic."

"Yes, Officer. That's the point."

"Are you in charge, Mr. uh . . ."

"The Rev. Wade Blank. I'm just here to hand out water and help them to the bathroom."

"Well, they gotta disperse or we'll arrest them."

"First, sir, a person who's severely disabled has the same right as you to pursue his happiness, or hers. And if that means getting arrested in front of a bus, so be it. Second, it's not going to come to that, is it? You're not going to arrest them."

"Hmmmph."

"Because your jail's not wheelchair accessible."

THE SUN BEAT down. Carolyn, Mel, Debbie, Kerry, Lori, Bob, Cindy, Renate, Mary Ann, Bobby, Jeannie, Jim, Glenn, Larry, Linda, Terri, George, Willy, and Paul went on singing and chanting. The 'jet set,' as some called themselves, swiveled and popped wheelies. They waved signs at the crowds gathering on the sidewalk. It was turning into a party.

Police put up barricades. Traffic cops diverted cars traveling Colfax and Broadway. Wade and the friends and family helped people up the curb when they needed a respite in the shade of the trees in Civic Center Park.

RTD officials came out to talk, their collars straight and ties cinched. *Gawd, I really can't stand those kind of guys.*

"You lost in court," said the head suit, RTD executive director John Simpson. Wade knew him too well. "Now what do you want?"

"Wheelchair accessible buses."

"Judge Matsch already told you no."

"That was last week. This is this week."

"Good grief. How many?"

"All of them. Every bus in Denver."

"Absolutely not. That'd cost millions. It's not happening. You know that, Wade."

"WE WILL RIDE!!" the gang shouted.

"Tell them to pipe down." The RTD suit ran a finger beneath his tight collar.

It's so great to see 'em sweat.

"FREE OUR PEOPLE!!"

The RTD suits retreated to their offices. Protesters passed around sandwiches, slurped colas.

"Don't let the bastards get you down," Wade encouraged, worried about the heat.

"Not a chance," said George. "We're just getting warmed up. Literally."

RTD officials came back from their air-conditioned offices, cool and collected.

"We are sympathetic to your plight," said one, probably the PR guy, his mouth turned down in contrived concern. The others nodded, gravely.

Lord help us. Pity. Like that's gonna accomplish anything. Wade held his tongue.

"We would like to help," said Simpson. "But have been unable to ascertain where the handicapped people want to travel to and from."

Wade hid his exasperation, very poorly. "Anywhere you might want to go, they want to go. Anytime you might want to go somewhere, they want to go."

"Lifts upset the regular schedules."

"Adjust the schedules."

"The hydraulics are slow and noisy. It annoys the other riders."

"If they're so annoyed, they can drive their own cars," Wade said, "Severely disabled people don't have that option."

"The lifts break down."

"Fix 'em."

"The drivers don't like operating the lifts."

"Lots of stuff I don't like I gotta do, like talk with you."

And so it went. Hour after hour. When things got boring the Gang of Nineteen sang. Ragged voices belted out an off-key rendition of 'Ain't Gonna Let Nobody Turn Me Around.' And turn around they didn't. Evening rush hour came and went, Denver's busiest intersection, shut down.

The sun set. Still they didn't move. RTD executives were confounded. The police were confounded. Sleeping pads and pillows appeared. The protesters slipped out of their wheelchairs onto the street, snuggling into down bags. It had been a long day. Now it would be a long night.

Wade and family and friends took turns staying awake through the night, on guard.

"Reverend Blank." He heard a woman's voice behind him. "I have something for you." That voice sounded familiar. He'd heard it on TV news. Wade turned.

U.S. Representative for Colorado's First Congressional District, Patricia Schroeder, handed him a doughnut.

He laughed. Took a bite, swallowed. "I didn't expect to see you here."

She licked sugar off her fingers. "I didn't expect to see you here, either. You could have at least issued a press release."

"This was a sneak attack."

"It sure was."

"Bam! Total power!" He rammed a fist into the air, the one not holding the doughnut.

A voice came from inside a sleeping bag on the pavement. "Hey, stop holding out on us! That lady got any more of those?"

The U.S. Representative went out into the street with a box, kneeling down beside each sleeping bag, handing out treats to the gang.

Wade licked his lips, reached inside his bag, feeling for something to wipe off the rest of the sugar. His fingers found the two halves of the geode. Crystals poked his skin. The scene in front of him swirled, dissolving. *Am I delirious? Like this morning?*

Humid air replaced the arid Colorado evening. Hot sun slammed his shoulders like it was midday again. *Weird.* The Colorado State Capitol steps, just behind him, transformed into even bigger, grander steps. The U.S. Capitol? In D.C.? The Gang of Nineteen multiplied into a crowd. He saw hundreds of people, hundreds in wheelchairs.

Did Pat spike the damn doughnut? This is one hell of a trip.

༄

"You started it, man. Shot heard around the world. That's what they come to call the bus protest. Hell's Angels of the disability movement, that's what they call ADAPT. You win. In the end. Mostly."

Who's there? Must be one of Schroeder's aides.

"I'm Mancio," says a man, grabbing his hand, shaking it like a politician. "A prophet. Like in the Old Testament. Or a heavenly messenger, if you prefer."

This is crazy. Delayed heat stroke?

"I'm released from that geode thing Mike gave you," says the strange man. "To show you the future."

Wade looks the man in the eye. *What's the harm in playing along? Life is full of weird shit.* "That future better include fully accessible buses in Denver."

"Wade, Wade, Wade," scoffs Mancio. "A future of all fully accessible buses *in the United States*."

Wade laughs.

"I'm serious."

"Sure you are. And how long does it take?"

"Longer than you'd like."

"Everything takes longer than I'd like. How far in the future are you going to show me?"

"You're experiencing 1990. D.C. There's a little girl here. You bring her. Jennifer Keelan. She isn't even born yet when the Gang of Nineteen takes down RTD. But she's the star today. Watch. Listen."

The little girl from the morning hallucination. He remembers that high voice. Her blonde hair is wrapped in a red, white and blue ADAPT sweatband, and she needs it. Shiny from exertion, she's pulling herself up the concrete steps with her elbows, shouting at the cameras, "I'll take all night if I have to!" She can't be more than eight years old.

Looks like over a thousand people gathered. More drop out of the wheelchairs, throw down their canes, push over their walkers, and crawl up the capitol steps. Some scooch up backwards. A few are hauled, willingly, by their shoulders. Others drag their own crutches. They're yelling.

"What do we want? ACCESS! When do we want it? NOW!"

Wade squints. Counts the steps. Eighty-two. *Geez.* "What the f...what the freak is going on, Mancio?"

"The Americans With Disabilities Act is stalled in Congress. ADA it's called. A bill of civil rights for people with all kinds of disabilities. It's a big deal barrier-breaker, with some bipartisan support. But it's not passed yet, and these people won't let it get watered down. This is the 'Wheels for Justice' demonstration."

Far out.

"Tomorrow they'll chain themselves together in the Capitol Rotunda. A hundred will get arrested."

"Badges of honor. Does it accomplish anything?"

"Certainly. The ADA passes. It mandates accessible buses everywhere, accessible restrooms, concert venues, and restaurants. Disabled people are no longer banned as 'fire hazards.' Interpreters sign for the deaf at public meetings. Braille signage is installed for blind. What you started at Colfax and Broadway, it changes everything. Civil rights for disabled people in all fifty states."

MANCIO SNAPS his fingers. Now they're standing on a lawn, hot as hell. Another crowd, better dressed.

Wade overhears a patronizing whisper, "It would be unfortunate if anyone got sunstroke."

Then came a defiant reply, "We have as much right to sunstroke as anyone else!"

Wade looks for the rebel, to offer a high five.

"You're in the future, Wade. You see her; she can't see you," Mancio explains.

A fountain sprays in the background. Thick floral scent fills the air. The Rose Garden? A gray-haired man sits at a table with a row of silver pens lined up in front of him.

Wade shades his eyes from the glare. "Is that George Bush?" He looks to Mancio, "What's the CIA got to do with this?"

"It's not 1978 anymore. In 1990 it's President Bush, the first one."

"The first one?"

"Never mind."

President H.W. Bush starts his remarks. "Together we rejoiced when the Berlin Wall fell. Now I sign legislation which takes a sledgehammer to another wall . . . Let the shameful wall of exclusion come tumbling down."

The signing starts, silver flashing in the sun. Souvenir pens are passed around. An armless man takes one from Bush's hand with his feet.

Wade turns to Mancio. "Who would have thought a bunch of rag bag crips from Denver could have started something that would have grown this big? What's the rest of the story? How did we get here, to this ADA thing?"

"A LONG STRANGE TRIP it's been," begins Mancio. "Your bus theatrics at Colfax and Broadway are just the beginning. Next week the ADAPT folks disperse, screwing up traffic at bus stops all over the city."

"I know. Already have that planned."

"Then twenty folks occupy RTD offices. Get carried out, kicking and screaming, literally. ADAPT gets increasingly obnoxious, but you win. RTD gives it up. Promises all accessible buses."

"Far out. Those chairs are awesome weapons. They were beat before we even started."

"Not really. RTD reneges in 1980, but you don't let up, and they back down again, for good. All RTD buses are accessible for wheelchairs."

"Mission accomplished."

"I recognize sarcasm when I hear it, Wade. We both know Denver's just one city. Not good enough. ADAPT takes its show on the road, making a big fuss wherever the American Public Transportation Association meets. San Diego, San Antonio, L.A., Cincinnati, Phoenix, San Francisco, St. Louis. You guys get arrested in all the best cities."

"And along with fighting for lifts, we gotta fight against the curbs. Curbs stop people from even getting to the bus stop."

Mancio waves his hands in front of Wade. A new vision materializes. Two men in wheelchairs on Colorado Boulevard, taking turns thwacking a curb with a sledgehammer.

"What a visual! Disabled guys vandalizing public property! Made for TV! Gotta whack all 44,000 curbs in Denver."

"Wade, Wade, Wade," scoffs Mancio. "All curbs *in the United States.*" Mancio waves his arm again.

As if by magic, because it is, they're standing in front of Union Station in Denver. Wade barely recognizes what he's always dismissed as just a moribund old train station, now bustling with people going in and out. A couple in vacation garb pull rolling suitcases over a curb cut. "Denver leads, but the ADA requires municipalities all over the country to slope their curbs," says Mancio. A woman in a business suit scooters past over a curb cut. "In the twenty-first century, which you're seeing, curb cutting continues, making them even better." A man pushes a baby in a stroller over a sloped curb. "Because they benefit everybody." A woman in a motorized wheelchair disembarks from the Mall bus and rolls past Wade and Mancio into a restaurant. "Not just people in wheelchairs, everybody."

"So this ADA, it lets me put my feet up on the beach? Content?"

"A radical is never content, Wade. The ADA is a tool, sometimes a weapon, and ADAPT is the army. Wherever there are barriers, there are protests. But after the ADA passes, ADAPT moves on to lobby for funding for personal care assistants."

"To get people out of those f . . . those freaking nursing homes."

"Exactly."

"Well, Mancio, this vision or hallucination, or whatever it is, has been a hell of a trip, but the present calls. You got me fired up. I gotta get back to my people. There's work to do. Send me back."

THE SUN RISING behind the golden dome of the Colorado State Capital brings to Wade's mind his seminary paper on Psalm Forty-Six.

He stretches, massages his neck and back, sore from a night on the hard park bench. He sets the geode on the grass beside the bench and goes out into the street to help the protesters out of their sleeping bags. They're rubbing sleep from their eyes, still in high spirits, ribbing each other, waving signs.

The two buses are still pinned down. He and the friends and family who stuck it out through the night push the protesters to restrooms, one by one. They hand out coffee and egg sandwiches, what few doughnuts are left from Rep. Schroeder's box. Another rush hour comes, the city core still tangled up.

'The nations are in uproar, the kingdoms totter; he utters his voice, the earth melts,' as the psalm says.

RTD is tottering. He can feel it.

Ten o'clock a.m. July 6, 1978. Twenty-four hours are passed. It's time to pack up, go home, get ready for the next protest.

As the poet Mike once wrote, 'As he drowned in the music of the heavens, he finally found his answer – and was happy.'

Epilogue

Wade Blank lived long enough to see for himself the transportation transformation he started at the intersection of Colfax and Broadway in 1978. Disabled ridership on regular RTD buses, which was virtually zero in 1978, was already 8,000 *per week* in 1989. He was happy with, if not delighted by, the ADA (radicals are never satisfied), which brought wheelchair accessible buses to cities throughout the country.

Wade got married in 1983 and adopted his wife's daughter, Heather, who had spina bifida. Wade and Molly had two children together, Lincoln and Caitlin.

Wade died in 1993 while vacationing with his family on the beach in Todos Santos, Mexico. He drowned while trying, unsuccessfully, to save 8-year-old Lincoln from the undertow. Over a thousand people attended his funeral. One of them yelled, "If heaven isn't accessible, God had better watch out!" His death was commemorated in the Congressional Record by the Honorable Patricia Schroeder, who said, "Wade Blank, a man with many dreams and visions, made Denver, CO, and the United States a better place to live." His casket was draped with an American flag, its stars formed into the shape of a wheelchair.

Justin Dart, Chairman of the President's Council on the Employment of People with Disabilities, eulogized: "Wade understood that love is not just smiling at nice people, but passionate, lifelong action to preserve and enlarge the joy, the dignity, the quality of every human life. He understood that love does not smother with criticism, care and control; it encourages, emancipates and empowers... Let us join in one voice to shout his shout: 'Free our people.'"

Today, accessibility for people who use wheelchairs is taken for granted. The *Denver Post* once editorialized that it made no sense for RTD to make buses accessible when so few people in wheelchairs rode buses. Today the loopy logic makes people guffaw, but in 1981, when that editorial was published, the irony was less obvious. The editorial board, like everybody else, including then Governor Dick Lamm, assumed that people who used wheelchairs never wanted to go anywhere. Wade and ADAPT proved that wrong.

Wade's dream was far bigger than buses. When he died, Senator Tom Harkin of Iowa wrote in the Congressional Record: 'The fight for consumer-driven personal assistance services continues. Today, an intolerable number of people with disabilities who want to live independent lives are forced into nursing homes and institutions and a life of dependency. We will continue Wade's fight for consumer-driven personal assistance services.' Today, in the second decade of the twenty-first century, the great majority of Medicaid spending for young disabled people goes toward freeing them to live outside of nursing homes and institutions. An increasing number of older people are eschewing long-term nursing home lives as well. In 2015, for the first time, the majority of Medicaid Long-Term Services and Supports (LTSS) shifted from nursing homes to

Colorado Phantasmagorias 110

independent living. Nursing home residency (incarceration, Wade would say) has declined so much that the industry has shifted its primary focus to short-term rehabilitation.

It's easy to underestimate how bad it used to be. Before the ADA, restaurants could bar a disabled diner for being 'too disturbing to look at.' Landlords could turn away a disabled person on the assumption she was 'a fire hazard.' Disabled people living in nursing homes were forbidden from having sex, even if they were married. Children they already had were placed in foster care.

Atlantis Community in Denver, co-founded by Wade and Mike Auberger, a former bobsledder who became quadriplegic from an accident during a 1972 Olympic time trial, pioneered the concept of personal assistance in place of residential care. Atlantis continues to provide resources for housing, assistant services, life skills and vocational training to hundreds of disabled Coloradans every year. The headquarters broke ground on a new building in 2019. When complete in 2020 or 2021, the new building will have brand new offices for Atlantis and over 100 new, fully-accessible apartments. And today, Atlantis is only one of many Independent Living Centers throughout Colorado and the United States.

It's also easy to overestimate how far we've come. ADAPT, which Wade co-founded with Barry Rosenberg, continues to protest barriers and injustice. In 2017 ADAPT protesters held control of Senator Cory Gardner's Denver waiting room for 57 hours, insisting they would not leave until he vowed to vote against cutting Medicaid funds for disabled people. That protest failed, as police dispersed them, arresting nine in the process, and the Senator rebuffed them in his vote.

Just the Facts, Ma'am

Two good books on the disability rights movement are ***Enabling Acts*** by Lennard J. Davis and ***The Disability Rights Movement: From Charity to Confrontation*** by Doris Zames Fleischer and Frieda Zames.

Lives Worth Living, a film by Eric Neudel, a PBS Independent Lens documentary, tells the story of the disability rights movement. At the time of this writing, it was not available streaming, but the DVD can be obtained through library loan. Produced in 2011, Bob Kafka is spokesperson for

ADAPT. It features vivid footage of the Capitol Crawl, the occupation of the Capitol rotunda, signing of the ADA, and still photos of bus protests.

Shorter videos of the **Wheels for Justice** demonstration, which came to be known as 'The Capitol Crawl,' can be found by searching Youtube for Cultural Agent: Capitol Crawl or The Capitol Crawl 1990. The now grown-up Jennifer Keelan remembers that day in an interview that can also be viewed on Youtube; put her name in the search bar.

It should be noted that **RTD** has come full circle. In 1978, the board and executives considered Wade Blank enemy #1, but now count him as the district's hero. Every new RTD employee gets a tour of Atlantis and learns the history of ADAPT and accessible transit. Today, in addition to fully-accessible buses on all regular routes, RTD offers Access-A-Ride for those who can't get to the bus stop.

There's a colorful story, often told, that Wade came back from a Grateful Dead concert with Heritage House residents to find himself fired and his office packed up. Although he did take residents to concerts, it was money, not music, that got him fired. In his own time, Wade opined that the nursing home was only 'cashing in' on deinstitutionalization, and moving people to their own apartments took away the cash. "The initial success of the youth wing ran into the wall of profit motive," he said. Wade's own perspective can be best gleaned at the Western History Department of **Denver Public Library,** which has organized thirteen boxes of Wade and his wife Molly Blank's personal papers. These boxes hold the primariest of primary sources, containing everything from Wade's seminary essay to Michael Patrick Smith's poetry, plus lots of newspaper clippings and photographs.

Although Wade Blank's activism benefited people with all levels of disability, he served the most severely disabled people, the ones who, in his words "slobber, can't speak clearly, are crass, dirty and slimy." He did far more than organize protests. He drove a van and pumped gas, hauled luggage, hoisted wheelchairs and wiped butts. He would have been loath to admit it, but he also did a lot of boring stuff like meeting with bureaucrats and pushing paper. At his ordination in 1966, the scripture readings included Mark 10:43—'Whoever wishes to become great among you must be your servant.' Wade took that to the extreme, like everything he did.

Just for Fun

When Wade Blank took young Heritage House residents camping in the mountains, it was a radical act. Today, you can Google "**accessible hiking trails**" and many options pop up, from Rocky Mountain State Park to city trails. **Wilderness on Wheels** (on Highway 285 an hour west of Denver at the base of Kenosha Pass) has been providing wilderness experiences for people with all kinds of disabilities for over thirty years. The wheelchair accessible boardwalk trails are beautiful. Able-bodied hikers are welcome, but no bikes or motor scooters. Cabins and tent spaces are available. Be generous with your donation. See: https://www.wildernessonwheels.org/.

Colorado is also active in promoting winter sports for disabled people. The **National Sports Center for the Disabled (NSCD)** is headquartered in Denver and Winter Park. More than 4,000 children and adults with disabilities participate in more than 18,000 lessons in a variety of sports. Disabled athletes include those with developmental diagnoses, autism, cerebral palsy, Down Syndrome, brain injuries, spinal cord injuries and amputations. Alpine skiers are the most visible NSCD athletes. Anyone who skis at **Winter Park** sees disabled skiers whooshing down the slope. But NSCD athletes also river raft, ride horses, rock climb and more. For all the details, check out www.nscd.org. For those who prefer Nordic, **Ski for Light** offers week-long events for visually-impaired and mobility-impaired athletes. Headquartered in Minnesota, Ski for Light hosts events in Colorado. See www.sfl.org.

Indoor entertainment more to your liking? **Josh Blue** is a Denver-based, nationally-renowned comedian, known for his self-deprecating humor centered around living with his cerebral palsy. He was born in 1978, a few months after the Denver RTD bus showdown. It's the saddest thing that Wade didn't live to laugh with Josh. To catch Josh's act live, check out his schedule on www.joshblue.com. If he's not in Denver when you are, get a laugh from any number of his acts streaming over Youtube, including his winning set from the TV show 'Last Comic Standing.'

Catch other talented disabled performers at Denver's award-winning **Phamaly Theatre Company**. Each season this troupe of actors with cognitive, emotional, intellectual and physical disabilities puts on about four different plays at venues around the city. For a current schedule, locations and tickets, go to https://phamaly.org/.

It's hard to know whether to put the 1990 movie **When You Remember Me** under fun or facts, because it's a little of both. This compelling made-for-TV drama tells the story of Wade 'Black' (guess who) and a Michael 'Mills' (Michael Patrick Smith). Kevin Spacey plays Wade, Fred Savage plays Mike, and Ellen Burstyn is Mike's mother. Although details were changed to enhance the drama, both the real Michael's mother and Wade himself endorsed the movie as 'essentially true.' Although it's out of distribution (not easily found in either DVD or streaming), you can find the movie in its entirety on Youtube, provided you're willing to put up with degraded audio and video.

Atlantis holds the country's largest archive of artifacts and documents from the Disability Rights Movement. At the time of this writing, Atlantis is raising money for an upgraded **Disability Rights History Museum** to be housed in their new building. Check on their progress or give a donation at http://atlantiscommunity.org/.

There's a small monument to the July 5-6, 1978 bus protest near the southeast corner of Colfax and Broadway by the bus stops at **Civic Center Park** in downtown Denver. It's not worth a special trip, but if you're walking past, take a minute to read the plaque, look around, imagine the havoc of twenty-four hours, and be grateful for what Wade and the Gang of Nineteen accomplished.

Barney L. Ford
1822 - 1902
Escaped Slave, Entrepreneur, Civil Rights Pioneer

THE OLD CATERER, as Barney Launcelot Ford has lately nicknamed himself, clears a path to his restaurant, his mustache and goatee frosted white as his surroundings. He doffs his hat to other early-risers, his neighbors trudging through the snow in dark woolen coats and lace-up, fur-lined boots.

The Colorado mountains in winter are a long way from Georgia, where he'd been born as another man's property, not even owning his own body. These days he is a free man of wealth and influence, with a reputation as a shrewd businessman. Today he'll cash out yet another profitable investment. But first he has to make it through the snow.

He scoops another load. His shovel lifts a rock. Almost unnaturally round the rock is. He picks it up, brushes off the snow, notices a crack running through it. *Ah, the geode that saucy little boy brought to the party last night. He must have dropped it. I shall have to return it.* The two halves fall apart in his gloved hands. Inside, lavender crystals mimic the mountains that surround Breckenridge. *Beautiful.* He takes off one glove and rubs the miniature peaks. Suddenly he feels woozy.

This snow will be the death of me yet.

His sight blurs, as if looking through ice. Gone are his familiar neighbors in their dark woolens, replaced with a flurry of people sporting puffy jackets in shiny magenta, cerulean, and jade colors. He squints. *What's on their feet?* The clunkiest shoes he's ever seen, fastened with metal clasps, in similar unlikely colors. They carry large, long boards. *Perhaps the apparatus used by mountain mailmen and those Norwegians miners?* He waves and doffs his hat, but the strange people clunk past, chattering as if he's not there.

Suddenly, his familiar mountain-town surroundings dissolve completely. He sees a golden-dome, rising into the blue Colorado sky. Then the cold air warms, as if heated by a radiator. He feels jostled, as if by people knocking him about with books and bags. Even through his blurry vision, he detects the space is opulent. Onyx. Marble. *What's going on? Where am I?*

He sees a woman, her skin even darker than his wife Julia's, speaking from a lectern. A man of their race stands on a raised dais before a stained-glass window. Sun streams through the golden glass, illuminating the form of a black man leaning on a walking stick. *Is that an image of myself?*

He shakes his head clear and takes a deep breath, slipping the rock into his coat pocket. The warmth and opulence dissolve. Cold and snow, wooden buildings, and woolen-wrapped neighbors reappear.

No time for a phantasmagoria today. He has oysters to fricassee, and another fortune to make.

༶

Breckenridge
1889

THE AROMAS of popcorn and hot apple cider greeted Mr. B. L. Ford as he unlocked the door of his Saddle Rock Restaurant. Last night had been one of the Fords' special parties for the children of Breckenridge. His beloved Julia stayed at home today, to recover. The thin air was trying for his wife, even after years in the mountains. They would have to move back to Denver soon. Today's business deal would help make that happen.

But first, he shed his top hat and black woolen coat, replaced his boots with shined leather shoes, and set the geode on a sideboard. His housecleaners bustled in and began sweeping, dusting, wiping down. His cook arrived, slapping on an apron and readying the oysters. Lastly came the waiters, laying the tablecloths, setting the silver, stacking the menus. There was a time, many years before, when he'd done all these tasks himself, for the profit of his master, a man who owned him. That was before he'd made himself free, and got himself rich.

Mr. Ford straightened his collar and tie, smoothed his mustache and goatee, polished a smudge from his shoes, and turned over the sign. *Open.*

WHEN THE LUNCH crowd had cleared out, The Old Caterer readied a long table for his special guests—his partners in the Oro Group gold mining company and the businessmen who would buy them out. Today's deal would make him rich—again. He and Julia were comfortable, a lovely home, thriving business, three fine children, all grown up now. He'd come a long way from the shack of his boyhood, but he'd also been richer at times in the past, and he looked forward to becoming richer yet again.

A man in a silk top hat walked through the restaurant door, the first of the businessmen he was expecting for the meeting. The man removed his hat and gloves, extending a hand. "I'm honored to make your acquaintance, Mr. Ford!" he exclaimed. "At long last."

Mr. Ford was his formal name, befitting a man of his accomplishment, affluence and reputation. Julia called him Barney, the name his mother had given him, as did his close friends. The newspapers wrote B. L. Ford. He called himself 'The Old Caterer' because that's what he was, and self-deprecating humor made for good advertising.

"Pleased to meet you, as well," he said to his guest. "Please, make yourself comfortable."

It had always come down to this, making his fortune providing comfort to the well-heeled. Food, drink, and hospitality. Today would be a day far more profitable than most. He poured a whiskey for the man, passed him a plate of oyster snacks.

His guest swigged the whiskey. "Smooth, with just the right bite." He gulped a fricasseed oyster. "Delicious!" he exclaimed.

The Old Caterer chuckled. "We had some children here for festivities yesterday. I overheard one little boy say that oysters tasted like, dare I repeat it . . . boogers."

The guest smacked his knee. "Out of the mouths of babes! One shudders to think how the little fellow came to that comparison. He clearly has not a refined palate." The man swallowed another oyster, licked his lips. "You're more than a restauranteur, I know. How long have you been in the gold prospecting game?"

Was he making conversation or mining for information? The Old Caterer mulled his response. Such a long life he'd lived, with so many twists and turns. How much to divulge?

"I first learned sluice mining when I was a boy, in Georgia," he answered.

The man chuckled, "Georgia!"

"Auraria, Colorado, is named after a town in Georgia where gold was mined." The Old Caterer omitted more personal details. Any gold he had found as a boy in Georgia had not profitted himself. Indeed, he was searched each day, scrubbed down sometimes. Any flecks he picked up, or even that stuck to his skin, went into his master's pockets, for he'd been enslaved.

"And the restaurant game? When did you get into that?" the man asked.

The Old Caterer stroked his goatee, reminiscing, "I gained my first experience in the hospitality trade on a Mississippi riverboat, called *The Magnolia Blossom*, when I was a young man of twenty." Just a little white lie. His first experience had actually been as a boy, cooking, polishing the silver, and setting the fine china in his master's Big House. He omitted another detail as well. His owner had hired him out on *The Magnolia Blossom*. His riverboat wages had not been his own to keep.

"You're well spoken. For a Southerner," said the man.

The Old Caterer knew what he meant, but kept his thoughts to himself. "An actor on *The Magnolia Blossom*, hired to entertain our guests, coached me on elocution. Taught me Shakespeare. 'Be not afraid of greatness,' he taught me. That's from *Twelfth Night*. And 'To thine own self be true, and it must follow, as the night the day. Thou canst not be then false to any man.' *Hamlet*, Act I, Scene 3."

He stopped, chuckled. "Can you believe I still recall that after all these years?"

But of course, he would never forget. He had followed those words his whole life, the words learned from the man who helped set him free, actor J. Anthony Preston.

It had been quite the production. Preston smeared pale theatrical pancake makeup on his face. Dressed him in clothing borrowed from one of the actresses on board. Tried to stuff his feet into the lady's shoes, but had to give up on that.

When *The Magnolia Blossom* docked in Illinois, a white woman in bonnet, blue dress and long white gloves, shy behind a folding fan, sashayed down the ramp. Coins sagged her—his—pockets and purse. His wages had not been his own, but tips had been slipped to him to keep. He also disembarked with a more valuable treasure: knowledge and skills that could not be taken away.

Once on dry land, free land, he shed the bonnet, blue dress, gloves and folding fan and hid them where the actress could find them. He washed off the make-up and put on the men's clothing he carried in his valise. He was on his way.

Colorado Phantasmagorias

Two dollars bought barber lessons. Nobody who sat in his barber chair imagined for a second he'd ever been enslaved. He quoted Shakespeare like a Yankee and discussed politics like a man who read the *Chicago American* newspaper every day, which he did. For that he thanked his mother, the dictionary and book thief, who risked her life to make him literate.

Barbering took up too few hours of the day, so his new friend, H.O. Wagoner, put him to work in his livery business and on the Underground Railroad, ferrying folks from Missouri through Illinois and north toward freedom in Ontario.

Wagoner also introduced him to the most beautiful woman in the world. *Julia.*

They married, and then the gold bug bit him. As it would, again and again. And yet, no matter where the hunt for gold led them, his fortunes always ended up coming from food and hospitality.

Today's business guest was becoming impatient, drumming his fingers, looking about the restaurant, shuffling papers on the table. The Old Caterer must go on with his story, answer the question. How had he got into the restaurant game?

"My first restaurant and hotel were in Nicaragua," he told his guest.

"Nicaragua!" exclaimed the man. "In South America?! That is a story worth hearing! Do continue, Mr. Ford. It appears as if the others are delayed to our meeting. Perhaps waylaid by the snowfall."

"Please, take another," he offered, pouring his guest another shot of whiskey.

THE HEADLINES SCREAMED 'Gold Discovered in California!" It was 1849, and he and Julia were one year married. There was no forgetting the tiny bits of glitter he'd held so briefly as a boy in Georgia. Shoveling gravel into a sluice box was backbreaking work, but better than hoeing fields or driving smelly pigs to market. Even so, having to turn over to the master each flake, no matter how small, had been excruciating.

Now, here was an opportunity to prospect for himself and Julia. And forget flakes, in California there were nuggets to be found! Real wealth. Julia took some convincing, because his barbering and livery work were providing a comfortable living in Illinois. But gold sang a siren song. They saved up their funds and left for California, the long way around, east by train to the Atlantic, then south and west by sea voyage. It cost just forty-five dollars for steerage.

On a stopover in Nicaragua a mosquito got him. First it was just an itch, but soon he felt lethargic. Not at all himself. Malaria, they told him. He was in no shape to travel. Julia found a place to rent. Expensive and inadequate, but that's all there was. He recovered, looked around, and saw paradise. Flowering vines perfumed the air. Brightly plumed macaws, parakeets and parrots flitted and cawed. But even in paradise, a man must have some money. He considered the terrible room and board offered to the people coming and going on the ships.

"If a man here can make money putting people up in sorry accommodations and feeding them revolting comestibles, then a man such as you, trained in cookery and hospitality on *The Marigold Blossom*, could make a fortune," Julia suggested. He agreed, at least until they'd saved up enough for another try at gold prospecting.

The U.S. Hotel, he called the place. He and Julia made sure the beds were soft, the floors swept, and the sustenance delicious. *Tortillas and frijoles* were filling, but the U.S. Hotel offered far better. Surrounded by local fruit, he and Julia concocted recipes for breadfruit, coconut palms, oranges, lemons and bananas. Farms just upriver raised cabbages, eggplants and tomatoes. He ordered them shipped down the San Juan in bongo boats. Julia supervised the maids and waited tables.

In this way they made a fortune pleasing the hopeful 'Forty-Niners' on their way to the California gold fields. They took in even more from the dispirited 'Go Backers' spending their last dimes retreating home. The arithmetic could not be denied. They were well-off, but homesick. It was time to head back to Chicago. He gave up his golden dreams and sold the hotel, a handsome profit having been made. Five thousand dollars. Not bad for four years' work.

Back in Chicago, H.O. Wagoner put him back to work at the livery and on the Underground Railroad, yet another detail he left out of his recital to today's guest. He made the acquaintance of the firebrand abolitionist John Brown, participated in the famous Christmastime raid, liberating eleven from Missouri and transporting them north to freedom in Canada. He was even introduced to Charles Sumner, the anti-slavery Senator from Massachusetts.

Then the gold bug bit again. The newspapers reported gold strikes in Colorado. No malaria would stop him this time. It was 1858. He was ten years free, thirty-six years strong. He left Julia in Chicago and worked his way west, a general helper and cook on a wagon train. First tried his hand

Colorado Phantasmagorias

at the gold 'diggins' in Denver, Auraria and Mountain City. When he went to file a claim, the clerk took one look at his café au lait complexion and turned him down. Never mind, the prospects were not rich enough, anyway. He aimed higher. He considered his favorite verse from the Bible: 'I will lift up my eyes unto the hills from whence cometh my help.'

French Gulch, Breckenridge, Summit County. The peaks of Summit County took his breath away. Surely here, among the Shining Mountains, he would find his fortune. How to file a claim? Time to get creative.

A white lawyer agreed to file on his behalf in exchange for twenty percent of the bounty. Problem solved. He set to work in French Gulch with a few friends. Soon enough they'd accumulated a respectable vial of gold dust and even a few nuggets. Not a fortune yet, but enough to invest in better equipment. They took their dust and nuggets to the assayer, and the cash to the equipment supplier.

Word got back to the lawyer. The Sheriff showed up. "This here claim don't belong to you," the lawman announced. "I got papers here from the rightful owner, the man whose name is on the claim. You got twenty-four hours. Get out." Right's right and wrong's wrong, but a wise man does not challenge a badge with a gun on a horse.

Back to hospitality, he went. Back to Denver. Julia came out with their baby boy, Louis Napoleon, and they opened up a barber shop and lunch counter in a shanty he threw up next to a gambling hall on Blake Street. Gamblers, fresh off their winnings, want to look spiffed up and are usually hungry, too. He and Julia raked in cash at a pleasant and profitable pace until fire razed all of Blake Street, including their shanty, which turned out to be a blessing.

Banker Kountze refused his plea for a loan to rebuild what was lost. Better, bigger, and fire-safe, Kountze insisted. The banker would loan nothing less than nine-thousand dollars for a fine, two-story brick building. He accepted the challenge, sketched plans, concocted a business plan, and watched as the structure rose, brick by brick, from the ashes of Blake Street.

The basement became a barbershop and ladies' hair salon, 'wherein competent artists are ever pleased to wait on customers in first-class style.' At street level, The People's Restaurant offered a full menu, including oysters, lemons, and Havana cigars. A second-story saloon topped it off. Customers crowded in. A few months later he'd paid off the loan (a good thing, considering the exorbitant interest Mr. Kountze was charging). He was soon earning the fourteenth richest income in Denver. Mr. William Byers published that fact in *The Rocky Mountain News*.

But no amount of income could make up for the fact that too many of Colorado's territorial leaders, Territorial Governor Cummings excepted, wanted to deny him the right to vote and to sit on a jury. Disappointed and angry, he went by train to Washington, on his own dime, to lobby Senator Sumner and make sure Colorado didn't become a state until his race was guaranteed all the rights of citizens.

The Old Caterer's guest interrupted the story. "I did hear you were to blame for holding up our statehood." He slapped him on the back. "No hard feelings, my good man. All's well that ends well."

The wily Senator Sumner made sure President Andrew Johnson kept in mind that should the president's unpopularity result in impeachment, a State of Colorado would send to Washington a pair of anti-Johnson Senators eager to vote for conviction. He also reminded the president of the territory's small population, and that Territorial Governor Cummings opposed statehood, even as his territorial legislature overrode him. With a letter on his desk from Gov. Cummings, B. L. Ford and others, President Johnson vetoed Colorado statehood, quoting Cummings: "By the laws of the United States, negros and mulattoes are citizens and subject to the duties, as well as entitled to the rights, of citizenship."

Not to mention the right to make a fortune as a hotelier. B.L. built the elegant Inter-Ocean Hotel in Denver, "the finest and best appointed hotel west of Saint Louis," the *Rocky Mountain News* called it.

But he didn't give up politics. Even if the people pushing for statehood didn't appreciate his energy and knowledge, the Party of Lincoln surely did. Some years the Territory allowed him to vote, other times not, but he served as an Election Judge, and was called to sit on a Grand Jury. He served as a delegate to the Arapahoe County convention.

The whites-only contingent finally gave in. The clause denying voting rights to 'negroes, mulattoes, or black persons' was shelved forever. The Colorado State Constitution would guarantee voting rights regardless of race. With that, the well-respected hotelier B. L. Ford gave his blessing. Colorado entered the Union in 1876.

"So it's to your credit we are known as 'The Centennial State'," said his guest, "and not the '1867 State,' which has far less ring to it."

FORD'S FELLOW ORO GROUP members, his partners in a gold mining investment, started arriving at the Saddle Rock, brushing snow off their coats and hats. With them came his guest's business partners, who were there to buy the Oro Group. The Old Caterer offered more plates of oysters and whiskey to warm up their insides. They pulled out pens from their vests, shuffled papers into order.

The Old Caterer's gold lust would, at long last, pay off.

Julia had been exasperated when he proposed returning to Breckenridge again, nine years ago, to hunt for gold. "Barney, really, *again?*" she'd scolded. He'd proven himself a genius at making money selling food and hospitality. Why not stick with that? She'd been quite right, for a time. When the rocks didn't yield gold for him, profits from Ford's Chop Shop and then the Saddle Rock built them their fine new home with its bay window and a comfortable living.

But. *Gold.* It was beautiful. And very, very valuable. Even just the possibility of it.

"LET THIS MEETING come to order," pronounced the President of The Oro Group.

Mr. B.L. Ford's astute four thousand dollar investment in The Oro Group gold prospecting company was about to turn into forty-four thousand dollars. Negotiations had been going on for months. The buyers needed only lay down their money. He'd made other fortunes selling his hotels and restaurants through the years, but this felt different. It wasn't exactly like hitting a gold strike himself, but at his age, sixty-seven, it was close as he might get. Julia didn't care much about gold, she just wanted to move back to Denver.

He signed the ownership transfer papers with a flourish, as did his partners. They pocketed their money. Handshakes all around.

When the transaction was done and the men departed, he went to the sideboard and picked up the boy's rough geode, the thing dropped outside after last night's party. How different had been that gathering from this afternoon's meeting. Children, giggling over their apple cider, spilling popcorn, stumbling about blindfolded to pin the paper tail on the paper donkey. He looked forward to grandchildren. In the meantime, he would secure his profit in the office safe, then return the boy's souvenir on his way to tell Julia the good news. He cracked open the rock again, to admire the crystalline peaks one more time before returning the stone to the boy.

The room spun.

༄

A MAN MATERIALIZES at the front door of the Saddle Rock. *Where did he come from?* He wears one of those shiny and colorful jackets from the morning's hallucination.

"May I help you, sir?" asks The Old Caterer, ignoring his customer's inappropriate dinner attire.

The man stomps his clunky boots clear of snow, leans two long boards against a corner. "A fine day on the slopes, couldn't hardly bear to leave, but the lifts closed."

"I do not understand you at all, sir. Speak plainly."

"Skiing. Nice day for skiing."

The Old Caterer tilts his head, inquiringly.

"I'm a soothsayer. Apologies for the casual twenty-first century ski garb. Mancio's the name. Released from your geode to show you the future."

What? Twenty-first century? Released from the geode? Like the genie in the Aladdin tale?

The Old Caterer decides to ignore the ridiculous statements. He engages in business instead.

"Were you saying you would like a libation?" he asked. "Perhaps a plate of fricasseed oysters?"

"As delicious as that sounds, Mr. Ford," says the strange man Mancio, "you and I have bigger fish to fry today."

With no further ado, the Old Caterer finds himself and this Mancio whooshed onto a park-like space. A dome glittering gold, rises into the sky. The man who calls himself Mancio leads him up granite steps, past an engraving that reads 'One Mile Above Sea Level,' then into the unfamiliar, opulent onyx and marble chamber of his morning's phantasmagoria.

Is this a malaria hallucination? Like in Nicaragua? It doesn't seem so. His vision and hearing are clear. The place is a-bustle with men and women, elbowing each other and nattering in undignified fashion. It feels as chaotic as his Inter-Ocean Hotel restaurants right after a train full of passengers disgorges all at once. Mostly white people, but black people and brown people, too. The women wear skirts above their knees, the men sport suits

Colorado Phantasmagorias

of a peculiar cut. Mancio's attire is magically transformed into something more dignified, too.

If not a malaria hallucination, am I having a stroke? The children are capable of taking care of themselves, but Julia, I don't want to make her a widow.

"You're not having a stroke, Mr. Ford, and you haven't contracted malaria," says Mancio, reading his thoughts. "This is the Colorado State Capitol in the twenty-first century. I mean to show you what you helped accomplish. You'll return home soon enough."

A gavel bangs the horde to order.

Just behind the gavel-banger, oranges and blues of sunlit stained-glass attract his notice. The window from the morning vision. *Is that supposed to be me? Surely it is! In front of my Inter-Ocean Hotel.* Rendered in glass, his image holds a paper that reads: 'Colorado Free State Black Vote.'

"Twenty-first century? That's very hard to believe," he whispers to Mancio.

But is it true? Or a phantasmagoria? *Could I truly be seeing the future?*

"You may speak aloud, Mr. Ford. You see the future. The future does not hear or see you."

He chooses to believe, clears his throat. "Mr. Mancio, why is my picture here? In the Capitol?"

"A grateful state honors you, Mr. Ford, and others like you. You fought the good fight for civil rights. Thanks to you, Black Coloradans, men and women, have served their constituents in the legislature. George L. Brown served nineteen years in the General Assembly before being elected Lieutenant Governor. Terrance Carroll was Speaker of the House. Peter Gross, President of the Senate. Coloradans elected Joe Neguse to Congress. Denver has been led by two Black mayors, Mr. Wellington Webb and Mr. Michael Hancock."

"If what you say is true, I am heartened to know that my party has seen fit not just to embrace the vote for my race, but to nominate and elect us to high office."

"Today's Black leaders are mostly, not quite entirely, of the other party, Mr. Ford."

"Democrats?! No! Say it isn't so!"

"In politics, a lot changes in a hundred years."

Mr. B. L. Ford studies the glass a bit more.

"1822 to 1902, it says. Today is 1889. Then I have a few years left. Will I leave Julia alone?"

"No, Mr. Ford. You return to Denver. Julia appears in the Social Register, the first woman of her race to do so. She dies of pneumonia, a few years before you."

"What finally does me in?"

"Shoveling snow."

"I knew it."

Epilogue

Barney Launcelot Ford died clearing snow in front of his residence in Denver in 1902. He and Julia are buried in the historic Riverside Cemetery in Denver. They had three children, Louis Napoleon, Sara Elizabeth, and Frances (Frankie). Ultimately, they left no descendants. Frankie gave them one grandchild, Edith, who died in the 1906 San Francisco earthquake.

Just the Facts, Ma'am

The Black West by William Loren Katz, includes a section on Barney Ford. Older sources include *Mister Barney Ford: A Portrait in Bistre* by Forbes Parkhill, *Barney Ford: Black Baron* by Marian Talmadge and Iris Gilmore. Talmadge and Gilmore borrow heavily from Parkhill. Both are dated in their approach and might be almost as fictionalized as this account. No time travel, though! Barney Ford is featured in James Crutchfield's *It Happened In Colorado: Remarkable Events That Shaped History*. For younger readers, *Barney Ford: Pioneer Businessman* by Jamie Trumbull is part of the Great Lives of Colorado History series.

Any historical tour guide or historian will tell you that the people who made the fortunes in the Gold Rush were not the miners themselves, but the people who sold them stuff. B. L. Ford proves their point. Build a popular restaurant or hotel, sell at a profit, do it again, was his successful business model. His enterprises included Ford's Chop House, the People's Restaurant, Sargeant's Hotel (renamed Ford Hotel) and Oyster Ocean, all in Denver. In Breckenridge, he opened Ford's Chop House and then the Saddle Rock. The crown jewels of his career were his opulent **Inter-Ocean Hotels** in Denver and Cheyenne, Wyoming. At its opening, the *Rocky Mountain News* described Denver's four-story Inter-Ocean's 'bronze chandeliers, rich velvet drapes trimmed with satin . . . chairs of black walnut and russet leather, a dove-colored Brussels carpet . . .wires to every room

Colorado Phantasmagorias

and speaking tubes on every floor.' It stood at the corner of 16th and Blake for a hundred years before being demolished in 1973.

As with any businessman who takes risks, sometimes B. L. Ford won, sometimes he lost. His enterprises were destroyed by fire several times, which wasn't at all uncommon in the days of wood cook stoves, candles and gas lights. In today's dollars, he was a multi-millionaire for most of his business career. He also bought and sold commercial real estate and made business investments. The sale of the Oro Group alone netted him over a million in today's dollars.

The saga of Colorado Territory's flip-flopping on civil rights for African Americans is crazy confusing. What's clear is that the persistence of B. L. Ford, the obstinacy of Territorial Governor Alexander Cummings, and the integrity of Senator Charles Sumner of Massachusetts—not to mention the territory's small population and President Andrew Johnson's impeachment problems—led to Colorado becoming **The Centennial State**. If not for their insistence that Colorado guarantee equal rights, Colorado may have become a state as early as 1864 instead of 1876.

A self-educated and well-read man, B. L. Ford gave back to the Black community, which was only about one percent of the population during his time (compared to about 4.5% today). After the Civil War, he and three friends set up adult education classes for people newly freed from slavery. He taught government.

B. L. Ford gave back to the business community as well, serving on the Board of the Dime Savings Bank along with William Byers, publisher of the *Rocky Mountain News*, and other Colorado luminaries. He was influential in improving Denver infrastructure. In 1873 the *Rocky Mountain News* reported that the city received a petition for a new sewer from "B. L. Ford and forty-seven others."

News reports from the time verify his vigorous involvement in Arapahoe County politics (Denver was part of Arapahoe County at the time). He reportedly hosted a party for Republican Presidential Candidate Ulysses S. Grant in 1868. He lobbied in favor of the **Colorado Civil Rights Act**, which prohibited discrimination in 'hotels, restaurants, churches, barber shops, public conveyances, theaters, or other places of public . . .

amusement.' It passed the Colorado General Assembly in 1885. He did not, as is sometimes reported, serve as a member of the General Assembly. The first Black legislator elected in Colorado was **Joseph H. Stuart** in 1895.

Just for Fun

The Barney Ford Museum, 111 E. Washington in Breckenridge, is a lovely, restored Victorian home. He and Julia had it built in 1882 and they and their daughter Sarah ('Sadie') lived there. Interesting trivia: the kitchen in the rear was a later addition. Being a restauranteur, Mr. Ford saw no need to have a kitchen in his house! A small donation is suggested. The Ford home is part of the charming **Breckenridge National Historic District.** Take a walk on your own, enjoy a beer or a coffee or shop for clothing, sporting goods and gifts. Guided historic tours are available. Check out https://gobreck.com/ for more information.

Mountain bikers enjoy spectacular views on the **Barney Ford Trail** near Breckenridge: https://www.mtbproject.com/trail/5563314/barney-ford. Bring your own mountain bike or rent one from one of the shops in Breckenridge.

Oysters were kind of the 'burgers and fries,' of the nineteenth century, enjoyed by rich and working class alike. Served simply, they were popular and cheap bar food. Gussied up with fancy preparation, they made an entrée fit for the high falutin'. Most were canned and shipped from Chesapeake Bay, which was loaded with oysters back then. B. L. Ford was reported to travel by train to Baltimore to negotiate favorable terms for his oyster supplies. Here are a couple nineteenth century **recipes** for you to **cook** at home:

> **Fricasseed Oysters:** Take a can of oysters, drain them as dry as possible, put a piece of butter, size of an egg, into your spider [A spider is a cast iron pan with short legs], heat it until brown; put in your oysters and as soon as they commence to cook add as much more butter which has been previously well mixed with a tablespoon of flour, let it cook a moment and add one egg beaten, with a tablespoon of cream; let this cook a moment and pour all over toasted bread. Serve hot. *Mrs. E.K. Bennett.*

Spiced Oysters: Empty the oysters with the broth into a kettle; salting well, cook them until they plump, then skim them immediately into cold water which blanches them; strain the broth through a cloth, put it back into the kettle, adding whole black pepper, whole allspice, a few blades of mace and a dash of cayenne pepper. Drain the oysters in a colander, then pour the broth boiling hot over them, adding four tablespoons of vinegar. It is better to prepare them the day before using. Keep in a cool place. *Mrs. C.H. Roberts*

Wanna catch gold fever yourself? Gold is still mined commercially in Teller County, Colorado (that's where the gold for the capitol dome came from), but Summit County mines 'played out' (became financially unviable) long ago. There are, however, **old mines** where you can take a **tour** or **pan for gold** in the summer. You're not going to strike it rich, but panning is a weirdly hypnotic experience for adults and fun for kids. Washington Mine, Country Boy Mine and Lomax Placer Mine are three. Country Boy, which was active until 1971, is the real deal, where you'll experience not just quaint history, but see the giant slag heaps (more properly known as spoil tips or gob piles) left over from mine operations. Choose your experience by typing 'gold panning Colorado' or 'gold mine tour Breckenridge' into your search engine, or visit https://gobreck.com/.

The largest gold nugget ever found in Colorado is the 13.5 pound **Tom's Baby**, found at the Gold Flake Mine near Breckenridge in 1887. It's on display at the Coors Mineral Hall at the **Denver Museum of Nature and Science**, open every day from 9 a.m. to 5 p.m. at 2001 Colorado Blvd., Denver, 80205. See www.dmns.org for more information about exhibits.

These days, **skiing** is the 'cold, white gold,' of the Breckenridge economy. The ski area opened in 1961, so it's not something Mr. Ford would have done, at least not in the modern sense. The resort offers five huge peaks, 2,908 skiable acres, a 22' Superpipe, four terrain parks, eleven bowls, and the highest chair lift in North America.

The building B.L. built for his **People's Restaurant** at 1514 Blake Street in Denver is, at least at the time of this writing, a sushi restaurant. It's a stop on the Denver **Lower Downtown (LoDo) Walking Tour**. Visit https://historicdenver.org/ for more information on the tour, or go there for a bite of sushi.

The gold-domed **Colorado State Capitol**, 200 E. Colfax Avenue in Denver, was constructed starting in 1890 and opened in 1894. B. L. Ford would have seen it being built, as he and Julia moved from Breckenridge back to Denver just as ground was being broken. He was probably disappointed that the dome was covered in copper rather than gold. It was first gilded in 1908, after his death. It was re-gilded in 1950, 1980, 1991 and 2013. The most recent gilding was the first time only Colorado gold was used— sixty-five troy ounces of 24-karat gold was mined and donated by the Cripple Creek & Victor Gold Mining Company. The **stained-glass window** honoring B. L. Ford was installed behind the Speaker's platform in the chamber of the Colorado House of Representatives in 1976, a hundred years after statehood. **Free tours** of the capitol are offered 10 a.m. to 3 p.m. Monday through Friday. Reservations are not necessary unless you're bringing a group of 10 or more.

Enthusiastic docents at the **Black American West Museum**, 3091 California Street, will show you the home of Dr. Justina Ford (no relation), the first licensed Black female physician in Colorado; unique exhibits about Black cowboys and ranchers; photographs of prominent Black Coloradans (including a photo of B. L. Ford); and the history of **Five Points**, a cultural hot spot for jazz and Black culture starting in the 1920s (quite a while after the Fords' time). The museum is most easily accessed by hopping on the RTD Lightrail L line and just riding it to the end; the museum is across the street from the L Line terminus at 30th and Downing.

The Ford's brick Victorian at 1569 High Street, one of the last homes they lived in, is still standing, but privately occupied. If you're into cemeteries, and what history-lover isn't, **Riverside**, Denver's oldest cemetery, 5201 Brighton Blvd., is the eternal home of many prestigious Colorado pioneers, including B. L. and Julia in Block 20. Tours are occasionally available from Friends of Riverside Cemetery and other historic groups. Or you can just walk about by yourself. For more information, see http://friendsofriversidecemetery.org/.

Colorado Phantasmagorias

Ora Chatfield
1873 – 1936
and
Clara Dietrich
1865? – Unknown
Ladies in Love

With Clela Rorex, Jean Dubofsky, Chief Justice Luis Rovira

ORA SNUGGLES DEEP into her cousin's embrace. Clara smells delightfully of lavender. Outside the bed chamber window rise the twin summits of Mount Sopris, still clad in snow, like the bodice of a wedding dress. A sprig of cool mint freshens her breath for kissing. The percussive patter of snow melting off the roof drips a musical accompaniment.

Clara reads a poem:
"Honey nor bee! The tingling quest
Must that too be denied?
Deep in thy bosom I would rest,
O golden blossom wide!
The joys o'er which bees murmur deep
Your Sappho's senses may not steep."

She stops reading, slips from Ora's side and kneels. Her skirt, with its minimum of frills and a bustle only as large as necessary, drapes gracefully. Even so, Ora sees that beneath the black folds, Clara is on one knee.

"Marry me, Miss Chatfield, my most beloved Ora."

What? Oh, my goodness. Such a suggestion!

Ora responds with a caress to Clara's shoulder. "Nonsense. It would not be allowed."

"I'll dress as a man," Clara insists, rather loudly, because they believe they're alone in the house. "I'm somewhat masculine in appearance. We'll go to the Justice of the Peace in Aspen."

Marriage? You're Miss Clara Dietrich, a competent postmistress and storekeeper. I'm just Ora, a schoolgirl, less than a year accustomed to the corset!

"Oh, my dear Clara, where do you get such an idea?"

Clara reaches beneath her bed and pulls out a box. She cracks open the lid. Inside is a geode, one rock split into two halves with a gem-like core.

"Ora, my Treasure, I have the means to support us." Clara hands her the geode. "You see these purple crystals? They are more beautiful than diamonds from South Africa. Please. Accept this engagement gift. Say yes to my proposal."

Ora takes the rock from Clara, brushes the crystals with her fingertips. She swoons. Weird shapes swirl before her eyes, like images from the magic lantern of a phantasmagoria show. She gulps for breath. "Clara, get the smelling salts!"

Clara lunges for the bottle on the dresser. "It's empty!" she cries, smashing it against the floor in frustration.

"I need air!" gasps Ora. "My corset is too tight! I can't breathe!"

Clara starts unfastening the tiny buttons down Ora's front. Nimbly, but there are twelve in all.

Ora's eyes lose focus. She grips the rock as strange visions and voices invade her senses. A pair of men, holding hands, stand before a counter, as if in a government office. They're speaking to a young woman, an official clerk perhaps, large wire hoops dangling from her ears.

The government counter dissolves before Ora's eyes. Now she envisions rows of people sitting on polished pews. *A church?* Here's a different woman, this one wearing the jacket of a man and a skirt so short it exposes her calves! People listen from a high bench. They're all wearing black robes. No crosses or stoles. *Not a church, a courtroom!*

Clara keeps ripping apart Ora's buttons. She's not working fast enough. Ora's visions grow even stranger. A woman in a white gown and a person in a tuxedo, another woman, discernable from the shape beneath the lapels. Ora perceives words. *Love and cherish?* Wedding vows! Farther afield two men embrace, a flag the colors of the rainbow flapping overhead. Then two women, both in white lace, kiss and toss flowers.

At last her dozen buttons are released. Clara slips off Ora's bodice and rips apart the strings that pulled the corset too tight. Ora drops the rock, inhaling a mountain-ful of air. The delirium disappears. Her corset falls to her hips. Clara holds her, cupping her fingers over the thin chemise covering Ora's breasts. They sink to the floor.

Weeping in relief, neither hears the click of the lock or the squeak of the hinge. Only the smell of bear grease alerts them to danger.

It's Mr. Chatfield's hair tonic.

"What in God's name is going on here?" Ora's father bellows.

※

Emma, Colorado
(Near Aspen/Basalt)
May, 1889

TWO WEEKS SHE had lain abed, imprisoned under her father's lock and key, tormented by confusion and guilt. *Why, oh why did I betray dear Clara?*

> *How could I bear to see,*
> *Her from my bosom torn*
> *Myself departed be*
> *And left alone to mourn . . .*

Ora tossed and turned, her stomach shrinking ever smaller as her appetite disappeared. Soon she'd not be able to find a corset small enough to fit. If she survived her anguish, that is.

Every day she relived the frightful drama. Her father, barging into Clara's home. She, scrambling to cover herself. Too slow. He witnessed the hand on her breast and spotted the inflamed red mark on her neck. Clara's signature of ardor had, up until then, been secreted carefully beneath her high collar.

"She bit me!" Ora had cried, terrified of her father's wrath.

Clara stayed silent.

"Why are you out of breath? And nearly unclothed?" her father demanded.

"She squeezed me nearly to death! I'm afraid of her!"

He turned to Clara, eyes blazing. "Niece, what is the meaning of this?"

"I love your daughter more than life itself," Clara had proclaimed, eyes ablaze.

Ora had struggled to set her attire back to rights again. As soon as she managed to secure the final button through its buttonhole, her father grabbed her and pushed her out of Clara's house. He dragged her onto the road, yanked her onto the wagon and hauled her back to the ranch.

There he had ransacked her room, tossing clothes and toiletries every which-a-way. He found what he was looking for—her locked box. "Where's the key?" he demanded. "Give it over."

She had fumbled around, pretending not to know where it was, opening one drawer after another, in a daze, feigning befuddlement.

"Where can I have put the key?" she wailed.

Her father had not been fooled. He held his fist in a frightening manner. He threatened to call the Sheriff. Only when he brought in an axe from the barn did she relent and dig out the key she had jammed between the floor and baseboard.

He unlocked the box, dumping the contents. A landslide of letters and poems spilled over the floor. Clara's declarations of devotion sullied amidst the dust.

He picked up one paper and read the handwriting aloud. His low voice had growled out the words, not at all like Clara would have done:

"I love you more than words can wield the matter,

Dearer than eyesight, space, and liberty;

Beyond what can be valued rich and rare,

No less than life, with grace, health, beauty, honor;

As much as child 'ere loved, or parent fond,

Beyond all manner of such loves

I do love thee."

"It's Shakespeare!" Ora protested. "That we read in school. *King Lear*!"

"You think I'm a fool? That I can't tell the difference between a schoolbook and a love letter? This is insanity! Bewitchery! Pick these up! Pick it all up."

His large body had loomed over her as she gathered the papers back into the box, the odor of his hair tonic making her sick.

"Give it all to me! Now!"

Trembling, she handed over the boxful of letters. He stormed out, slamming the door and locking it behind him. She feared he would burn it all. She would learn he was planning worse than a bonfire. Much worse.

MY LIFE, RUINED! Ora wept into her pillow. *And I deserve it!*

Caught between her sweet lover and angry father, she'd chosen wrong. Amid the chaos of discovery she had claimed to be afraid of Clara, when it was really her father she feared. *Bumbling immaturity!*

Weeks now spent prisoner in her father's home, released only to scrub clothes and wash dishes and use the outhouse, foreshadowed life with a man for a husband. Not to mention the string of babies that would come from a conventional union. She didn't know exactly what happened in a birthing room, but she had heard it involved screaming and lots of blood. And sometimes an obituary notice in the newspaper. *I could die!*

Ora yearned for freedom and education. Clara offered both and she'd reciprocated with disloyalty and deceit. *What will become of me now?*

One tiny glimmer of hope intruded into her despair. Right after Clara had declared her love, while Mr. Chatfield's back was turned, she had whispered, "Keep up the act, dear Ora. I'll make a plan."

'MAD INFATUATION,' was the headline in the *Aspen Daily Times*. Her shame on newsprint, wedged between grocer advertisements and news from the silver mines. Black ink stained her hands as she read. Halfway down the column, she leapt from bed and pounded on the door with what little strength she had left.

"You gave my letters to a newspaperman! How dare you?!" she screamed, banging the wood until her fist ached. "Those precious lines are mine! They're private! How dare you!"

If her father heard, he did not respond. She put her back against the wall and slid to the dusty floor. *The newspaper questions our sanity. The Sheriff is involved! And what has happened to Clara? Where's her plan? What's taking so long? Has she given up on me?*

Bereft, Ora kept reading down the column.

Apparently, during Ora's confinement, Clara had been corresponding with Mr. Chatfield. The newspaper quoted a letter Ora had never seen: "The fact that my love for your daughter exists, however, just as strong as the love of man ever was for woman, is beyond question, and I am ready to prove it with my heart's blood."

Ora gasped. There was hope. Clara still loved her.

WORD REACHED THE RANCH that Miss Clara Dietrich was engaged to be married to a gentleman. Upon hearing the news, Mr. Chatfield released Ora from constant vigilance.

Over a month had elapsed since the scene in the bed chamber. Ora had missed weeks of school, and now it was summer. Sun warmed even the highest meadows. Mt. Sopris still wore her gown of snow, but the ranch had greened up. Spring-born calves were putting on weight. Love letters began arriving again, sneaked in by Ora's half-sisters, an earlier carrier-pigeon idea having proven impractical.

'My devotion is as purest silver,' Clara wrote. 'My heart pounds like stampeding horses. Expectation once more to see your face burns hot as the sun.'

One sunny July morning, Ora went for a stroll and just kept walking. Three miles it was to the train station in Basalt. Her shoes pinched, but sweet anticipation was potent tonic against discomfort. For standing on the train platform was Clara. Even from afar, Ora recognized her instantly. In spite of the disguise. Clara's postmistress attire was covered by a long, white apron. A frilly white cap perched on her head. Quite becoming, actually. One hand held a valise, the other a cloth face mask.

Ora yearned to rush into her arms, but instead tucked herself into a corner of the station. Only when she saw Clara alone on the platform did she approach.

"You're a tubercular on your way to a sanitarium in Denver and I'm your nurse," Clara said, handing her a ticket and the mask. "Put this on. If anyone starts asking questions, cough a few times. That'll keep people from getting too nosy."

They boarded the Colorado Midland train just as it pulled out of the station, leaving Basalt for Denver at ten sharp. The train chugged past trees, through the Hagerman tunnel, and stopped in Leadville.

As Clara predicted, the other passengers gave the nurse and her tubercular patient a wide berth. Ora wished to embrace, but discretion limited them to holding hands, and if anyone looked their way, nurse Clara patted her in a palliative manner. They changed trains in Colorado Springs.

Ora didn't remove the mask until they arrived at Denver's Union Station, where the bustle of strangers provided blissful anonymity. Aspen's eight thousand souls were as nothing compared to this metropolis of one hundred thousand. They checked in at the Inter-Ocean Hotel on Sixteenth and Blake. The bronze chandeliers and velvet drapes were a far cry from the ranch house in Emma.

Clara treated Ora to a late snack. They clasped hands over a plate of oysters.

"Free, dear Hubby! We're finally free!"

Denver
July 6, 1889

'LOVELORN GIRLS,' shouted the headline in the *Denver Times,* 'Sensational Elopement of the Two Girls Who Come to Denver.'

At least the *Aspen Daily Times* had used pseudonyms. The *Denver Times* printed their real names, and even mentioned their famous uncle, the

Honorable I.W. Chatfield, representative to the Colorado General Assembly. The article also set forth excruciatingly complete physical descriptions of both of them and warned that reporters were searching the city 'in all directions.'

Denver was not safe after all.

The paper shook in Ora's hands, great blobs of tears smearing the ink. Clara took it from her and replaced it with the geode engagement gift. She wrapped Ora's hands around the rock. "Remember my promise to you. It will be all right. I'll get us tickets to Kansas City." Ora nodded and wiped her face.

As the door clicked behind Clara, Ora opened the two halves of the geode. The purple crystals reminded her of the view from her family's ranch. She imagined she would never return. She had chosen love. She had chosen Clara. *But at what cost? And why is everyone so worked up, anyway?*

She brushed her fingers over the crystals. A woozy feeling overwhelmed her, like the hallucination on the day Clara proposed. Ora was too bereft to search for smelling salts. She took as deep a breath as her corset allowed.

༄

"GOOD MORNING," says a woman's voice.

Ora starts, jumps from her seat. "Who's there?!"

"My name is Sybylla."

There in the room stands a woman Ora had never before laid eyes upon.

"Who are you? How did you get in here?"

"I'm a seer. I've come to show you the future, a prophetess released from your geode, the genie in the story of Aladdin you read about in school."

Ora is too drained to respond or be afraid.

"This newspaper article, this *Denver Times* reporter, immortalizes your story," Sybylla says.

Ora knows she should be afraid, but instead she feels soothed, like she's taken a dose of laudanum.

"You provide hope for future generations. There comes a time when the kind of love you feel, the marriage you seek, becomes accepted, or at least legal. It's a long journey, but you and Clara took the first steps."

In spite of all hopelessness, Ora rises from her seat.

The prophetess takes her by the hand. "Follow me on the journey."

With no further ado, they are magically transported outside the hotel, into the lobby of a very officious building.

"Where on earth are we?" she asks.

"Boulder," says Sybylla.

Ahh, the city where I had hoped for an education. I did not expect it to look like this. "Everything looks so terribly strange. Is this the university?" asks Ora.

"No, dear. This is the Boulder County Courthouse, far into the future—1975."

Ora gawks. The walls are made of sharp-cornered blond blocks. A red and gray geometric pattern decorates the floor.

The newspaper had speculated that she and Clara followed the occult. Ridiculous! she had thought when reading it, but now wonders. *Could this be a spell? Am I bewitched?*

Sybylla tugs her sleeve to get her attention. "Let's go down the hall. The people we come to see are in the clerk's office."

They walk through a large door, toward an office labeled 'Clela Rorex: County Clerk and Recorder.' Two men stand in front of a long counter. A young woman wearing hoop-shaped earrings is waiting on them. *The people from my vision!*

Ora senses great affection. *If this is a spell, it's benign.* She listens.

"We want a marriage license," says one man.

"The County Clerk in El Paso told us you might help us," says the other man.

The young clerk wrinkles her face, but her eyes shine in a friendly way. "Well, this is a first. I'll have to look into it," she says, extending her hand.

The men shake the clerk's hand. So courteous and professional. If only she and Clara had found a nice lady clerk like this! As the gentlemen walk past, Ora says to one, "That is what Clara sought for us. A marriage license like you asked for." But neither man acknowledges her.

"You can see the future. They can't see you," explains Sybylla. "Ms. Rorex does look into it. She keeps her promise. The Boulder district attorney tells her that Colorado law allows marriage between two persons. These men, being persons, qualify. So she calls them back and gives them the license. Five other same-sex couples come to her for marriage licenses, including two women. Unfortunately, the Colorado Attorney General then orders her to stop."

Ora shakes her head, woe turning down the corners of her mouth. "I do not understand it. Where's the harm? Why make her stop? Why does everybody get so worked up, anyway?"

"It gets better, my dear," says Sybylla, patting Ora's hand. "Our journey's not over."

Again they are transported by benevolent magic. "Colorado Supreme Court," says Sybylla. "1993."

There's the woman in the business jacket and calf-exposing skirt! The one she saw in her delirium back in Clara's bed chamber.

"May it please the Court," Ora hears the woman say, followed by a plea using a perplexing jumble of words: Amendment Two, anti-discrimination, equal protection, fairness under the law.

"I can't make sense of this."

"This lawyer is Jean Dubofsky. This is the highest court in Colorado. The man in the center is Chief Justice Luis Rovira," says Sybylla. "She's arguing to nullify Amendment Two.

"You see, in 1992 the citizens of Colorado vote to stop cities from passing laws to treat men who love men and women who love women, such as you and Clara, in the same way they treat other people. Boulder, Aspen, and Denver all have such equal rights ordinances. Amendment Two is meant to prohibit such protections.

"The amendment is a setback for gay men and lesbians, but the fight against it leads to greater progress and equality, eventually, thanks to Ms. Dubofsky and Justice Rovira—and many others."

Ora is confused. *Doesn't gay mean happy? And what's a lesbian?* Clara once explained 'tribade.' Perhaps it's the same thing. She'd like to ask questions, but can't manage to form thoughts into sentences as long as the prophetess keeps nattering. 'Church bell' is the word people use for talky ladies like Sybylla.

"Judge Rovira nullifies the amendment with his order of the court," Sybylla continues, "but it gets appealed all the way to the United States Supreme Court. Ms. Dubofsky convinces them, too, that women who love women and men who love men are entitled to the same rights as everyone else."

"So they can get married!" Ora claps her hands like an excited child.

"Not quite," says Sybylla. "We're not there yet."

Ora puts her hands down, disappointed again.

"It takes until 2015 for the Supreme Court of the United States to bring about marriage equality," Sybylla says. "Not just for Coloradans, but for all Americans. But it is the Colorado opinion written by Judge Rovira that sets the precedent that points the way."

Ora does the simple arithmetic in her head. Well over a hundred years it takes. That seems like forever, maybe longer.

"Now, perk up that long face," Sybylla encourages. "Our next stop is celebratory!"

Finally the seer stops talking. In a whoosh, they land in an outdoor venue. The air is perfumed with lavender, like Clara's perfume. Ora can't tell exactly where they are, but the brilliant blue Colorado sky is unmistakable.

A woman in a white gown and a person in a tuxedo, another woman, stand beneath an arbor promising to love and cherish until death do they part. *Wedding vows!* Just like in the bed chamber delusion. Sybylla touches Ora's arm and redirects her attention. Across a grassy meadow two men embrace, a flag the colors of the rainbow flapping overhead. Beyond them another pair of women, both in white lace, kiss and throw bouquets of flowers. *Those visions in Clara's bed chamber, they were prophecies!*

"I'm so happy for them all," exclaims Ora. "But what of me and Clara? What happens to us?"

Sybylla shakes her head. "I've shown your legacy. Your life is yours to live as it must be lived. It would not do for me to meddle. I cannot show the immediate future."

And with that, Ora finds herself back at the Inter-Ocean Hotel. The door swings open and Clara walks in. "The train to Kansas City leaves in two hours," she announces. They pack a bag.

Epilogue

Before the month of July 1889 was up, Pitkin County Sheriff John White brought Ora back home from Kansas City under orders from her parents. She had just turned sixteen, still a minor. A year later, Ora was reported to be among a 'merry party on the Rio Grande going down to their ranch at Emma.'

Ora married Charles Shaw in 1898. They had one son before divorcing. She died in 1936 in California.

Postmistress and storekeeper Clara Dietrich disappeared from Colorado history.

Just the Facts, Ma'am

There's no question that Colorado's LGBTQIA+ community counts Ora and Clara as pioneers in the long struggle for marriage equality. A version of their story has been retold by ***Outfront* Magazine** (June 16, 2015) and the Denver entry in the **GLBTQ encyclopedia**. These modern retellings are based on the *Denver Times* article published on July 6, 1889, which was subsequently picked up by national and international news sources, including the *New England Advertiser* (September 17, 1889) and the *Brisbane (Australia) Courier*, (September 2, 1889).

The local historical record in the ***Aspen Times*** (May 11, 1889) and ***Aspen Chronicle*** (July 6 and July 8, 1889) tells a more complicated and contradictory story. The local reporter noted the age difference (Ora was fifteen-going-on-sixteen and Clara was probably twenty-four, maybe older) as much as the fact that they were both female. And while later reports described their love as mutual, not so the first. The retelling in this book acknowledges the contradictions and uses imagination to reconcile them.

Ironically, lifelong committed relationships between women were relatively common in the 1800s. So-called 'Boston marriages' were accepted as 'enlightened' unions between 'chaste' women. This made sense to conventional Victorians, who considered 'well-bred' women 'passionless' and therefore lesbian lovemaking was incomprehensible. Or at least, that was the polite pretense. Regardless, the nineteenth century taboo against speaking or writing about sex of any kind flummoxes today's historians. The consensus is that some Boston marriages were pragmatic arrangements between career women, others were romantic but asexual, and others were physical. Books on the subject include ***Surpassing the Love of Men*** by Lillian Faderman and ***Disorderly Conduct*** by Carroll Smith-Rosenberg. ***Charity & Sylvia*** by Rachel Hope Cleves tells the true story of a loving Boston marriage.

Ora and Clara made at least a couple mistakes that catapulted their story into national and international fame: they made the sexual aspect of their attraction obvious, and sought a legal marriage rather than just cohabitation.

Their timing was off, too. The last decade of the nineteenth century was the beginning of the end for the 'don't ask, don't tell' Boston marriage. Male sexologists began a campaign of persecution against both gays and lesbians. Acceptance continued to sink until it reached its nadir in the 1950s. Very slowly, attitudes became more accepting after that.

In 1975, Boulder County Clerk Clela Rorex was among the first to knowingly issue a legal marriage license to a same-sex couple. When word got around, she ended up issuing licenses to four more gay couples and one lesbian couple. She got death threats and a weird visit from a cowboy who brought his horse to 'marry.' Ms. Rorex explained the law: eight-year-old Dolly the horse would need a permission slip from her parents. Rorex obeyed the Colorado Attorney General's order to stop issuing same-sex licenses, but always felt that it had been the 'right thing to do.' In 2018, the Boulder County Courthouse was recognized on the **National Register of Historic Places** for its significance to LGBTQIA+ history. (Colorado Heritage, Winter 2018/2019)

Appealing for Justice by Susan Berry relates the compelling story of how attorney Jean Dubofsky and Judge Luis Rovira turned Colorado's Amendment Two into victory and progress for LGBTQIA+ Americans.

Judge Luis Rovira is also remembered for being the first Hispanic Chief Justice in the United States.

Love Unites Us: Winning the Freedom to Marry in America, edited by Kevin Cathcart and Leslie J. Gabel-Brett is a compilation of essays and articles tracking the marriage equality struggle from 1970 through 2015.

Just for Fun

The stunning Art Deco **Boulder County Courthouse** is in the Downtown Historic District just off the **Pearl Street Mall**. It was built by unemployed Boulderites during the Great Depression after the original burned down. The six same-sex marriage licenses issued by Clela Rorex are memorialized on a plaque just to the left of the front door to the courthouse. Also note the bronze statue of a red-tailed hawk winging over the flagstone plaza. The plaque below it reads: 'A witness to countless changes over time, she flies from the past, embraces the present and gazes into the future.'

Colorado Phantasmagorias   143

For more history, stop at the octagonal Visitors' Center in front of the Courthouse and pick up **Boulder Historic Neighborhoods Walking Tour** guide. Or just stroll the historic Pearl Street pedestrian mall where you can find fine dining, pizza, or falafel; fine art, local handicrafts, or university souvenirs; handmade fashions, outdoor gear, or t-shirts; coffee, tea, or beer.

The **Aspen Historical Society** offers a variety of fun ways to experience the Aspen/Basalt (Emma) area, including downtown walking tours, tours of the historic Wheeler Opera House and Hotel Jerome, pub crawl, historic mansions, and the Holden/Marolt Mining and Ranching Museum. Go to https://aspenhistory.org/ for details.

The historic **Wheeler Opera House** at 320 East Hyman Avenue in Aspen was being built in 1889, just as Ora and Clara were escaping to Denver. Since then it's become Aspen's premier venue for concerts, movies, festivals, and lectures. To find out what's on the schedule and buy tickets, go to https://www.wheeleroperahouse.com.

The Aspen Historical Society preserves the **Ashcroft Ghost Town**, which was built, populated and abandoned in the late nineteenth century. It's eleven miles up Castle Creek Rd. from the roundabout at the west entrance to Aspen. A docent leads tours during the summer. Admission is $5 for adults; children and active-duty military get in for free. A self-guided honor system provides access during 'closed' hours and during the fall, winter & spring. Get more information at https://aspenhistory.org/.

The Aspen/Basalt (Emma) area is generally known for its silver mining history and its glitzy celebrity-studded present, but the Chatfields were ranchers. **T-Lazy-7 Ranch** offers a fun and modern ranch experience, with winter snowmobile tours, summer horseback riding, fly-fishing, and venues for special events. The Deane family raises all-natural beef, honey, and hay on their working ranch. Visit https://www.tlazy7.com/ to find out more.

Ora's uncle I. W. Chatfield is the namesake of **Chatfield Reservoir** south of Littleton. The Colorado state park offers boating, fishing, hiking, biking, and camping. More information can be found at: https://cpw.state.co.us/placestogo/parks/Chatfield.

Denver PrideFest is held every June in Civic Center Park between the Colorado Courthouse and the Denver City and County Building. Recognized as one of the top ten pride events in the country, Denver's PrideFest is a celebration of community, heritage, family and culture. Produced by the Gay, Lesbian, Bisexual and Transgender Community Center of Colorado, more than 250,000 people from Colorado and surrounding areas come out to enjoy the parade, rally, music, entertainment, food and much more. Admission is free. Visit https://denverpride.org/ for details.

When Ora and Clara lived in Pitkin County, they would have thought of skiing as something you did to check the cows or deliver the mail. Skiing for fun was still in the future. Today, of course, Aspen is a world-renowned ski destination. Starting in 1977, Aspen began hosting a **Gay Ski Week**. For more information on ski activities, dining, dancing, and drink, visit https://gayskiweek.com/.

Adolph Coors
1847 – 1929
Brewer

VERRÜCKT. CRAZY. That's what this Prohibition is. Banning beer? What German could imagine such a thing? *I'm American now,* he reminds himself, *my children grew up in Colorado.* Still, this is *verrückt.*

Adolph Coors combs his hair carefully, knots his tie neatly, laces up his polished shoes, and goes to the table to share breakfast with Louisa. She says little. He says little. No different from most mornings.

The ridiculous *Denver Post* headline taunts him: *'S' Long John, Take Keer of Yourself! Is Farewell Shout in Denver as the Hon. Mr. Barleycorn Packs Grip and Hops Car to Oblivion.'* He shoves the paper aside. There's nothing amusing about Prohibition.

When his egg and toast are reduced to bits and crumbs, he stands. On the buffet sits a brown rock.

"What is this?" he demands of Louisa.

"One of the ladies brought it to yesterday's tea. A conversation starter. It's a geode, very beautiful inside. She left it behind by mistake."

The outer surface feels grainy. Mr. Coors cracks it open, exposing purple crystals. He starts to swoon, as if he'd had several beers too many, which he never does. The room's coffee aroma is transformed into the familiar fruity smell of beer. He hears the laughter of women not his wife or his daughters. *Die Sinnestäuschung.* His senses are playing tricks on him. He sets the rock down. The *halluzination* fades.

No time for such *Verrückheit.* He has beer to dump.

☙

Golden
December 31, 1915

CLEAR CREEK FLOWED past Adolph Coors's galoshed feet, just the same as it had over forty years ago when he'd first walked these cottonwood-lined banks. So much had changed over the decades. Everything, really, except this creek.

Clear Creek had surely been flowing just like this when he was born in Germany, when his parents died of tuberculosis, when he first hired on as an apprentice at Wenker Brewery in Dortmund, when the Kaiser came after him for the draft. He had never heard of Colorado back then.

Thump, thump, thump . .. The first of his last barrels of lager rumbled down the bank toward the creek. His workers opened the spigot. A fringe of ice along the bank crackled as the barrel hit the water, spewing his beautiful, golden-hued brew into the creek, returned from whence it had come. He would weep, but a Coors doesn't cry. His eyes remained dry, as cold and blue as the Colorado sky overhead.

This creek had been flowing just like this the day he sneaked inside the ship bound for the United States, where he had hidden in a cubby, thankful to be escaping the Kaiser's endless wars, dreaming of making beer for Americans. *The best beer. Clean and crisp and pure.* This creek would be the secret ingredient, he just hadn't known it yet.

Coors stamped his feet to keep them warm, pulled the collar of his overcoat up around his neck. A second barrel came rolling down—thunk, thunk—behind him. Like the first, its beloved contents sloshed into the creek – *schwappen*.

Five hundred fifty-eight barrels to go.

Clear Creek—the same creek that had delivered those shiny, enormously valuable yellow specks to dreamy-eyed miners in the Gold Rush—had been flowing just like this when he worked off his ship passage in New York in 1868. It kept flowing when he headed west to Chicago, still flowing during those long days when he'd made small wages laying bricks, chiseling stone, feeding coal into the maws of steam engines, back when he was a young man, strong and willing to do whatever it took to realize his own golden dream.

The barrels came rumbling down faster now, his workers opening the spouts one after another, his beer adulterating Clear Creek and being adulterated by Clear Creek. *Panschen,* the worst thing a brewer can do, and here he was, letting it happen, barrel after barrel after barrel. How had it come to this?

Women.

When he had first discovered the pure water from the springs along Clear Creek in 1873, the ladies of the Women's Christian Temperance

Union were already making a big fuss around the country, but back then the women and their male allies claimed to like beer. "Liquid bread" was better than hard liquor, they argued, "a safe substitute for drink of a more ardent nature," as the *Golden Transcript* put it. Perfectly true. He'd seen little harm in the temperance ladies' efforts back then, appreciated the free advertising for the benefits of beer over whiskey and gin.

All that commotion had been barely a consideration when he and his benefactor Jacob Schueler bought the old Golden Tannery. He had put up two thousand dollars and years of brewing experience and the candy seller Schueler had entrusted him with eighteen thousand. He turned their money into Golden Brewery. Built a three-story malt house, which became, as it turned out, on account of the temperance ladies, perhaps his most prescient investment.

He put out three thousand barrels of Schueler Coors Golden Lager the first year. Seven years later it was time to buy out Schueler, which he had done. Just thirty-three years old then, newly wed, and fast on his way to becoming a millionaire. *Der Amerikanischer Traum*. The American Dream. Today the dream was a nightmare. All this beautiful beer, wasted.

The irony was, he believed in temperance. Then and now. That is, he believed in moderation. Self-discipline. *Der Selbstbeherrschung*. A solid German value. Then came Carrie Nation.

Women. There are three places women don't belong — politics, business and saloons.

That crusading prohibitionist Carrie Nation had gone storming into saloons with her hatchet, hacking the bars to pieces, soaking her dress in beer. Unseemly behavior for a lady, to say the least. She was hysterical, and the press gobbled it up. 'The famous and original bar room smasher,' they called her. Then the crazy woman went around the country giving speeches and making money selling souvenir hatchets to hordes of other women. Carrie Nation and her ilk were not temperance. *Verrückt.*

Following on her heels came the Anti-Saloon League. That was a clever name. The problems with saloons were pretty hard to miss. Convivial places for men to gather and relax after a hard day's work, a place without women, not counting the occasional prostitute, a masculine enclave, but even he felt sickened by the sight of these men stumbling through the swinging doors, vomiting on the public thoroughfares, going home to beat their wives and children, too hung over to make it to work some days. Their minds corrupted by whiskey, some men became petty thieves and vandalizers.

But the Anti-Saloon League had had no intention of stopping at just closing saloons and sobering up drunks. Their enemy was all alcohol of any strength in even the most responsible amount. They burned 'John Barleycorn' in effigy. Tricked the alcohol men into doing battle against each other, turning the whiskey distillers against the gin men, the wine men against the brewers. All the while marching steadily on toward total prohibition. *Verrückt*.

No matter that Presbyterians and Baptists and Methodists went around preaching, prohibition was not the answer. The answer was, Coors could explain to anyone who cared about common sense, *der Selbstbeherrschung*. Self-control. A man who dresses his best has no desire to spew all over his clothing. A man who takes pride in his labor puts his earnings toward his family, not all into the saloon's till. A man who is on time for dinner with his wife and children every evening—6:25 on the dot at the Coors household—would not have time to become a sot. A pint of lager after work, a glass of Rhine wine on Sunday, he was himself living proof that a man who drinks in moderation can prosper very well.

But here we are. Pouring good beer down Clear Creek.

Coors and the Citizens Protective Union of Colorado had fought the prohibitionists manfully, but sense held no sway over passion. In spite of all good reasoning, Coloradans voted 'dry' in 1914, giving him a little over a year to figure out what to do. Some assumed he'd pull up stakes and take his brewery to a wet state. He refused. Colorado was his home, where his children had grown up, the place that had made him rich. A millionaire two times over. And move to where? A dozen states were already dry, plus six more going dry at the same time as Colorado. Nineteen and counting while there was serious talk in Washington of banning alcohol in all forty-eight states.

His investments were all here. It made no good business sense to waste his resources and rebuild somewhere else, all to maybe, probably, be legislated out of business yet again. He and his sons Adolph Jr., Herman and Grover would stay in business. Here. In Golden, Colorado.

He and Grover would make malted milk. A drink made for infants and invalids. *Sheesh*. But it required malted barley, and they had plenty of barley and that three-story building to malt it in, his most prescient investment. He tried not to think of their other beverage, Mannah, dreck that looks like beer, smells like beer and tastes like, well, a word a gentleman does not utter. *What's the point of it?*

Colorado Phantasmagorias

Adolph Jr. and Herman had already set their minds to perfecting Coors ceramics, running the pottery 'overtime and on white heat,' as the *Colorado Transcript* put it. He felt only a little bad that they had tragedy to thank for that. The pretty little tea sets the company made probably wouldn't have amounted to much, but then the Kaiser sunk the passenger ship *Lusitania*, killing 128 Americans. *Dummkopf*.

In retaliation, the U.S. Department of Commerce embargoed German ceramics—the highest-grade ceramics needed to safely contain chemicals and dyes in scientific experiments—and issued a challenge. A business opportunity. Figure out how to make high quality ceramics here in the U.S. He and Adolph Jr. and Herman had been up to the challenge. They would show the president and the Kaiser what American ingenuity and a German pedigree could put out.

Coors Ceramics would surely make money, so might Grover's malted milk, possibly. In the meantime, his family would soak up all the positive press they were getting from going along with the ridiculous Prohibition. 'Most commendable,' said the *Salida Record* of his and his sons' adaptations. 'Great success,' was predicted. 'Old Mr. Coors is for prohibition,' reported the *Colorado Transcript*. *Lächerlich*. The press coverage would be laughable, if the whole thing weren't so tragic.

Rumble, thud, splash. The last of his barrels spilled their lager. Hundreds of barrels of beer made the creek smell like a German beerhall on Oktoberfest, but without the merriment. His beer, his passion, was a business *kaput*. The craziest thing of all was that Coloradans could still buy and drink beer, just not his. Make a phone call to Cheyenne, Wyoming, and a distributer up there would send down a shipment of inferior Wisconsin beer that Coloradans could still buy legally, and drink legally, provided they mailed their payment across the border and stayed home to drink it. At least until the whole country went dry. *Verrückt*.

A good citizen, Coors would obey the letter of the law, no matter how crazy. He had brewed and sold as much pure, quality beer as he could before time ran out. His last shipments had gone out in trucks this morning, to stores selling to Coloradans stocking up their private cellars, more to the saloonkeepers and hoteliers getting ready for Colorado's final festive New Year's Eve. Then the saloons would all close their doors, at midnight or when the booze runs out, whichever came first.

The last of his beer washed down the creek. His workers began rolling the empty barrels back to the brewery. It was time to go home, shed the galoshes and get back to work.

HIS BELOVED GARDEN was dead, too. Through the window of his dining room he saw his flowers, dry and broken. Like his brewery. The difference was, his garden would come alive again in the spring. His beer, though, was gone forever, he thought.

It was as if Colorado's voters had ordered him to rip out his roses and plant dandelions. No, not dandelions, you can make wine from that. Milkweed, it's like he'd been reduced to growing milkweed in ceramic pots.

On the table the morning's *Denver Post* headline continued to mock him:

> *'S' Long John, Take Keer of Yourself! Is Farewell Shout in Denver as the Hon. Mr. Barleycorn Packs Grip and Hops Car to Oblivion*
>
> *Lo, and a few hours and the bright brass rail shall gather mould, the glasses on the back bar shall swipe no more across that shining place of solid mahogany where rested the seidel o' beer and the good ol' shot in the arm.'*

Colorado dry tomorrow, the whole country soon. A Constitutional Amendment was in the near future. He just knew it. Once that happened, there would be no going back. He'd learned about the Constitution when he had studied to become a citizen. Nothing in the Constitution had ever been crossed out. Ever. Coors beer was over. Forever.

SILENCE WAS SOLACE. He sat heavily, considering what task to undertake next. The burden of the day weighed down on every limb of his body. Louisa had left him alone with his thoughts.

The grainy rock sitting on the buffet seemed to call to him. He picked it up and pried it open.

≈

HE SMELLS FRESH BEER again, feels sunshine on his shoulders, hears women laughing and the crack of a baseball bat and the roar of a crowd. He's no sports fan, but baseball is not played in December, even he knows that. *Die Sinnestäuschung* again. His senses are playing tricks on him, just like at breakfast.

Colorado Phantasmagorias

A man appears. Coors somehow understands, instinctively, that the man is not an intruder. Still, his presence is disconcerting. Coors means to be alone.

"My name is Mancio," says the man. "I'm a soothsayer, sent to show you the future."

Coors puts no stock in soothsayers.

"*Raus hier*," he says. "Get out of here."

"The future is not as bad is it seems today," says the man.

Harrumph.

"Times change," says the man.

"I'm not interested," says Coors. He needs to get to work. This *halluzination* must be dealt with. He shakes his head to no effect. He waves his arms. The man is still there.

"Your brewery becomes the largest single-site brewery in the world. Twenty-two million barrels a year." says Mancio. "In the future."

"You're drunk."

"I am not."

"As of today, my brewery puts out zero barrels a year, not counting that unfermented dreck, Mannah." Coors makes a face.

"Trust me. Millions of barrels. A whole menu of brands. Real beer, with alcohol in it. They name a baseball stadium after you. Sell Coors beer there. You should see it. Come, get out of your funk here. It'll be summer where we're going. Warm. Louisa won't even know you're gone. I promise."

"Why are you pestering me with this lunacy?"

"I don't really know. I'm sent to pester a lot of people. You're on the list."

Harrumph.

"You pig-headed old German. If you won't follow me, I'll drag you into the future against your will."

HOT SUN SLAMS Coors' shoulders. He stands outside a brick stadium. He looks up. Enormous white letters spell out his name. COORS FIELD. He's surrounded by men, women and children scurrying toward entrances. Mancio magically whooshes them past the turnstiles. It's cooler inside, dimmer, but still warm. Carts and food stands crowd a concourse around a baseball field. His name is everywhere. In lights. On cups. On cans and bottles.

People slosh beer on his trousers as they walk past. Women. Women in very immodest dress carry clear glasses of beer. He can tell by the color and the bubbles and the aroma. They're laughing. The female laughter from the hallucinations.

"Get me out of here!" says Coors. "I'll take no part of this. I don't enjoy baseball. These women disturb me. I'd lock my daughters in the house if I ever saw them drinking in public or dressed worse than harlots. It's beyond immodest."

"My apologies. The future is too much to take in all at once," says Mancio. "Let's retreat to The Sandlot."

Coors objects, but it makes no difference.

The Sandlot feels like a cross between a German *Bierhalle* and saloon, but not really. The shamelessly dressed women are drinking beer here, too, but show no apparent interest in soliciting customers. If they are prostitutes they are unambitious ones. At least he can sit on a proper chair at a table. Mancio brings him a tall glass

"Coors Banquet," says Mancio. "Brewed with one hundred percent Rocky Mountain Water Since 1873." He points to the wall. "Says so right on the sign."

Coors takes a drink. Light, less malty than he considers ideal, but with flavor undeniably clear and crisp. He holds the glass to the sky. The color of Colorado sunshine.

Mancio's drink is something else altogether. It's labeled 'Blue Moon Mango Wheat Brewer's Select.' A cloud passes over.

Coors feels annoyed, but he is not without curiosity. "What is mango?"

"It's a fruit, Mr. Coors."

"That's not beer in that can, I trust. Beer is pure. Hops, barley, water and yeast. *Reinheitsgebot*. That's it. That's beer."

"Not anymore."

"Anything else is abomination. Mango. Whatever that is. Not permitted."

"Times change," says the man. "Blue Moon Mango is one of the many beers brewed by your great-grandchildren," says Mancio.

"Is Clear Creek still flowing?" asks Coors.

"As it always has."

"Then not everything changes. Beer doesn't change. Beer doesn't use. . . fruit."

"Better mango beer than no beer," says Mancio, taking a deep swig.

"*Falsch!* A man must know right from wrong. There is a right way to brew beer and a wrong way, indeed many wrong ways. Mango is a wrong ingredient."

"Loosen up, man," says Mancio. "Enjoy that Coors Banquet of yours, no fruit in that. Then we'll talk some more."

"I don't believe it. I don't believe any of this. This morning's activities have made me take leave of my senses. Take me home. It's clouding up. Looks like rain."

"Not until we've finished your great-grandson's brew."

"If this— this future—is real, I suppose I'm dead by now."

"Yes, sir."

"Then let me rise up out of my grave and kick my great-grandsons in *den Hintern.*"

"I can't let you do that, sir."

Harrumph.

After enough silence had passed, Mancio continued. "You predicted right. A Constitutional Amendment eventually passed, in 1919, and the whole country went dry."

"*Verrückt.* So what are we doing? Violating the sacred American Constitution?"

"The American people soon came to recognize that Prohibition is as crazy as you know it is. The Amendment doesn't last. When it is repealed, your sons are among the first to get back into brewing. About fifteen hundred breweries go bust when the nation goes dry. On the first day beer becomes legal again, Coors is one of only thirty-one beers available. Your legacy, high quality beer brewed from the springs of Clear Creek, that legacy is a lasting one."

"But the women, The WCTU and the ASL, they insisted the saloons be closed down so the husbands, the undisciplined ones, would quit beating their wives and children. How did that work out?"

Mancio sighs. "That's a problem never fully resolved. Prohibition didn't stop drinking, and it didn't stop abuse, either."

"I am most unhappy to hear that, but not surprised. So how were the women then satisfied? The Carrie Nation types."

"We let good women in. The male-only saloon culture never comes back. Why relegate women to tippling at home alone? Hiding in the bathroom sipping 'medicine'."

"Not proper. These women drinking in public, they are . . . disreputable."

"Not at all," Mancio says. "Fine women deserve a bit of relaxation, too. Ironically, Prohibition rid us of saloons, but introduced speakeasies, where we discovered that mixed company is more fun. There was no going back after that."

"And that's how we ended up with mango beer, I suppose," says Coors. "*Women.*"

Droplets of water, clear water, fall from the Colorado sky. Coors drains his glass of non-mango lager. Mancio takes him back inside the stadium. The Colorado Rockies are ahead. A double rainbow arches over the scoreboard.

"See the rainbow? That's a symbol. The future is promising," says Mancio.

"Rainbows are a dime a dozen in Colorado," says Coors. "It means nothing. You are not a *Wahrsager*. You are not a truth-teller. You're a liar."

"I'm hurt," says Mancio, not sounding very hurt and continuing regardless. "Things started off a bit slow when Prohibition ended, but eventually there came a beer renaissance. A brewer became governor of Colorado in 2011."

"My grandson?"

"Would you believe me if I said yes?"

"No, I wouldn't."

"Well, then, I might as well tell the truth. No, not your grandson, not even the same political party. But a beer brewer, which is something, although not really very surprising. In the twenty-first-century there are hundreds of breweries in Colorado. Most are small. Craft beer, micro-breweries, mostly," continues Mancio.

"How many so-called craft brewers make mango beer?" Coors says it like he's spitting poison.

Mancio laughs. "Mango, pumpkin, blueberry, coffee, carrot even. Name the flavor and somebody is either brewing it or doing their best to try. India pale ales, English ales, German dunkels. Irish reds. Coors makes a nice Irish red. I once tried an elderberry beer. Not bad. If it contains alcohol and tastes good, somebody wants to brew it and somebody else wants to drink it."

"Abominations!" Coors slams his fist on a stadium pillar. "Take me home. I am done with *die Phantasterei*. You speak lies and nonsense. I believe none of it. My family makes malted milk for children and ceramics for scientists. That is what we do now, and I must get back to it."

BACK HOME in Golden, Coors thrusts the geode from the buffet into the hands of his wife.

"Who was it left this thing here at your tea party?" he demands.

"Mrs. Brown, I believe."

"Is she a dry? A crusader against alcohol?"

"I don't know. That's not a thing a lady guest would mention in our home."

"Get the d--- get this thing out of my house. Out of my sight!"

Epilogue

Adolph Coors Sr.'s life story does not have a happy ending, as Coors family stories tend not to have. He committed suicide in June, 1929, four years before Prohibition ended. He jumped from the balcony of his sixth story room at the Cavalier Hotel in Virginia Beach, Virginia, where he was either vacationing or recovering from the flu, or both. Some speculate he may have been murdered, but the more commonly accepted explanation is that he was 'unhappy, lonely, and without anything to occupy his time.' Other than instructions in his will to pay his hotel bill in full, he left no note. His body was brought home to Colorado and buried at Crown Hill Cemetery in Wheat Ridge. The Great Depression had not yet started, but Prohibition had been in effect throughout the country for a decade, even longer in Colorado. His sons were managing the malted milk and ceramics factories.

The Eighteenth Amendment, which prohibited "the manufacture, sale, or transportation of intoxicating liquors" throughout the United States, was repealed by the Twenty-First Amendment in 1933. Coors's sons resumed brewing beer immediately, his grandsons and great-grandsons continuing the business. Coors did not believe women should be in business and the males-only tradition help up until very recently.

The Coors family saga has been rife with tragedy since the founder's death. Most infamously, Coors' grandson and heir, Adolph Coors III, was murdered in a kidnapping gone badly awry in 1960.

The Coors family and Coors businesses are a huge presence in Colorado. Starting as a regional beer, Coors Brewing continued growing after

Prohibition until the brand became available in all fifty states in 1991. It is now part of Molson Coors. CoorsTek, manufacturer of 'engineered technical ceramics' for science, semiconductor and medical research applications, is less visible but arguably even more successful. The malted milk business, however, disappeared with the end of Prohibition.

Just the Facts, Ma'am

Adolph Coors Sr. focused his energy on making beer and raising his six children. He was not a publicity hound. The relative void of contemporaneous accounts of his life (not counting the carefully-crafted public relations statements the company put out) may have provided opportunity for mythmaking after his death. The fact that he was a stowaway on a ship was a family secret kept hidden until 1970. The story that he was able to save up $2,000 (approximately $40,000 in today's dollars) from three years of 'meager earnings' as an itinerant laborer cutting stones and laying bricks seems a little far-fetched. But maybe.

With all that in mind, ***Coors: A Rocky Mountain Legend*** by Russ Banham is a readable account of his life with some lovely historical pictures. ***Citizen Coors*** by Dan Baum tells the story of the later generations' involvement in evangelical religion and conservative politics. ***Colorado Vanguards: Historic Trailblazers & Their Local Legacies*** by Phyllis J. Perry includes a short biography of Coors. ***Death of an Heir*** by Philip Jett is a true crime story of the abduction and murder of Adolph Coors III.

Ken Burns tells the fascinating story of the temperance movement in his three-part documentary series ***Prohibition,*** which can be streamed on Netflix or purchased on DVD from PBS. There are many historical accounts of Prohibition in print, including ***The War on Alcohol*** by Lisa McGirr and ***Last Call*** by Daniel Okrent.

Just for Fun

The behemoth **Coors Brewery** in Golden still sits along Clear Creek exactly where Adolph Coors put it. **Tours** are open to all ages. Park at 13th and Ford in Golden. You'll get a shuttle tour through the city of Golden past the Territorial Capital and other historic buildings. The tour inside the brewery is a combination of visual displays and audio, with real people along the way to answer questions and to keep you from getting lost. The

Colorado Phantasmagorias

highlights are the really cool copper kettles and the canning conveyor belts. (Interesting trivia: Adolph Coors' grandson Bill invented the recyclable aluminum can in 1959. No matter what brand of beer or soda you drink, if it's in a can, it's Bill Coors' can.) **Beer** samples (not the tiny tasters of brew pub fame but a full eight-ounces) for adults twenty-one and older (bring a valid ID) and free soda for the kids ensure that everybody leaves happy. Go to https://www.millercoors.com for the latest accurate information on tour days and times.

Walk, run or ride a bicycle along the 20-mile long **Clear Creek Trail**, which stretches from downtown Golden, along the brewery boundary, past Tabor Lake, through several suburban parks and into downtown Denver. It's mostly flat and wooded, a cool ride for a summer's day.

You can also tour **Coors Field** in downtown Denver, but better yet, catch a **Colorado Rockies** game. Go to https://www.mlb.com/rockies to find information on tours and games.

Colorado was and remains a leader in craft brewing. Once you've had your Coors Brewery tour, be sure to take some time to check out some of the hundreds of smaller **craft brewers** in the state. There are organized tours that will take you from brew pub to brew pub, or you can explore on your own. It won't take long to find one, or a dozen, brew pubs, each with their own handcrafted ales and lagers. Just to give you an idea of the wide variety of brewers making beer in Colorado these days, check out the Colorado Craft Brew website at https://www.coloradocraftbrews.com for a list and a map.

Give the kids and yourself a taste of delicious **malted milk**, a beverage that has fallen out of fashion but remains available. Carnation and Ovaltine still make it. The dried powder is made from milk, wheat and malted barley. Although it contains no refined sugar, malted barley is naturally sweet. Mix the powder with regular milk to create a creamy, desert-like beverage. It's available in regular grocery stores next to the hot cocoa mixes. If your kids are put off by the grainy aroma, offer Whoppers or Maltesers, two brands of chocolate candies made from malted milk.

Carl Howelsen
1877 - 1955
Ski Pioneer

"MR. HOWELSEN! Mr. Howelsen! Are you all right?!"

A boy is shaking Carl Howelsen by the shoulder. *Why is he shouting at me in English?* A big tumble off the ski jump has jangled Carl's brain. *Oh, yes, right. I live in America now.* He comes to his senses, checks for broken bones. *Uff da!* Everything seems in its proper place. "I'm quite all right, my boy," the ski jump coach assures his terrified young student.

"Over a hundred twenty feet, you jumped, Mr. Howelsen! Wowee!"

It's not Carl's first fall or worst fall, and most assuredly won't be his last. The first thing he teaches his students is how to fall properly, the most important skill in ski jumping. He takes a deep breath, stands upright. His woolen coat lists to one side. *Oh, yes!* That silly geode rock the child gave him as a gift. He'd stuffed it into his pocket and forgotten about it. It must have thrown off his balance going down the ski jump. He takes off his woolen gloves to retrieve it.

Just as the jagged crystals of the rock scrape against his bare fingertips, his familiar mountain surroundings transform before his eyes. Huge white tracks slash through the forest on Storm Mountain to the east, like a giant lynx has clawed it in a frenzy. Closer in, the ski jump he just slid down and flew off (landing with such uncharacteristic indignity), is multiplied several times over. He counts three jumps. No, five! Wait, seven!

Carl doesn't know the English word for seeing things you know aren't there, but in Norway it's called a *hallusinasjon*. Perhaps he needs another second to set himself to rights.

He shakes his head to clear it, hands the rock to the boy. "Put this aside where I won't forget to take it home." The boy puts the split halves back together and places it on the heap of coats and scarves left by the other children.

Carl's *hallusinasjon* disappears.

Colorado Phantasmagorias

"What's that saying you ranching boys use," Carl asks, leaning over to scrub snow off his woolen knickers.

"Gotta get back on the horse that threw ya?" the boy guesses.

"Yes, indeed. Let's do it again. But better this time."

And they climb back up the hill.

PINE TAR'S BITTER, smoky aroma, left over from tarring the bottoms of his skis, greets Carl as he opens the door to his ranch house. It's not a very pleasant smell, but it's redolent of memories. It makes him smile.

Carl nurses the bruises from his fall. Quite minor. Not at all as bad as the injury that sent him packing out of the Barnum & Bailey Circus a few years ago. Jumping all over the country with the Greatest Show on Earth. Most famously at Madison Square Garden in New York City, sliding down a jellied slide and taking off in front of twenty thousand spectators. Over elephants! My goodness, that had been fun!

'Ski Sailing: The Perilous Scandinavian Winter Sport in All Its Wild and Wondrous Daring' the advertising posters had proclaimed next to his picture.

But the back injury had been a godsend. Without it, he would not be settled here now in beautiful Colorado, on a ranch in Strawberry Park, resting up from an invigorating day coaching the local children, training for his own competitions, surrounded by the best snow in the whole world.

He takes a dip of chewing tobacco in his mouth, relishing the spicy bite on his palate, before opening the letter from his good friend, George Cranmer of Denver. He sets the letter on the table as he searches for a pen to respond. A draft threatens to blow the paper away. He reaches for the geode rock to weight it down.

Another *hallusinasjon* appears. Before his eyes he sees legions of creatures wearing all manner of colorful contraptions buckled to shiny, monster-sized feet. *Is my tobacco tainted? Or am I still jangled from the fall?* The creatures have giant bald heads of all colors—red and green and yellow and blue—and glowing garments to match. And great single-eyes, like Cyclops. Thousands upon thousands there are of these creatures. Maybe millions. Some stand in long lines upon the snow. They climb into metal compartments that dangle from cables. Others schuss down white slopes. Mythical creatures on outlandish skis!

Maybe it's a Norwegian *nisse* playing a trick, he laughs to himself, but he doesn't really believe in goblins.

He sets the geode halves face down on George's letter. The *hallusinasjon* disappears again.

No time to waste on such foolishness. He must reply to his friend, tell him of the great honor his neighbors will bestow on him, invite him to the christening of Howelsen Hill.

৯

Steamboat Springs
March 1917

SNOW SUGARED from the sky as Carl Howelsen's skis slid through fresh powder knee-deep on Rabbit Ears Pass. Flakes piled up in blobs on the limbs of the pines, like dollops of whipped cream on a layer cake. His breath crystalized on his blond mustache like rock candy. Cold nipped his nose and hardened his cheeks, but otherwise he felt quite toasty. Thick woolen stockings snugged his legs and toes, like the knit cozies his mother wrapped around the kettle back in Norway.

"God, it doesn't get any better than this!" he cried, reverently, to the trees.

Well, that wasn't quite true. Sailing off the end of a ski jump, flying a hundred feet and farther through the air. Landing on two feet, hearing the satisfying slap and swish. Feeling the weight of a winner's medal around his neck. That was even better.

He stopped and turned, admiring the straight tracks he'd just cut through the snow, inhaling a deep breath of crisp, chilled air. There was nothing more refreshing than a day on newly fallen snow. It smelled clean, of nothing and therefore of everything.

Carl waited, listened carefully. The world lay swaddled in silence. Stillness. *Stillhet*, in Norwegian.

Then, very softly, he heard some huffing. The sound grew a little louder, then louder yet. His flatlander friend George came puffing along the trail.

"Have some mercy, Carl! I'm just a lowly Denverite!"

"Buck up, Denverite, there's a steep climb ahead."

"Lord have mercy," said Cranmer, gulping in what little oxygen he could find at nine thousand feet elevation. "Where does a small man like you get all his stamina?"

"You can do it! You've done it before!" Carl encouraged him.

Colorado Phantasmagorias

"You know what would be great? A cable car for the uphills," George wheezed.

Carl laughed.

"I'm serious. The trick to making ski sport popular is a way to carry skiers uphill. A funicular, like the one at Red Rocks Park."

Such an American idea, thought Howelsen.

"People would gladly pay for such a convenience. It could be a money-maker. Millions of dollars."

Cranmer the stockbroker, always thinking about money. "Now, where would be the sport in that?" Howelsen asked.

"Why, the thrill of making turns in the snow. Jumping, as you do. Somersaults, like that crazy Hans Hansen does off your roof. All of that is good sport. You wonder why more Coloradans aren't ski experts. It's all the trudging uphill, that's why. It's just too hard for most people. They work at jobs that don't keep them as fit as you. And they live in Denver where there's, there's … there's just much more air!" This speech has made George breathless. "Colorado has millions of dollars ready for taking!" he continues, in between gasps. "I'm not referring to gold or silver, but this wonderful winter playground."

"Perhaps someday you'll make that happen, my good friend," said Carl. "In the meantime, we have a hill to climb!"

THE NEXT DAY'S Hill Dedication was quite auspicious. There was a band, and banners, speeches and other hoopla. Carl had the place of honor on the podium. George Cranmer, fully recovered from their *langlauf* traipse over Rabbit Ears, was in the audience. Marjorie Perry, the woman responsible for introducing him to Steamboat Springs, sat next to George.

The mayor of Steamboat Springs concluded his remarks and the large audience applauded enthusiastically, the sound muffled by the thick mittens they wore on their hands. Spectators sat and stood next to Carl's famous ski jump, on the hill that would now and forevermore be called 'Howelsen Hill.' *What an honor!*

Carl had heaps of medals at home. Some from his ski conquests in Norway and more from his career in America. Baubles tarnish, perhaps even get lost over time. But a mountain named after him! Why, that was immortality! His name to be printed on maps forevermore! The speakers claimed he earned the designation through his countless hours teaching children and adults alike the joy of ski sport. It wasn't like that had been hard work. He knew hard work. Laying bricks all day was hard work! Skiing was fun.

A BOY GROWING up in Kristiana, Norway, didn't expect much. The place was cold, dark, and very poor. Whatever toys Carl had were useful—a fishing rod to supplement the family's meals, a bicycle for running errands in the summer, skis for winter. But little Karl Hovelsen, as he was known back there, did not let utility get in the way of fun. Skiing fast was fun. Skiing off a big jump was even more fun. The more you did it, the more you won, the more you won, the more fun you had.

In his twenties Karl won the King's Cup, a fifty-kilometer race, clocking four hours, twenty-six minutes and thirty seconds. Then he won the Gold Medal at Holmenkollen. He got to shake the Prince Regent's hand after winning the Prince's Silver Cup. The *Norwegian Sports Journal* called him a 'Skiing Hero.'

But you can't eat medals.

He had no money for school, so he learned how to lay bricks. Which would have been a fine career if anybody in Norway had the money to put up brick buildings or even brick fireplaces. Unemployment was simply no fun at all.

He heard of a building boom in Chicago in the United States of America. So at twenty-eight years old he got on a boat, disembarked at Ellis Island, Americanized the spelling of his name, and headed to the big city in the middle of the country. It was as if the entire population of Norway was stuffed into a single city, and what a grimy place! But there were bricklaying jobs to be found, and more importantly, other immigrant skiers. As soon as the first snow fell on the dirty streets, Carl formed the Norge Ski Club of Chicago.

There was never enough snow for real skiing, but the club made the most of what it had. The *Chicago Daily Tribune* noticed, printing a picture of Carl and a friend sailing off a ramp on skis. That caught the attention of the Barnum & Bailey Circus. The Greatest Show on Earth knocked on his door with an offer he could not refuse. Two hundred dollars a week! Why, he was pretty sure the Prince Regent of Norway didn't even get that much.

The circus ballyhooed his jumping as 'A perilous pyramidal, prodigially proficient reproduction of the most dangerously diverting sport in the wide world. A lightening dive, dash and glide, on skimming skis down a declivitous incline: a sweeping, soaring, sensational flight through space, across a gruesome gap, and a final landing on a resilient landing platform.'

He called it "a little stunt."

He did his little stunt in front of four million Americans in one hundred forty-six cities in six months. Then he wrenched his back. He would have to go back to bricklaying, but not in Chicago. Now that he'd seen the width and breadth of America, he chose Colorado. In 1909 he signed on as a member of the Denver Local of the Bricklayers and Masons International Union.

When he wasn't mixing mortar and slapping it between bricks, he skied (mostly in the winter of course, but there was snow to be found even in the summer if you knew where to go, like St. Mary's Glacier.)

In winter, the Moffat Railroad took him over the mountain pass and down to the snows of Middle Park. One day in 1911, he and a friend skied to the open plain by Fraser and admired Byers Peak. They skied on to Hot Sulphur Springs and built a jump for the town's Winter Carnival. They leaped off it to the delight of the townspeople. The Hot Sulphur Winter Carnival was where he met Marjorie Perry. She told him about an even better hot springs town with even more snow. Steamboat Springs.

He lived in Denver for work, taking the train up to the mountains as often as he could. When he couldn't get out of the city, he made use of what snow there was. After a blizzard in January 1913, he skied the few blocks from his home on Sherman Street to the hill in front of the State Capitol and skied down that. *The Denver Post* put his picture on the front page! Then he went skiing through the park, where he met a stockbroker a few years younger than himself. George Cranmer thought skiing looked fun, and asked Carl to teach him. Of course he would teach him! That's how they became friends.

What puzzled Carl, though, was why all Coloradans were not ski experts. Colorado had the highest mountains, most magnificent snow! Why were Denverites not all in the mountains every chance they could get, like he was?

Well, if there was anything at all he'd learned from the circus, it was the value of promotion and spectacle. In January 1914 he built a ski jump and put on a ski jumping exhibition at Denver's Inspiration Point, for the entertainment of National Western Stock Show guests. A crowd of fifteen-thousand, maybe even more, watched him fly one hundred thirty feet.

'He went through the air like a rocket,' *The Denver Post* reported.

That oughta get 'em enthused. And it did.

But Denver wasn't the best town for skiing. The Rocky Mountains were calling Carl home. He bought a ranch near Steamboat Springs, raised Timothy grass and clover, and put want ads in the *Steamboat Pilot* seeking work for a bricklayer. When he wasn't laying bricks or caring for his animals, he coached skiing and jumping free of charge to any locals who wanted to learn. He got the whole town so excited they wanted to name a hill after him. That's how he ended up on the podium next to the mayor.

WHEN THE HOWELSEN HILL christening folderol concluded, George and Marjorie and Carl celebrated with a visit to Strawberry Hot Springs. A sleigh carried them as far as the horses could manage. They strapped on skis for the rest of the way. Carl carried Marjorie's bathing costume in his knapsack. Marjorie glided next to him on the eight-foot wooden skis he'd handcrafted just for her.

"This is all your doing," he said to her.

"Certainly not," she responded, modestly.

"I had never even heard of Steamboat Springs that day we met at Hot Sulphur," he said. "I wouldn't be here if not for your introduction to the place. 'Where the hills are steeper and the snow deeper,' you told me."

"Surely you would have found it on your own accord eventually," she replied. "A high-flying ski jumper like you would not rest until he's found the steepest and deepest."

True enough, true enough.

Steam blurred the green pines and barren aspens on the hillside sloping down to the hot springs. Marjorie retreated into a little tent to change into her bathing costume. George and Carl took off everything but their long johns and jumped in. Marjorie came out of the hut, hands hugging her arms.

"Careful! Don't slip on the ice!" called Carl.

Hot steam rose from the bubbling pools, got swept by the breeze and settled back down on the rocks, freezing instantly. It was treacherous. Marjorie stepped quickly but carefully. She'd been here before. She submerged herself chin deep in the deepest pool, the skirt of her bathing costume ballooning about her waist.

"Ahhhh," she said.

"Ahhhh," said Carl and George together.

Strawberry Hot Springs was the perfect relaxing conclusion to the action-packed, thrill-filled Fourth Annual Winter Carnival. Henry Hall's record-setting jump, off of Carl's ramp on the slope newly christened Howelsen Hill, had been the highlight of the event for most spectators. The ranchers, though, cheered most raucously for the Ski-Joring competition. Horses whose job it was to herd cattle three hundred sixty-four days a year took a day off to pull skiers down Lincoln Avenue. Then there were toboggan races and a cross-country ski marathon. Half the Steamboat children and a lot of their parents were having fun on skis. It was perfect.

After a few minutes letting the heat seep deep into his bones, Carl fished his surprise treat from the hot springs. Hardboiled eggs and sausage, cooked to perfection. He offered them first to Marjorie, then George, and finally took a share for himself. Delicious! And great fun, too, this little cookery trick.

"Has George told you of his crazy idea?" Carl asked Marjorie, licking the sausage grease from his lips. "He thinks we need a cable car to haul skiers uphill."

"Mmmmm," said Marjorie, immersed in relaxation. "I've heard of rope pulleys in Germany and one in California, too, that tow skiers up the hill."

"It seems a little like cheating," said Carl. "The uphill is part of the sport."

"Ropes and pulleys! Bah!" exclaimed George. "This is the twentieth century. We can surely improve upon that. Besides, those rope tow things are reported to wear down gloves. The main beneficiaries of that will be the glove-makers." He paused. "Perhaps I should buy some stock in a glove manufacturer."

Such an American. Such a capitalist! But a good fellow nevertheless.

"The conveyance should involve a chair, comfortable for men and women," said George. "It will cost money, of course, to build and operate such a convenience. I am convinced that such a funicular or cable car is what is needed to turn ski sport into something big, really big, for Colorado. The velocity of the dollar is increased greatly where sports are active!"

"You're a man of money, George," Carl reminded. "Don't turn skiing into something a poor bricklayer can't afford!"

"You're right, of course. Ski sport is for all. A skiing place should be a public park, for both the wealthy and the poor, as well as the vast majority in between."

"Ideally, there should be a ski mountain closer to Denver," said Marjorie.

"There's a fine mountain along the Moffat Road in Grand County," said George. "Forested, with thrilling vistas."

"There are fine hills by Aspen, although that's not closer to Denver, I suppose," mused Carl, imagining a state overrun by ski sport enthusiasts. "Leadville has good skiing. And Summit County. All over!" He lifted his torso from the hot bath to cool himself. Snow fell from the sky. He caught a couple flakes on his tongue. "But there's no place quite like this!"

"I'm about cooked," said George. The trio exited the hot springs. After drying off they would celebrate with other well-wishers at Carl's ranch house, then the Denverites would head home by train.

AFTER THE PARTY, tidying up took a bit longer than Carl anticipated. Such was the plight of a man beloved by so many friends. They'd come by ski and sleigh, and polished off his cocoa and doughnuts. *Who am I to complain? They named a hill after me!*

That hill wouldn't pay the bills, though. Cash awards for ski jump wins he happily accepted, but those weren't enough, either. It was time to get back to reality. He took down from a shelf the plans for the First National Bank in nearby Craig, which he would be building as soon as the weather warmed. He unfurled the architectural drawings across his table, planning to set to calculating the manpower and mortar that would be needed. It was hard to focus, though, after all the excitement of the day.

He placed the two halves of his geode on opposite corners of the architectural plans to weight down the curled paper. The geode's embedded crystals reminded him of the alpenglow over Storm Mountain. Now that was a ski mountain for the ages. Perhaps someday the town would rename Storm Mountain, too. He kept thinking of the prediction made by the *Steamboat Pilot*, that someday, 'undoubtedly,' they wrote, the honors he had gained would be 'wrested from him by younger men.'

His fingertips brushed the tips of the crystals. The room tilted and spun, as if he were crashing off a ski jump.

༄

"WRESTED, NO. AUGMENTED, yes," Carl hears a man say. *Who said that? A latecomer to the party? How does he know my thoughts? Is he a nisse? Of course not, such superstitious Old World nonsense that idea is!*

A man stands at his door. "I'm not a goblin," says the man, reading his mind again.

This man seems both very strange and oddly familiar. He wears a coat of bright reds and yellows, stands on giant, shiny blue feet. Could those be—boots? Why, the man looks rather like the monster creatures in that crazy *hallusinasjon*! Except he has a normal head and two eyes, not one.

"May I come in?"

It would be rude to leave the man out in the cold. Carl remembers the fur trapper who once invited him into his cabin for a hot meal on a day he was skiing on Rabbit Ears Pass. Carl had been a stranger to that man, although not so strangely dressed, and had been welcomed inside. It would be kind to do likewise tonight.

"Come in out of the cold, sir," Carl says. "Close the door behind you."

The man tromps in with his giant boots and sets on the table a rounded, head-sized object and a transparent contrivance like Cyclops eyes. The colorful, bald monster head from the *hallusinasjon*. Just a costume!

"What brings you to Strawberry Park?" asks Carl.

"My name is Mancio. I'm a prophet, a seer if you will, released from your geode to show you the future of ski sport."

Carl chuckles. How absurd!

The absurdity transforms into reality. Although Carl knows in his rational mind that he is inside his home and the sun has already set, he feels warm sun on his face, sees the blue Colorado sky above, hears the crunch of snow beneath his feet. He is surrounded by the creatures with the giant feet and Cyclops eyes he saw in his *hallusinasjon*, which he now realizes are just people wearing hardhats and really big spectacles.

He looks up to the mountain. It feels like Storm Mountain, but it can't be. Hundreds, maybe thousands, of people whoosh down the slope on what must be an odd sort of skis. Some skid so close he feels the spray of snow on his face. He jerks away.

"Don't worry," says Mancio. "They can't see you or hurt you. You're not really here. We're observers of the future. This is ski sport in the twenty-first century."

Some people are standing on oddly colored boards, which are very wide and much too short. Others carry what looks like a small toboggan with giant buckles attached. They hop onto a contraption that swings them up the hill. *Is this what George had in mind?* Enclosed cars hanging from a cable fly overhead. This is all very confounding. And it looks like the entire population of Colorado is here.

"Mr. Mancio, please help me make sense of all this. Where are we? What is going on here?"

"We're standing at the base area of Steamboat Ski Resort on Mt. Werner. Over a hundred years in the future. I know that every time you come to town, you look at Storm Mountain and imagine a track from the top to the bottom. Now, here it is!"

It's true. Carl does think that's a fine idea.

"This mania for recreational skiing you started," Mancio continues, "it keeps on growing. The first skier from Steamboat Springs to compete in the Olympics is John Steele, a boy you'll start coaching next year. Later, a young man not yet born, Buddy Werner, becomes a world champion and Olympian. The town renames Storm Mountain in his honor."

Carl sifts through this information, trying to decide what to believe and what not to believe. It feels like a dream. "The Olympics are a summer event," he scoffs.

"In 1924 Winter Olympics are added."

"Ah. Good idea," says Carl. He feels delighted by that. So this is not a nightmare, but a good dream, yet still bewildering.

Mancio continues talking. He explains about helmets and goggles. Carl appreciates the need for those things, having conked his head recently, not to mention the time he went snow blind for three days. Mancio talks about chairlifts and gondolas, which are easy enough to understand. Mancio's explanation of twenty-first century ski gear, which involves a lot of unpronounceable English words he's never heard of, makes no sense.

More fun to hear about are the many new and different types of ski sport, like snowboarding and freestyle aerials. Carl doesn't understand at all the single, fat board with two boots attached, but he's not at all surprised that his friend Hans Hansen's obsession with 'aerial flip-flop' has become popular. Mancio takes Carl up the slope to watch experts on skis and boards spin and flip and seemingly fly into the clouds. He gawps. It's astonishing! What would The Barnum & Bailey Circus be willing to pay these brave fellows?

Mancio keeps jabbering about all kinds of other ski sport, none that Carl recognizes except for what Mancio calls "backcountry," and, of course, ski jumping. Carl's astonished by the number of people participating. And the children! So many children on skis. He smiles. Many aren't very skilled, but once a child gets on skis it does not take long until they can manage them pretty well.

Colorado Phantasmagorias

Mancio keeps talking. "A hundred years and more in the future Colorado has about two dozen ski resorts throughout the mountains. Your friend George Cranmer builds one of the other big ones in Grand County, at the west portal of the Moffat Tunnel."

"Moffat Road," Carl corrects.

"In the 1920s a two-bore tunnel is cut through the mountain, one bore for the train, another to send water to Denver. By then Mr. Cranmer has quit the stock broker business. He pursues his passion for the outdoors and convinces the City of Denver to build a ski area at the west portal. There are lifts to carry the skiers uphill, of course."

"Of course." George is not the kind of man who quits before he gets his way.

"Governor Carr comes to the dedication of George's Winter Park ski area in 1940. It grows and becomes very popular. Three thousand acres more or less, about a million skier visits every year."

"There aren't even a million people in Colorado!" Carl exclaims.

"Not in 1917, but a hundred years from today Colorado has almost six million residents, not to mention the people who come here from all over the country, all over the world, to ski and snowboard. Together, Colorado ski areas count seven to thirteen million skier visits every winter, depending on the snow that falls that year, more than any other state. This is something you predicted would happen. Didn't you write in the *Steamboat Pilot*, 'Skiing is a clean, useful and healthful sport. It is a sport for all the people. We have many already who are taking an active interest in it. There will be many more. It may take a little time, but they sure will come.'

"Well, not this many more! How could I expect so many people would come? More than all the people in Colorado. It's so crowded! So . . . mechanized . . ."

"It started rather small, with your Howelsen Hill, then Winter Park and Aspen, during the 1930s. Things really took off when the Tenth Mountain Division returned from World War II . . ."

"Wait," Carl interrupts. "Two?! World War II? We just got into the world war in Europe! One is not enough?! There's gonna be a second?" He's aghast. Odin, the Norwegian god of war, is run amok!

"Let's stick to ski history, Carl, and what happens here in Colorado. Anyway, the U.S. War Department decides it needs to train soldiers to fight in the Alps."

"The Alps? So it's the Germans again?" Carl can't get his mind off the idea of this second world war. "Coloradans fight in the Alps? On skis?" He's not sure he likes the future, anymore, but he's curious. "Who wins?"

"We win, Carl, the battle and the war. The U.S. and our allies win the second world war and liberate Norway."

"Liberate Norway? What are you talking about?!?"

"Focus, Carl. We're talking your greatest love in the world, skiing. Anyway, nine thousand outdoorsmen and ski racers from all over the country come to Leadville for combat training. Fast forward to the end of the second world war, and these men can't wait to come back. Peace brings the former ski soldiers back to the greatest snow in the world. They develop dozens of recreational ski resorts, including Steamboat, and the biggest resort of all, Vail. These men are the moving force behind improved ski technology, chairlifts and gondolas. Recreational resorts with snow."

Carl's feelings are all jumbled up. He's happy so many thousands—millions—of people are sharing his joy in ski sport. He's always known, in his heart, that George was on to something with his cable car idea. Trekking uphill is just too hard, and not enough fun, for a lot of people. Still, skiing uphill is part of the sport. So is *stillhet*, peace and quiet. He shakes his head.

It seems Mancio reads his mind, for just like that, the hubbub disappears and, by magical transport, they're both suddenly sunk knee deep in powder on Rabbit Ears Pass. Nobody else is around. It's quiet. Snowflakes tickle his nose, stick to his mustache. Then he hears swish swish, a sound almost imperceptible at first, but it grows. Swish, swish, swish. The familiar pulse of skis cutting track. He turns. People wearing stocking caps are coming toward them. Skiing uphill!

Mancio grins. "Twenty-first century backcountry ski gear is better than anything you ever imagined, but the technique is not so different. Not all future skiers go to resorts with mechanical lifts and gondolas. Quiet trails like this are scattered all over the mountains."

Carl is always working on improving the performance of his gear, so he wants to talk with these skiers and inspect their remarkable skis and poles, but Mancio reminds him that he can't be seen. The people swish past. Silence again. Until the chatty Mancio starts up all over. "There are other new kinds of ski sport you need to see. Now we go to Howelsen Hill."

Whoosh, the magic transports them again. To the Ski Touring Center at Howelsen Hill, Mancio says. The Yampa River flows past. In the farther distance is Storm Mountain, or Mt. Werner as Mancio calls it, looking clawed up. Ah, yes, just like in that *hallusinasjon*. He understands that vision now. But what he doesn't understand is how the snow beneath their feet is so flat and hard-packed. *And what manner of supernatural being is able to cut such perfectly straight grooves?*

Mancio, ever the mind reader, explains about the mechanically cut ski grooves of classic Nordic. He tells the story of the American who invented skate skiing, a technique perfected by Norwegians, which turns into yet another separate ski sport. Classic skiers use the cut tracks, skater skiers the wide, packed trail. "In addition to the big resorts with the chairlifts and so on, Colorado also has many groomed ski trails in Nordic ski areas such as this one," Mancio concludes.

Carl has completely lost track of all the different kinds of ski sport that people do in the future. But there's one Mancio hasn't mentioned.

"What about jumping?"

"Not so popular as in your day," he responds. "But you'll be pleased to know that kids still learn to ski jump here on your hill. Jumping is still an Olympic event. More Olympic jumpers are trained on Howelsen Hill than any other place in America. Indeed, more winter Olympians have come from Steamboat Springs than any other place in America. Buddy Werner of Mt. Werner fame trained on Howelsen Hill. That's your legacy."

The Olympics symbolize friendship and peace through sport. Carl likes that.

Mancio takes him to the ski jump area. He counts the ramps. Seven. Just like in his *hallusinasjon*. He's itching to actually jump. By magic, the most magnificent skis appear on his feet. He's transported via enchantment, yet again, this time to the top of the highest jump.

Mancio says just three last words. "Go for it." Then he disappears.

Carl sails down the ramp, flies into the air, and lands back at his real life.

Epilogue

Carl Howelsen intended to live out his life in Colorado. Once he'd left Denver and settled in his Strawberry Park ranch he said, "Here I shall stay if nothing happens to keep me from it." But something did keep him from it. He fell in love.

In 1921 he went on vacation to Norway, met a woman, married, and never returned to the U.S. He and his wife had one son, Leif. After Norway surrendered to the Nazis in World War II, Leif, age nineteen, became a Norwegian resistance fighter. He was captured and imprisoned by the Gestapo for two years, including several months in solitary confinement. Leif was released in 1945.

Carl never lost touch with his American friends. He corresponded with George and others via international post. George quit stock-brokering in 1928, a year before the infamous stock market crash that led to the Great Depression. In the midst of the depression, Mayor Stapleton appointed George to be Manager of Denver Parks and Improvements and he was responsible for the development of both Red Rocks Park & Amphitheater and Winter Park Ski Resort.

In addition to the hill named for him, Carl Howelsen left a lot of brickwork. Two of his buildings are listed on the National Register of Historic Places: First National Bank Building in Craig and Solandt Memorial Hospital in Hayden.

Carl lived long enough to watch Steamboat Springs skiers, including Gordy Wren and Buddy Werner, compete in ski races near his home in Oslo, Norway. He was on hand to greet the U.S. Olympic Team to Norway in 1952.

Carl was inducted into the U.S. Ski Hall of Fame in 1969. Carl and his friend George were inducted into the Colorado Ski and Snowboard Hall of Fame in 1977. Marjorie Perry was inducted in 1988.

Just the Facts, Ma'am

Carl Howelsen did not introduce skiing to Colorado. Mail carriers, doctors, and pastors used skis to get around for decades. Norwegian miners near Breckenridge were known to use skis (see the reference in the Barney Ford chapter of this collection). What Carl did was to introduce recreational skiing—skiing just for the fun of it.

Carl's son Leif Hovelsen (he used the Norwegian spelling of his last name), wrote the definitive biography of his father, entitled ***The Flying Norseman*** (1983). It's very entertaining, and a popular souvenir for visitors to Steamboat Springs. It can also be purchased online or borrowed through a Colorado library. A short biography is published online by the U.S. Ski Hall of Fame at https://skihall.com/hall-of-famers/carl-howelsen/

The most complete history of skiing in Colorado is *Ski Style: Sport and Culture in the Rockie*s by Annie Gilbert (2004). She focuses almost exclusively on downhill skiing (what she calls the 'cosmopolitan' style originating in the Swiss Alps), making only a glancing reference to less commercial (Nordic) and non-commercial (backcountry) skiing (what she calls the 'working class' style originating from Norway). Other than that common bias, the book is a must-read for anyone interested in the origins of Colorado ski culture.

Just for Fun

Where to start? If there was ever an influential Coloradan who wanted people to have fun, it was Carl Howelsen. Any kind of activity on the snow pays tribute to him, but there are far too many choices to list all of them individually.

Howelsen Hill touts itself as the oldest continuously-operating ski area in the country, so that's the most obvious place to start. Historical 'Then and Now' pictures decorate the walls of the traditional, shabby-chic log cabin lodge just outside of downtown Steamboat Springs. The giant ski jump ramps are Howelsen Hill's signature feature. Jumping is not undertaken casually without training. To watch adults and kids who know what they're doing, ask about the schedule at the lodge. Howelsen Hill also has a small downhill ski slope (yes, with lifts) as well as Nordic trails. Groomed trails require maintenance, so expect to pay a small trail fee. Enjoy far views of mountain peaks, mid-range view of Mt. Werner and the town of Steamboat Springs, and close-in views of rock outcroppings, aspen groves and the Yampa River. For details: http://steamboatsprings.net/131/Howelsen-Hill-Ski-Area.

For more thrills and amenities on skis or snowboard, of course there's **Steamboat Ski Resort**. https://www.steamboat.com/ or George Cranmer's **Winter Park Ski Resort** https://www.winterparkresort.com. or any of the 23 resorts belonging to **Colorado Ski Country** USA https://www.coloradoski.com, plus all four Colorado areas belonging to Vail Resorts https://www.vail.com/.

Colorado Phantasmagorias 174

Colorado has at least seventeen Nordic ski areas in addition to the one at Howelsen Hill. These are a compromise for those who want a more natural and peaceful experience than the downhill resorts, but aren't keen on breaking trail. Ski rentals and refreshments are available at Nordic centers. Carl is reported to have skied through the areas now covered by **Snow Mountain Ranch** in Grand County, the **Steamboat Nordic Trails**, and **Frisco Nordic Center**. But knowing how he got around, he may have hit any of the areas listed at https://www.coloradocrosscountry.com.

For an even more solitary and get-away-from-it-all experience, **Rabbit Ears Pass** offers some of the best backcountry skiing in Colorado. Expect. Really. Deep. Snow. Trails are marked, but it's a good idea to know some wayfinding skills of your own. Other backcountry trails are scattered about the Colorado mountains. A Google search of 'Colorado backcountry ski trails' will get you lots of locations and directions. You'll have to get your skis at a rental shop in the city or a nearby town and bring your own food and drink. Up for an overnight? The 10th Mountain Division Hut Association offers 34 simple huts accessible only from ski routes (hiking in the summer). Reservations must be made in advance at https://www.huts.org/.

Steamboat Springs is a real one-of-a-kind town. It has all the usual resort community t-shirt shops, bars, coffee shops, and art and crafts stores, but where else can you stand at a stoplight and watch ski jumpers fly right at you? Obviously they're far enough away not to create any danger to shoppers, but still . . . Look for the **life-size bronze statue** of Carl at 705 Lincoln Ave. (main street). **F.M. Light and Sons** on Lincoln Ave. has been in business since Carl's sojourn in the area, still offering clothing, hats, cowboy boots, toys and other whatnots. In the back is a small historical exhibit with a picture of Mr. and Mrs. Light skiing in their backyard in 1916. If you're around in February, Steamboat Springs hosts the longest running **Annual Winter Carnival** in the country. Carl started it in 1914 (or 1913, depending on who's counting). The famous Lighted Man fireworks spectacle was introduced in 1936. There are also ski races, jumping, ski-joring (skiers pulled by horses) and all manner of winter frivolity. For exact dates, contact the Steamboat Chamber of Commerce at https://www.steamboatchamber.com/.

Colorado Phantasmagorias 175

Cold enough? Tired yet? Nothing's warmer or more relaxing than soaking in a hot spring while snow falls on your head and drips off your lashes. And there's no place lovelier or likelier for that to happen than **Strawberry Park Hot Springs** about seven miles from downtown Steamboat Springs. Sorry, but nowadays food is forbidden at the springs, so don't bother bringing eggs and sausage like Carl used to do. Several different pools with sand and gravel bottoms offer varying temperatures. You'll soak beside beautiful and not-so-beautiful people, including kids during the daytime. After sunset it's adults-only and clothing optional. There's a fee to get in. The road is steep and mostly unpaved, so don't try it in the winter if you don't have a four-wheel-drive vehicle; call one of the hot spring shuttle companies instead. The admission fee is included in the cost of the shuttle if you go that route: https://strawberryhotsprings.com/.

In the heart of downtown Steamboat Springs is the family-friendly **Old Town Hot Springs**. In addition to eight pools, there's a water slide, climbing wall and exercise room: https://www.oldtownhotsprings.org/.

To see the kind of gear Carl and George and Marjorie skied on (you'll be amazed) and real Olympic medals, visit **Tread of the Pioneers Museum** at 800 Oak Street (one block off main street) in Steamboat Springs: http://www.treadofpioneers.org or the **Colorado Snowsports Museum and Hall of Fame** right off of I-70 underneath the Welcome Center in Vail: https://www.snowsportsmuseum.org. Admission to the Snowsports Museum is by donation; Tread of Pioneers in Steamboat Springs charges a fee.

Both are fascinating museums, but the Snowsports Museum in Vail is more specifically ski-oriented. Be sure to look up Carl in the Hall of Fame video directory. The ski fashions through the ages video is hilarious. There are also interactive exhibits, including one that shows all of Colorado's active and abandoned ski areas. The 45-minute movie about the 10th Mountain Division, *Climb to Glory* **by Warren Miller**, is not to be missed. It includes archival moving pictures of training at Camp Hale (now Ski Cooper) as well as recent interviews with the veterans. The bravery and suffering of the 10th Mountain soldiers will make your gripes about I-70 traffic and long lift lines feel trivial.

Colorado Phantasmagorias 176

Experience the slopes and trails used for training by the 10th Mountain Division at **Tennessee Pass Nordic Trails** and **Ski Cooper**, ten miles north of Leadville. One of Colorado's most laidback ski areas, this is a great choice for families, budget-conscious outdoorsy types, and World War II buffs. Stop at the entrance to see the **monuments** to the 10th Mountain Division and the Viking Battalion. The Viking Battalion was comprised of Norwegian-Americans and also trained at Camp Hale.

If it's summer or you're just not into snow, walk the High Line Canal trail through **Marjorie Perry Nature Preserve Park** at 6060 S. Quebec St. in Greenwood Village. It's named for Carl's friend, the "naturalist, outdoorswoman, and conservationist" who farmed this property in the 1930s: https://www.greenwoodvillage.com/352/Marjorie-Perry-Nature-Preserve.

Florence Rena Sabin, M.D.
1871 – 1953
Public Health Pioneer

"HAVE YOU ANY notion of the cost of this?!" Spittle swings from the man's mustache.

Dr. Florence Sabin hands the man the cost-benefit analysis of her public health plan. Her temperament is cool as a Colorado evening.

He squints at the figures, face reddening.

Men get so emotional, especially about money.

Dr. Sabin is the only woman in this conference room at the State Capitol. She's comfortable, in command of her statistics. One of the country's first female physicians, a world-renowned research scientist, she has spent decades working with members of the opposite sex. The men around the table, on the other hand, squirm with discomfort, unaccustomed to a woman in a professional setting. They flip through the report she commissioned on death from preventable diseases in Colorado. Questions alternate between hostility and gentility.

"Dr. Sabin," says another man. "Your reputation in the world of medical science is inestimable. We are honored to share your presence. But you are no longer in a laboratory back east. Coloradans see things from a different perspective."

I'm a Coloradan, she objects, silently, to herself. *Central City born. Educated in Denver. I rode an ore bucket into a gold mine with my daddy. I'm a mountain climber.*

She takes a sip of tea, stays professional. The genteel insult makes her heart beat just a bit faster than usual, still less than when summiting a fourteener. She presses forward with her case. "Governor Vivian coaxed me out of retirement to address the deplorable state of health in my *home state*." She enunciates "home state" extra precisely, then continues.

"Building modern sewage treatment and water sanitation plants is indeed an expensive endeavor. Paying public health doctors, building hospitals, it all costs money. The figures are there for you to see. But you must factor in the cost of babies killed by diphtheria. Or children orphaned because a sick parent can't get to a hospital."

Another of the men speaks up. "You have spent your career in big east coast cities peering at tiny bits under a microscope. What do you know about dairy cows and beef cattle? These . . . edicts. . . for pasteurization of milk and quarantining sick cattle . . ." He shakes his head. "Our cattlemen will revolt."

"Tiny bits under a microscope are what taint milk and sicken babies. Cattlemen have children of their own; certainly they care about health. *Brucellosis* bacteria are tiny bits that make people sick, but also cause cows to abort calves. Ranchers know the cost of calves lost. Properly explained, they'll see the value in this."

Colorado's rate of preventable death is among the most miserable in the forty-eight states. The challenge before these men is as obvious as snow on Pikes Peak. Still, they appear unconvinced that any action need be taken, any funds spent, to improve the health of their constituents. Several are scribbling irritably on the margin of the report. One appears to be calculating on his fingers while puffing a cigar, the aroma strong. The air grays. Dr. Sabin is a patient woman, but these legislators are really taxing her tolerance. She fiddles with the good luck charm in the pocket of her jacket, a geode she picked up as a souvenir from the Colorado Mountain Club.

All of a sudden she feels dazed, like the time she accidentally inhaled chloroform in medical school. The smoky air freshens, like at a garden party. The men's bare heads sprout sun bonnets, ornamented with ribbons, lace and silk flowers. *My, my, what manner of tobacco is in that man's cigar? Or is my tea tainted?* Their visages soften, whiskers disappear, drab suits transform into embroidered dresses, ties turn into golden chains and glittering gem pendants.

The hallucination mutates rapidly. Sun bonnets become mortarboards over the curls of women's tresses. The suits that became dresses are now lab smocks hanging loose over female figures. The ties turned necklaces become black tubes lying casually against women's breasts. Shiny round disks swing from the tubes. *Stethoscopes.*

The person seated next to her rises and extends a hand. Dr. Sabin stands and removes her hand from her pocket. The illusions dissolve in a flash, as quickly as they'd appeared. The female visions are gone. Once

Colorado Phantasmagorias

again she's surrounded with cigar smoke and male legislators in black suits and ties. She shakes the chairman's hand.

"We'll take your recommendations under advisement," he says, a platitude no better than patent medicine from a quack practitioner. She's no fool. He plans no advisement.

But that momentary vision, the fleeting hallucination, inoculated her with real inspiration. The antidote to their tight-fistedness and unscientific thinking is clear as the air on a summit. *Women.*

She will take her science to the wives and daughters and granddaughters. That's how she'll win the war on flies and rats, filthy water, sick cattle, and dirty milk.

༄

All Over Colorado
1945-1947

"LITTLE OLD LADY, my foot." Dr. Florence Sabin's sturdy boots thumped along the rocky trail. "Figurehead, my foot," she said, clambering over a rock pile. "The governor is not supportive. I'm told he did not expect me to work vigorously. He must not have done adequate research before putting me in charge. Even a cursory examination of my record would have revealed I am nothing if not a hard worker."

Florence's older sister lagged behind a bit. She waited for her to catch up before continuing. "I'll get these health bills passed through the legislature if it's the last thing I do. Which it very well might be."

"Conserve your strength," her sister Mary advised, catching her breath. "We're not as young as we used to be."

Florence felt invigorated, if a little winded, by this delightful tramp. Mary's suggestion was a good one. No harm in a rest. She seated herself on a chunk of granite, smoothed loose gray hairs from her face. She took off her round rimless eyeglasses, polished them with a handkerchief and placed them back on her nose.

"Oh, my," she said. "This is wonderful."

Mount Evans' snow-packed crags rose above. Tiny whitecaps on Summit Lake shimmered below. It was unlikely they'd summit today, as they had as younger women, but even a short climb revealed a stunning vista. "What a marvelous view. Remarkable."

Undulating green foothills cascaded eastward, eventually giving way to the golden grasses of the Colorado high plains.

"That disagreeable legislator intimated that because I studied cells I can't understand cattle." She used her boot to point at a pile of bighorn sheep scat. "This pile is a community of microscopic life we can't see with the naked eye." Her gloved hand gestured toward the distance. "Likewise, the cities and high plains are populated by people and cattle we can't see from here. But we know they're out there. And a lot of them are sick. Many more than need be."

"You're preaching to the choir, Florence." Mary stretched her legs on an adjacent rock. A furry brown marmot poked its head up inquiringly, then scooted away. "What I want to know is, what's your strategy?"

"I'm taking my twenty-four-carat charm on the road," she replied. Mary would appreciate the reference, their being daughters of a gold mine manager. Florence picked a golden, five-petal Alpine avens, twirling its stem between her fingers. "PTAs," she said, plucking one yellow petal. "Garden clubs," plucking another. "The AAUW, literary societies, ladies' benevolent societies." Pluck, pluck, pluck.

"This little old lady does not take no for an answer. Once they've heard my arguments, the women will inundate their representatives, and the governor, with appeals to good health for their children and grandchildren. They'll pester their husbands, who will telephone their representatives or collar them on the street. Please, please pass these bills, the husbands will plead, so I can finally get some peace at home."

Mary laughed. Neither of them had ever married, so had no first-hand experience with nagging or husbands.

"Of course, I must make some appeals directly to men's groups as well, Chambers of Commerce and so on," said Florence. "I must push, push, push this public health legislation. Like an ore bucket on a mine-car. Until I see the light at the end of the tunnel."

"Don't forget to employ your famous sparkly eyes and friendly smile."

"And more importantly, my data," Florence said, pulling her jacket close against the persistent wind.

Mary stood and gave her a hand up. "I can't imagine anyone more suited to this crusade. Your impeccable scientific credentials, your passion for teaching, charm. Now, get going, we've got more mountain to climb."

"DURING WORLD WAR II, three times more Coloradans died from preventable disease than died in battle."

It was a shockingly accurate statistic. A real attention-grabber. She kept her voice cool and rational. Some said her years back east had injected a bit of Katherine Hepburn into her Colorado accent. Not a bad timbre for delivering an alarming message.

"We think of our state as a health resort, yet we're dying faster than people in most states," she continued. The assembled ladies whispered excitedly, obviously taken aback, beribboned hat brims bobbing.

Dr. Sabin was hatless, her frizzy gray hair parted down the middle, tied back in a bun. She wore a plain silk dress and sensible black Mary Jane heels. In spite of her disinterest in fashion, she felt at home with these ladies. Before retirement, during vacations from her work in Baltimore and New York, Colorado society had often invited her to speak about her science. This time was different. This was a plea to step beyond erudition. She wanted action.

"Every community faces different health challenges. Some towns need sewage plants, others hospitals. We must fund public health authorities in every locality to identify and address hazards. We need public health training for doctors in our state medical school. The legislature is reluctant to spend money. Even Governor Vivian, who appointed me head of his Post-War Health Committee, seems not to appreciate the urgency. It is up to you ladies to educate and motivate your representatives to pass my health bills."

On that cue, a volunteer scurried about, passing out pink leaflets entitled "Basic Health Needs of Colorado."

The applause ranged from polite to enthusiastic. She smiled, shook the ladies' gloved hands, enjoyed the whiffs of Heaven Sent and Chantilly, complimented them on their gem pendants, nodded humbly when the ladies extolled her awards and degrees.

She gave as many as three speeches a day, wearing out her vocal cords.

PTA ladies heard about schoolchildren sickened from tainted milk.

Ranch wives got an education on preventing the spread of *brucellosis*, which they called Bang's disease, in cattle.

The gardeners and cooking clubs learned the danger of irrigating vegetables with polluted water.

Businessmen heard her analysis of employee productivity lost to illness.

She urged mothers to immunize their children and answered questions about polio, tuberculosis, diphtheria, and scarlet fever. These diseases were never far from the minds of those who had watched anyone suffer or die. Which is to say, everyone in Colorado.

Denver to Yuma. Sterling to Steamboat Springs. Brush to Westminster. Boulder to Glenwood Springs. Dr. Sabin took her 'Health to Match Our Mountains' campaign anywhere they'd let her in the door. What better way to spend retirement than driving the length and breadth of her beautiful home state? She experienced flat plains and steep mountains, soft evening light and the mad blind terror of a snowstorm.

She paid for her own gas and was glad she'd learned the anatomy of a car and how to change a tire. When engagements were too far flung, she engaged a pilot and an airplane. No sense letting money rot in the bank, and time was running out. She was seventy-four years old. No matter how much Colorado improved its public health, she wouldn't live forever.

"You've been a tremendous audience. Thank you so much," she concluded her presentations, eyes crinkling in a warm smile. "Let's give Colorado 'Health to Match Our Mountains.' Urge your legislators to vote yes on all the health bills."

Who could say no to the bespectacled old lady with the pudgy face, twinkling eyes, and the big stack of facts and figures?

A FEW TRIED. Grumblers brought up bad publicity. Housewives won't buy Colorado vegetables if they think our irrigation water is polluted! *Well, it is, and perhaps they shouldn't, until we clean it up.*

The nay-sayers were no match for the famous researcher and her posse of women riding herd on public opinion. The only fight between the Republicans and Democrats was over which party supported the Sabin Health Bills most enthusiastically.

When the legislature convened, she was in the gallery, listening as the gavel rang out again and again.

Bang! Passed.
Bang! Passed.
Bang! Passed.

Six more times. Dr. Florence Sabin had won. Nine bills passed. Only the cattle bills failed, but the dairy farmers had voluntarily agreed to pasteurize their milk.

Colorado Phantasmagorias

As the last bang of the gavel echoed through the chambers, she gathered together her purse and papers and headed home to her apartment by Cheesman Park. She planned a celebratory dinner party, then back at it.

There was more work to be done.

WHAT NEXT? Nine out of eleven bills passed felt like summiting Gray's Peak; now she'd have to descend the saddle before climbing Torrey's. Next session she'd get the *brucellosis* bill reintroduced for a win.

Then she would take on the rats in the City of Denver. Get funding for free chest X-rays and convince people to get examined for tuberculosis.

Allies were essential and she was becoming quite good at courting political friends. Governor William Lee Knous had replaced the fool Vivian who'd wanted a 'figurehead.' Her friend Knous called her a 'dynamo,' and an 'atom bomb,' but in the nicest way.

In Denver, she and the health-minded mayoral candidate Quigg Newton planned to unseat that horrible Ben Stapleton. Newton would clean up the city. Literally. Provide modern garbage pick-up and sanitation, for starters.

So much to do. So little time.

What next? For inspiration she contemplated the bouquet of yellow roses on her desk. Such an optimistic color, but the flowers inspired no fresh ideas. She picked up the geode paperweight from the Colorado Mountain Club, toyed with the split halves, musing on the purple crystals, like mountain peaks.

༺

"SORRY TO INTERRUPT." A strange woman appears beside her desk, thin briefcase slung over her shoulder, extending her hand. "My name is Sybylla."

Mary must have let the woman into their apartment. She shakes the stranger's hand. Any friend of Mary's is a friend of hers.

"Pleased to meet you. I'm Dr. Sabin. Make yourself comfortable."

Sybylla sets herself on a cushioned chair next to the desk.

"May I inquire as to the purpose of your visit?" It's Dr. Sabin's manner to speak formally to strangers, but she employs an amiable tone. This woman is Mary's guest, after all.

"This is going to sound quite insane, especially to a scientist such as yourself," Sybylla begins. "I am here to show you the future."

"What a clever joke this is. Mary invited a fortuneteller to see me!"

"I am a fortune teller," Sybylla responds, "but Mary didn't invite me. I sprang from your geode."

Dr. Sabin is nonplussed. The geode remark is nonsensical, but by her own admission the woman is an intruder. The sensible thing would be to call the police, but for some reason she feels no need to reach for the telephone.

"You really started something with your public health initiative," the fortune teller continues. "I'm here to show you how it turns out, your legacy."

The woman seems harmless, although perhaps in need of psychiatric care. "Are you quite all right?" Dr. Sabin asks. "May I get you something? Tea to settle your nerves, perhaps?"

Sybylla ignores the suggestion, opens the slim briefcase, pulls out a rectangular object. The object opens on a hinge. One half is a keyboard somewhat similar to a typewriter. The other is a screen showing colorful pictures.

"My word, such a tiny television. And in color! Mary and I don't have a set of our own, yet, but I've seen them through storefronts. Never one like this, however. So small it can be fit into a briefcase. Remarkable."

"This isn't a television. It's a laptop computer," Sybylla says.

Computer? Where are the vacuum tubes? Dr. Sabin has heard of such devices, which reportedly solve twenty-nine mathematical equations at once, quite miraculous, but one such device would fill an entire room. And it wouldn't display images. Dr. Sabin leans forward to see this little marvel more closely.

Sybylla types a few words and large black type appears on the screen: 'Colorado Second Healthiest State.' She types again. Fresh letters pop onto the screen: 'Colorado in Top Ten Healthiest States.' Again: 'Colorado Healthiest State.'

"Your prediction is that we achieve health to match our mountains. I do hope your prognostication is correct."

"I'm not predicting; I'm reporting," says Sybylla. "It takes some years. These headlines are from the twenty-first century."

Florence leans back and chortles. "That's preposterous."

Sybylla continues, "In sixty years the challenges change. By the time laptops—laptop computers—are invented, the country's main public health challenge is obesity. Colorado is among the healthiest states in large part because our people are active. The activity you and Mary enjoy so much. Hiking. It helps keep us healthy."

"All my campaigning for health legislation and it comes down to mountaineering?" Florence does not really believe she's seeing into the future, but this conversation is intriguing and the woman is pleasant company.

"You got the ball rolling on public health. Raised awareness. Not just in Colorado, but throughout the country. Thanks to you, cattle disease comes under control, most milk is pasteurized, cities build water treatment plants, garbage gets collected expeditiously. Air pollution is mitigated. Antibiotics treat tuberculosis, vaccines control polio and diphtheria. The diseases you fought to prevent become so rare people forget. That's the great triumph of public health."

This fortuneteller is certainly an optimistic sort.

Sybylla keeps talking. "But also its weakness. Twenty-first century people face different public health challenges, but the old ones threaten to reappear. Coloradans need to be reminded what happens when air and water get polluted, pathogens infect milk, and kids don't get vaccinated."

Perhaps not so optimistic.

"We could use a clone of Florence Sabin, perhaps," says Sybylla.

"You're speaking metaphorically. Plants are cloned. Not people."

"Not yet, anyway," says Sybylla. "In the meantime, education." She moves her fingers fast over the keyboard. Dr. Sabin sees a picture of herself. Her name has appeared in newspapers and magazines hundreds of times, her photograph many dozens of times. But she's never seen herself on a screen.

"This tells the history of The Colorado School of Public Health," Sybylla says. "The school traces its beginning to you. Your picture is on their website."

Before Dr. Sabin can ask what a 'website' is, Sybylla snaps the laptop shut, takes her hand and escorts her out the door of the apartment. Dr. Sabin is not sure why she allows this, except that a researcher is nothing if not curious, and this Sybylla is a most curious character.

Tenth Street looks both familiar and transformed. Dr. Sabin's head snaps left. Two blocks down the Pavilion at Cheesman Park stands as it always has, but the building across the street is unrecognizable. She turns three-hundred-sixty degrees, peering up. The trees are so much taller, the foliage thicker.

Could I really be seeing the future? Florence peers up and down the street. Strange cars line both sides. Sybylla opens the door to one. Flummoxed and unsure what else to do, she climbs in and they drive off.

"If this is the future, why isn't this a flying car?" Dr. Sabin asks. The popular press predicts flying cars in the not-so-distant future.

Sybylla sighs. "We've landed men on the moon, but we still can't figure out how to avoid traffic and potholes."

Well, that's a bizarre statement. Dr. Sabin decides to sit back and see what there is to see. In her early days as a cellular biologist, her direct observations had upended the medical community's understanding of the lymphatic system, a major breakthrough. Seeing is believing. All of today's peculiarities could be made sense of later. Right now she would do what she does best—observe.

Sybylla drives down shady streets, past men and women exercising in the park. Running on trails, kicking balls, playing catch. They turn onto Colorado Boulevard.

The sight alarms Dr. Sabin. She jerks up straight in her seat. Shocked. *What happened to the medical school? The University of Colorado Medical campus should be here on Colorado Boulevard.*

As if reading her mind, Sybylla explains, "CU School of Medicine outgrew its campus and moved out to Fitzsimons."

"The Army Hospital?"

Dr. Sabin gawks. Sybylla turns onto Eighth Avenue, steering farther and farther eastward. The city seems never to end. Eventually the blond brick behemoth army hospital becomes visible amidst a chaos of unfamiliar glass and red brick. Sybylla parks. The Fitzsimons edifice is the only thing Florence recognizes.

Sybylla escorts her through a sprawling complex. Dr. Sabin's mouth gapes open. She covers it with her fingers. She's in awe, but not about the buildings.

"What is the most remarkable thing you see?" Sybylla quizzes.

Dr. Sabin places both hands over her heart. "All the women." She takes a deep breath. "Look at all of them."

A stream of women, long hair swinging beneath mortarboards, white tassels bouncing along, walk past her. Their gowns and stoles tell her these women are medical school graduates. *Doctors.* Like herself.

Colorado Phantasmagorias

"It's commencement day for the School of Public Health," Sybylla explains. "No longer are women a small minority of doctors, in any of the specialties, including biomedical research."

"A woman who works hard can be anything she wants, is what I've always said," Dr. Sabin takes her hands from her heart, extends them to congratulate the graduates, both men and women. They don't acknowledge her at all.

"We're seeing the future, Dr. Sabin," Sybylla explains. "They can't see you."

Next, Sybylla guides her into a brick and glass structure that must be a hospital. Here there are objects she recognizes—gurneys, wheelchairs, and IV bags hanging from poles. Doctors are checking charts, discussing prognoses. Stethoscopes swing from the necks of men—and women.

The graduates wearing mortarboards, women doctors with their stethoscopes, these are the images from that hallucination in the capitol conference room!

Florence inquires about the many patients breathing through face masks tethered to blinking machines. "These masks look like those used to administer anesthesia," she says, "but these patients are not in surgery."

"They are ventilators, Sybylla explains.

"Ah, like the ones World War II fighter pilots used to breathe," says Florence. "What's going on?"

"We have moved a few more years further into the future. We're witnessing the year 2020. Those graduates you saw are now doctors and public health advocates. A new virus threatens to rival the pandemic you witnessed in 1918."

"That was a terrible, terrible year. So many unnecessary deaths. I hope that not all the lessons we learned were forgotten in a hundred and two years. Did Coloradans respond wisely?"

"We listen to our public health doctors, your legacy. Bars and restaurants close, concerts and all public gatherings are canceled, all to slow the spread of the coronavirus. Many people are able to use computers, like the one I showed you, to do their work from home. People even participate in meetings and attend church by watching and interacting through the computer instead of going in person. To save lives."

Florence can't imagine how a person could attend church through a computing device, but if it saves lives, she's all for it.

"This is your legacy," Sybylla continues. "You are a pioneer for women in medicine. You are a pioneer for public health. In the twenty-first century, the Florence Sabin Scholarship is still awarded to students committed to community health. There will always be fresh dangers to address. Thanks to you, Colorado counts itself among the healthiest states, and a public health leader in the country and the world."

RING, RING, RING.

Dr. Sabin is jolted back to her familiar mid-twentieth-century reality. She's back at her desk in her apartment near Cheesman Park. The strange fortuneteller is vanished. How she got back from Fitzsimons to Tenth Avenue is a mystery. The phone on her desk jangles loudly. She picks up the handset and untangles the cord. "Hello, Dr. Florence Sabin speaking."

"Evening. This is Quigg Newton," says a voice she recognizes well. "Let's talk about my mayoral campaign, getting rid of the rats, the big one in City Hall and the ones in the alleys."

Epilogue

Dr. Florence Sabin's favored candidate, Quigg Newton, defeated Benjamin Stapleton for Mayor of Denver in 1947, thanks in part to her endorsement and campaigning. She was almost eighty years old when Mayor Newton appointed her to head the Denver Board of Health.

At the state level, more of the Sabin Health Bills were passed in the succeeding legislative sessions.

When Florence died of a sudden heart attack in 1953, at age 82, *The Denver Post* announced it in a double banner headline across the top of the front page. She never married and left no descendants. Her estate, valued at $250,000 ($2.4 million in today's dollars) went to the University of Colorado School of Medicine. She is buried at Fairmount Cemetery.

Sabin Elementary School in Denver and Sabin Middle School in Colorado Springs are named for her, as is a dormitory at the University of Northern Colorado.

Six years after her death, Dr. Sabin was memorialized in the National Statuary Hall of the United States Capitol in Washington D.C. The bronze statue shows her seated, a textbook and a microscope by her side.

Although Dr. Sabin called for the establishment of a School of Public Health in her lifetime, no program by that name existed until the Colorado School of Public Health was created in 2008, merging existing programs in preventative medicine at the University of Colorado, Colorado State University, and the University of Northern Colorado.

Just the Facts, Ma'am

For more on Florence Sabin's childhood and career in medical research, read Elinor Bluemel's definitive biography: *Florence Sabin: Colorado Woman of the Century* or *Probing the Unknown* by Mary Kay Phelan. For young readers, there are *Florence Sabin: Teacher, Scientist, Humanitarian* by E.E. Duncan, *The Life of Florence Sabin* by Judith Kaye; and chapters in *Remarkable Colorado Women* by Gayle Shirley, *Hidden from History* by Kim Zach; and *Women Pioneers of Science* by Louis Haber. The most accessible summary of her life can be found at https://womenyoushouldknow.net/.

Florence Sabin artifacts are on display in the **Strauss Library**, 12950 E. Montview Blvd, at the Anschutz Medical Center, including her mortarboard and diploma from Johns Hopkins University, certificate from National Academy of Sciences (she was the first woman elected into the Academy), and just a few of the many medals she was awarded.

Dr. Sabin was wildly famous in her lifetime, and not just among fellow scientists. She was named one of the 'Twelve Most Eminent American Women' by *Good Housekeeping* magazine in 1931. Colorado reporters described her as 'America's most eminent woman physician,' 'Madam Curie of the United States,' and 'crusader for public health.' *The Colorado Transcript* likened her to Jesus. *Time* magazine profiled her in 1946, quoting a Denver health official, "Hot damn—that woman is wonderful."

Just for Fun

Hiking remains hugely popular in Colorado. Books and first-hand information can be found at **Colorado Mountain Club,** founded in 1912 by Florence's sister Mary and a few others. Find them on the third floor of the old schoolhouse on Washington Avenue between Ninth and Tenth in Golden. CMC shares the building with the **American Mountaineering Museum.**

Colorado Phantasmagorias 190

The hike described in this story is the **Mount Evans Trail** starting at Summit Lake Park. The scenic drive from Idaho Springs to Summit Lake, completed by Denver Mountain Parks in 1931, is **North America's highest auto road**. On your way, stop at the 1920s-era log-built **Echo Lake Lodge**. Down the road a bit is a park with picnic tables and a stone shelter courtesy of Denver Parks.

Before there was a road to the top of Mount Evans, when the sisters were considerably younger, Mary and Florence hiked from the bottom, got lost and camped overnight. Mary Sabin described that and other 'tramps' up **Gray's Peak, Long's Peak, James Peak** and **Pike's Peak** in a series of articles for *The Denver Post* in 1911. These peaks are still among the most popular climbs near the metro area. As Mary advised, wear thick socks and an 'impervious coat,' even in the summer. Summit winds can be vicious. Also bring a good map. Expect to clamber over rocks. These are not walks in the park. Details can be found at https://www.alltrails.com.

Mary Sabin's recipe for the ideal hiking food was:
    Nuts,
    Raisins, and
    Chocolates.
Today Colorado hikers call that 'gorp.'

If walks in the park are more to your liking, stroll **Cheesman Park** between Eighth and Thirteenth Avenues, Humboldt and York Streets in east Denver. The very first hike sponsored by Colorado Mountain Club in 1912 was to Cheesman Park. Who knows why CMC chose such a flat, urban venue for its maiden hike. Maybe it was the panoramic view of Front Range peaks from the Pavilion.

Just down the street from the Pavilion is the Art Deco blond brick apartment building at **1333 E. Tenth Ave.** where Mary and Florence Sabin moved in 1938. It looks pretty much the same as it did then. It is privately occupied.

Also still standing, virtually unchanged outside, and privately occupied, is the house where Florence Sabin was born at 110 Casey Street in **Central City**. Other than the nicely-preserved Casey Street, there's little of Central

City Florence would recognize, except for the dozen or so tailings piles visible on the mountainside overlooking town.

Today Central City and its close neighbor Black Hawk are gambling meccas, but the **Gilpin County Historical Society** at 228 E. High Street preserves Central City's gold mining history. There's even an ore bucket like the one Florence's father let her ride into his mine. Also of interest is the doctor's office exhibit. On display are an antique exam chair, prescriptions, medicines and a microscope, perhaps similar to the one Florence used in her medical research.

If you go to Central City, be sure to take the old route along **Clear Creek Canyon** (Highway 6 to 119). It will be impossible to miss the real legacy of Dr. Sabin: two enormous facilities, similar to hundreds of other less obvious facilities throughout the state—the North Clear Creek **Water Treatment Plant** and the Black Hawk/Central City **Wastewater Treatment Plant**.

Stanley Biber, M.D.
1923 – 2006
Gender Confirmation Pioneer

DR. BIBER ADJUSTS his glasses and takes a moment to admire his cattle in the distance, a majestic herd illuminated by the rising sun, back-dropped by the sunlit Spanish Peaks to the west. 'Breasts of the earth' the Utes call the twin mountains. Doctor-rancher Biber is an admirer, of these and the real kind. It was a recent astonishment to learn that some men want their own. Well, women in men's bodies want their own. Breasts and all the other bits, too.

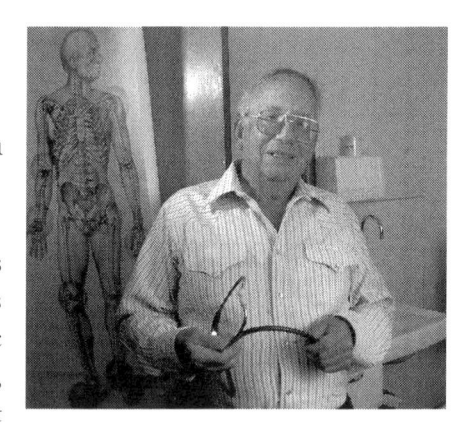

Who am I to judge?

The doctor's a bit of an odd duck himself, a Des Moines, Iowa, boy living in Trinidad, Colorado. A Mr. America weightlifting contender and a once-upon-a-time rabbi-wannabe. A short and stocky concert pianist raising cattle on the high plains. A Jewish surgeon treating Italian and Lebanese coalminers at a Catholic Hospital.

Still, his newest patient is a paradox the likes of which he's never seen before. What's a country doc to do?

The pocket of his jacket sags with the weight of a geode, a rock given to him by a little girl whose harelip he repaired. A geode's rough exterior hides what's inside, until someone does a little work to reveal the inner beauty. He takes the geode out of his pocket, jiggles apart the two already-broken halves, and admires the crystals inside. Beautiful, like the view from his ranch.

Suddenly, defying his five senses and all logic, he sees a mirage of women arising from the grasses of his pasture. Hundreds, no, there must be thousands of women. Their tresses swing like grass in the breeze. They smile at him, wave, laugh. He sees willowy beauties and grandmotherly types; women with delicate figures and others with the heft of pioneer women who set their muscles to the plow. Amidst them, a few bearded men laugh and wave as well.

What the hell is going on?

Dr. Biber is not the kind of surgeon who nips narcotics. He gets his high from his children, growing his herd of cattle, lifting weights, and helping suffering people feel better. He's healthy, in the prime of his career. There's absolutely no medical basis for this hallucination.

He positions the geode halves back together and stuffs it in his pocket. The mirage of women disappears, his familiar cattle once again the only beings in sight.

He climbs in his truck, steers toward the hospital. He has to scrub for surgery.

ဢ

Trinidad
1969

WHEN ANN FIRST came for a consultation, he assumed she was there to discuss the foster children she'd brought to him for treatment. She was a conscientious social worker, genuinely concerned for the wellbeing of her charges. Broken bones that needed to be reset, tonsils to be removed, harelips and cleft palates to repair, were brought to him. He was the town doctor in a place with too few people for a pediatrician.

"How's Becky doing with her new lip?" he asked.

"Very well, Doctor. The children aren't teasing her much anymore."

"That's great! Just great!" he beamed. If Dr. Biber had a fault, it was that he was a little too vain about his handiwork. And why not? It was damn good work he did.

Ann fidgeted in her chair; the vinyl squeaked. She seemed strangely nervous, more than he'd ever seen her, and they'd known each other for a while. "Is there something I can do for you?" he asked, real concern replacing his proud enthusiasm.

Ann hesitated. She pursed her lips. Her lipstick looked to be the same shade his wife wore. She combed through her hair with fingernails painted that same pretty color. He wasn't in any hurry, not like those guys in the big Denver clinics. He could be patient while she put her concerns into words.

"I'm wondering if you could do my surgery."

"Certainly I can!," he said, not knowing what she needed done. Overarching confidence is a surgeon's stock in trade, and it came naturally to Dr. Biber. He exuded a personality so big that his patients looked on his beefy frame of five-foot-two and guessed him to be five-foot-six, maybe even five-seven. "I was a MASH surgeon in Korea. I've seen it all! There's not an operation I can't tackle!" he exclaimed with trademark ebullience. "So, tell me, what is it you need done?"

"I'm a transsexual. I need a sex change operation."

Wait, what?

Now it was his turn to hesitate.

"What in hell's name is that?" he finally asked, feeling flummoxed for perhaps the first time in his surgical career. "You want to become a man?"

"No, Doctor. I'm a woman, always have been, inside, but my body is a man's body."

"Coulda fooled me," he said. She's pretty good looking, he thought, reddish hair, medium build.

After a long silence she continued. "I grew up pretending to be the boy everyone else told me I was, so I wouldn't get in trouble, like an actor who can't ever leave the stage, until I couldn't take it anymore. I've been under the care of Dr. Harry Benjamin for several years. He prescribes female hormones. That's how I developed breasts, and why my face and hair look like the woman I am."

"I'm not familiar with Dr. Benjamin."

"He works in New York and San Francisco. But he used to be friends with Judge Ben Lindsey from Colorado."

Ben Lindsey was a judge who blasted the coldhearted John D. Rockefeller after the Ludlow Massacre outside of Trinidad. That was 1914, long before Dr. Biber's time, but as the doctor to Trinidad's union coalminers, he knew the story well. Wives and children of striking coalminers died when their tents were torched. There was a monument to the tragedy north of town.

Ann continued, "Now I want to take the final step. Dr. Benjamin is not a surgeon. So I'm asking you. I've seen your work. I trust you."

"Well, I'll be damned." He didn't know what else to say.

"Dr. Biber, life has played a dirty trick on me. This thing I have, it does not belong to me; it must go. And a woman's body must be created in its place."

Dr. Biber wasn't exactly shocked. It was impossible to shock a MASH surgeon. But he couldn't help thinking, this won't be a surgery anybody is going to celebrate. Friends brought ice cream to his tonsillectomy patients;

Colorado Phantasmagorias

they signed the cast when he set a broken bone. Ann wouldn't have that support. He wouldn't get any accolades.

"German doctors did it before the war," Ann continued, "but Hitler banned it. The very first Nazi book burning destroyed medical texts that described how to do it."

Those goddamned Jew-murdering Nazis banned it? Well, then it's probably not such a bad idea after all.

"And, of course, there was Christine Jorgensen," Ann said.

"Who?" Dr. Biber didn't recognize the name.

"Christine Jorgensen!" Ann's eyebrows lifted, surprised. "The GI who went to Denmark and came back a woman. A singer. She performed in Las Vegas. She was famous! A sensation! Surely you remember."

"When was this?"

"The early Fifties, Doctor. Her picture was all over the newspapers. She's beautiful!"

"The early Fifties? I was very busy in Korea then."

"Just think about it, okay?" Ann stood, adjusted her skirt, and prepared to leave. "Dr. Benjamin wrote a book. Perhaps you'll understand better if you read it."

THE TRINIDAD CARNEGIE Public Library did not have a copy of Dr. Benjamin's *The Transsexual Phenomenon*, but Dr. Biber tasked his secretary with tracking one down. After many phone calls, a university offered to loan it out. Dr. Benjamin's book was quite recent, very eye-opening, and included an entire chapter about the conversion operation. But Dr. Benjamin was an endocrinologist and his description was woefully inadequate. Dr. Biber began making inquiries and found out the procedure had been accomplished by surgeons at Johns Hopkins Hospital in Maryland. He wrote a letter.

Soon enough he received back in the mail a packet of detailed handdrawings of each step in the procedure.

I can do this, he thought.

ANN SEEMED both more nervous and more at ease at her next appointment. She fidgeted and her eyes flitted around the office. But her answers came more quickly, spoken with greater conviction.

"Have you ever had suicidal thoughts?" he asked, as gently as he could.

"Doctor, don't ask a transsexual if she's had suicidal thoughts. Ask us how many times we've tried to do it."

That did it. This affliction, or whatever it was, could be fatal if left untreated. He was a healer. He could not say no.

"Let's do it."

ARMS SLATHERED up to his elbows with soap, he scrubbed vigorously, all the while reviewing in his mind each of the drawings from Dr. Hoops at Johns Hopkins. Biber was a man certain of his skills with a scalpel, but perhaps just the tiniest bit less certain than usual. He elbowed the tap off and held his sterile hands out in front of him. A nun slid gloves over them. Not a quiver. He was certain. He was ready.

The nurses were busy adjusting the lights and the table, arranging sterile surgical instruments on a tray. He had not made a big announcement about what he was going to do, nor had he cleared it with the board of Mount San Rafael Hospital. Better to ask forgiveness than permission. On the other hand, it was impossible to hide what he was up to. But he was Dr. Stanley Biber, one of the few physicians in Trinidad, its only surgeon for over ten years. The nuns, the nurses, the community, all trusted him to do what was right.

When it was over, if the board reprimanded him, what of it? It's not like he would ever be asked to do it again.

SHE SURVIVED. Not that he'd ever had any doubt. The nuns fluttered about Ann's room, checking everything, making sure Ann was comfortable. Tough broads, these Sisters of Charity. Who would've thought they had it in them? Compassionate and open-minded, truly impressive. He bid them goodnight, and headed out to his truck to drive back to the ranch.

The chill of the dry Colorado evening nipped his skin as he climbed into his pickup in the hospital parking lot. He reached over to grab his jacket. The pocket still sagged from the weight of the geode the little girl had given him. He took it out and placed each half face down on the dash so it wouldn't roll around. *I must remember to find a place for these.*

☙

"Good evening, Doc."

Dr. Biber jumps in his seat. A strange man sits beside him in the truck. *How did he get in here?* "Who are you? How did you get in my truck? What do you want?"

"Slow down, Doc. I heard you were the friendly sort. Apologies for startling you, after a long stressful day. My name is Mancio. I'm sort of like one of those messenger angels from the Jewish *Tanakh*. I've been released from your geode, like a genie, to show you the future."

Dr. Biber has never felt unsafe in Trinidad, but this Mancio gives him the willies. "Get out now. I have to go home to my wife and kids. Gotta feed the cattle, have dinner myself."

"This won't take any time at all, literally. It's magic. You'll see your legacy and be home in time for dinner."

Dr. Biber looks away from the stranger, takes off his glasses, rubs his eyes as if that will make the crazy guy disappear. It really has been a long day. He looks through the windshield. There in front of him is something other than the familiar hospital he just walked out of.

"Where am I?" he demands.

"Mount San Rafael Hospital, of course," says Mancio. "A new hospital is built in 1972. It gets another makeover in the twenty-first century, but many people credit you for the fact that it survived at all. A great many rural hospitals bit the dust at the end of the twentieth century, but not Mount San Rafael."

"You need a shrink. Let me refer you to a psychiatrist for evaluation. I know several who may be able to help you overcome delusional thinking."

"Neither of us is suffering from mental disease, Doctor. I'm just a messenger here to show you the future. Your legacy."

"The hospital survives. Got it. Now get out."

Mancio makes no effort to leave the pickup. "The hospital is the least of it. Your legacy walks the entire country, your legacy lives throughout the world."

"What the hell are you talking about?"

"Look, you and the nuns and nurses at Mount San Rafael prove something that once seemed almost impossible. That compassion can be had here in the United States. Transgender people don't have to skulk off to Casablanca or Tijuana or some back-alley quack for gender confirmation surgery anymore. And they haven't had to since 1969, thanks to you."

"You're using unfamiliar terminology, but I assume by transgender you mean transsexual? And what's gender confirmation? Do you mean sex change? Wait, why am I talking to a figment of my imagination?"

"I'm not a figment!" Mancio punches the doctor's arm in a genial fashion, as if joshing with an old friend. "If I were a figment I wouldn't use unfamiliar terminology!"

Dr. Biber thinks he must truly have gone crazy, because this Mancio makes a good point. He considers playing along. Why not? "Well, Messenger Mancio, how does my one single sex change operation do all that?"

"Not one, Doctor. You're gonna do five thousand."

"Holy shit!"

"Word gets out that you're a fine surgeon."

"I am!"

"Who doesn't cheat people."

"Of course I don't!"

"Who works in a modern hospital with an empathetic staff."

"Absolutely!"

"In an easy-going community."

"Trinidad's as good as it gets!"

"From today until you retire, you perform over five thousand successful gender confirmation surgeries, mostly male to female, a few female to male. Trinidad becomes the 'Sex Change Capitol of the World.' For several decades anyway."

"Not possible."

"Possible. And it started today."

MANCIO SNAPS his fingers. They are transported magically to Dr. Biber's office on the top floor, that would be the fourth floor, of the tallest building in Trinidad—the First National Bank Building.

"The twenty-first century is too big a leap all at once, Doc. I've taken you just a few months into the future. It's still 1969, but Ann is recovered and coming in for a post-op evaluation. Here's the deal. You, the time traveler will watch you the real doctor. Ann won't be able to see or hear you the time traveler. It's like watching yourself on TV."

Mancio vanishes. Ann is on the examination table. She's smiling, even laughing a little. It's fascinating watching himself, like a dream. *That's it. This must be a dream.*

"Thanks so much, Doctor," Ann says to Dr. Biber's double. "It works and everything! I could get married! I do hope so. And adopt children."

This is a very vivid dream.

Ann dresses and leaves. The stranger reappears.

"Messenger Mancio, it looks like hell, not at all up to my usual surgical standards," says Dr. Biber, "but she seems very pleased nevertheless."

"Eventually your skill in this particular procedure becomes so refined that even experienced gynecologists can't tell the difference."

The doctor chuckles. "Practice makes perfect, they say. Five thousand is gonna be a lot of practice."

WITH NO FOREWARNING, Mancio transports them again. Magic puts them in the balcony of an elegant, horseshoe-shaped hall, green carpet on the floor, well-dressed people leaning back in massive leather chairs. A woman is speaking in a pleasant, but unfamiliar accent. *British? No, not quite. Australian?*

"Mr. Speaker, I can't help but mention the number of firsts that are in this Parliament. Our first Rastafarian, our first Polynesian woman . . ."

Dr. Biber leans over to Mancio. "Where are we? Who is this?"

"New Zealand, 1999. Georgina Beyer. Your patient."

Dr. Biber starts listening again.

"And, yes, I have to say it, I guess," says the woman, lovely in an attractive red suit, swingy earrings, eyeglasses, and glossy black hair fixed with white feathers. "I am the first transsexual in New Zealand to be standing in this House of Parliament. This is a first not only in New Zealand, ladies and gentlemen, but also in the world. This is an historic moment."

"My patient?" Dr. Biber whispers. "From New Zealand? She came all the way to Trinidad?"

"Where else? Johns Hopkins did only a few before giving it up. By 1984, when Georgina comes to you, your reputation is known throughout the world."

Applause concludes her remarks.

"Are they happy, my patients?" Dr. Biber asks.

"The women you saw this morning in the hallucination, at your ranch. Did they look happy?"

"Friendly, certainly! Smiling. Pleased."

"Grateful, Dr. Biber. They are grateful."

MANCIO SNAPS his fingers again, and they're standing on a busy street corner. People walk by as if they're not there, because they're not. Dr. Biber thinks the people are wearing peculiar fashions. Some are chattering with friends, a great many are focused on shiny disks in their hands.

"Now what, Messenger Mancio? What's this? Now where are we?"

"We're nowhere and everywhere, Doctor, a half century in the future when transgender people just mix amongst everyone else, living as their true selves. That's your legacy. For a long time, you and Mount San Rafael Hospital cornered the market, doing two-thirds of all gender confirmation surgeries in the world. Finally, more doctors began offering comprehensive care to transgender people. Judgmentalists still get all worked up and pass laws about public restrooms and the military. But progress marches on anyhow. Surgeries increased four-fold between 2000 and 2014. Insurance coverage is more available. There's a spectrum, as you come to understand. Many need full surgery so urgently they'd die without it, others are satisfied with hormones, or are content to express themselves in the way that feels authentic, cross-dressing if you will."

Standing on this street corner which is both 'nowhere and everywhere,' Dr. Biber sees a world where gender lines are more fluid than he is used to, even in 1969, with all the long-haired hippies that live in the Drop City commune outside Trinidad. There's a man in a smartly tailored suit and bright pink shirt, hair tied back in a sloppy bun. A woman wearing camouflage combat fatigues, real ones, marches past. A boy cuddles a doll in his arms. Dr. Biber sees shockingly bright blue hair, hard to tell if it's on a man or woman. A small girl sports a buzz cut and a flower behind her ear. And the tattoos! On men *and women*. Dr. Biber spots more tattoos in five minutes than he's seen his entire life, not counting his years in Korea, perhaps.

Mancio continues. "Transgender people live and work everywhere now, as they always have, but openly. Some are even more famous than Christine Jorgensen. Olympic decathlete Bruce Jenner becomes Caitlyn. Chastity Bono . . ."

Dr. Biber interrupts, "Sonny and Cher's little baby?"

"Yes, all grown up as Chaz Bono, a man. Trans actors star on TV. Here in Colorado, the suburb of Arvada elects a transgender legislator to the Colorado House of Representatives." Mancio pulls what looks like a tiny TV from his pocket. He tells Dr. Biber it's a "smartphone," and flicks the screen a few times with his finger.

Glowing from the tiny screen is a photo of a curly-haired woman wearing a knitted hat striped pink and blue and white.

"Her hat is a representation of the colors of the transgender flag," Mancio says.

"They have a flag?"

The tiny TVs, transgender flag, little Chastity, the prospect of five thousand more surgeries; Dr. Biber feels overwhelmed, a feeling he's not used to. He just wants to go home to his ranch.

"Well, if this is truly the future, and not just a dream, and I've got more of these surgeries to do, on top of all the gallbladder operations, appendectomies, and prostatectomies, well, I really need a good rest so I can get right back at it tomorrow."

"And so you shall."

The strange Mancio disappears as magically as he appeared. Dr. Biber is back in his familiar truck. He turns the key in the ignition and presses his cowboy boot against the gas pedal. As he descends the hospital hill, he spots the basalt-capped Fisher's Peak rising in the distance above Trinidad. Vaguely phallic, it occurs to him for the first time, his mind now being fixed on such things. He turns northward toward his ranch, the summit in his rear-view mirror.

Epilogue

Dr. Biber performed gender confirmation surgeries up until 2003, when he lost malpractice insurance coverage due to his age (80 years old). Trinidad Mayor Joe Reorda proclaimed October 3, 2003 'Stanley Biber Day' in honor of his contribution to the Trinidad community. He continued to work for a couple more years, taking care of "friends who won't sue me," but turned over his surgical practice to Dr. Marci Bowers, a transgender woman herself (although not one of his patients). She practiced in Trinidad until 2010, when she returned to the west coast, where she continued to offer the surgery. Dr. Biber died in 2006, leaving his wife, ten children, and grandchildren. He is buried in the Masonic Cemetery in Trinidad.

Just the Facts, Ma'am

Dr. Biber's patients included movie actors, a judge, mayor, a train engineer, linebacker, and a Native American who brought along her own medicine man to bless the procedure. "Everything except a president of the United

States," he liked to say. Many people credit 'Biber's Girls,' as they were called, with keeping the local hospital open and solvent as they all paid in full, upfront, and in cash. Patients praised the high quality of care administered by the hospital and its staff of nurses, some of them nuns in the earlier years. The last Sister of Charity affiliated with Mount San Rafael Hospital retired in 1993, by which time Dr. Biber had already performed over 2,500 gender reassignments there.

Transgender people who came to Trinidad over the years were astonished by the casual live-and-let-live acceptance they received from the small community. "Everyone (almost) has been excruciatingly polite," patient Claudine Griggs wrote in her diary. "Why do the saints of Trinidad exist? Their presence on earth is an authentic miracle." Part of that casual acceptance came from a culture accustomed to diversity, where Hispanos (Spanish-speakers descended from sixteenth century settlers), Italians, Armenians, Greeks and Lebanese made up what *The Denver Post* called Trinidad's 'ethnic peculiarities.' Dr. Biber himself gets credit, too. Once he realized this would not be a one-time procedure, he gave a series of lectures explaining that "these are actually female people who've been female in their hearts all their lives." The town's religious leaders, including the local priest, "were very understanding and accepting."

Truth be told, however, some of the tolerance from the wider community came from the economic boost. Trinidad's population had shrunk by the time of Dr. Biber's first trans surgery and the average Trinidad salary was well below the state average. Dr. Biber's out-of-town patients brought in millions of dollars, not just from medical fees, but from hotel stays, restaurant meals and store purchases made by the families who accompanied them and stayed for a week or longer. "Listen, those people don't have a place in life, and he gives them a place in life," a dress shop owner told *Westword* in 1988. "What he does is wonderful." Nevertheless, not everybody was thrilled with the moniker 'Sex Change Capitol of the World.'

Westword was the best chronicler of Dr. Biber and his practice (September 21-27, 1988; August 27-September 2, 1998; November 27, 2003). Other media coverage included stories in **The Denver Post** (April 18, 1976; March 2, 1980; June 10, 1983), **The San Francisco Examiner** (July 26, 1984); **Gentleman's Quarterly** (December 1991), and the **Los Angeles**

Times (January 23, 1995). He appeared on Geraldo Rivera's TV show and was mentioned by radio talk show host Paul Harvey.

Claudine Griggs's diary, originally entitled *Passage Through Trinidad: Journal of a Sex Change*, later reprinted as **Journal of a Sex Change: Passage through Trinidad,** is a page-turner. Her story is brutal, but you cheer her along every step of the way.

Dr. Biber's protégé, Dr. Marci Bowers, is the subject of a documentary called **Trinidad** by **New Day Films**. Although Dr. Biber had passed away by the time it was produced in 2009, the documentary includes archival footage of an interview with him and a photo of Drs. Biber and Bowers scrubbing up together. The DVD can be obtained from certain libraries. Whether this is a plus or minus for you, know ahead that some of it is very graphic. A less graphic **Colorado Experience** documentary about Trinidad can be streamed at https://www.rmpbs.org/.

Back when Dr. Biber started in 1969, the difference between gender identity and sexual orientation was not widely understood, even within what we now call the LGBTQIA+ community. One of Dr. Biber's challenges was turning away gay and lesbian people desperate for a way out of the closet. Even today, many people conflate and confuse gender identity, sexual orientation, and gender expression. For those still confused, https://www.genderbread.org is a good place to start sorting it all out. **Being Transgender** by Robert Rodi and Laura Ross is a straight-forward and nonjudgmental book. Written for younger readers, it can also provide clarity for befuddled adults.

Dr. Biber worked with transsexuals (transgender people seeking a surgical conversion). He required his patients to have lived as their preferred gender for at least a year before he would operate. "By the time they get to me, they've already completed their gender identity change," he told *The Denver Post* in 1983. "I simply add the accouterments of anatomy." The 'accouterments' typically included removal of the penis, creation of a functional vagina and clitoris, and sometimes breast implants and a tracheal shave to reduce the size of the Adams apple. He did only a few female to male operations.

Dr. Harry Benjamin's 1966 book *The Transsexual Phenomenon* is outdated, but in it he issued a challenge: "Whenever, in the future, a conversion operation will be recognized as a legitimate surgery, perhaps even as a specialty within a specialty, and then becomes respectable therapy, improved techniques are bound to follow and with the improvement, perhaps more regularly obtained good results." Dr. Biber's legacy is that he took up the challenge and succeeded.

Just for Fun

Trinidad is a must-see for history fans. First stop should be the **Trinidad History Museum** at 312 E. Main Street, open 10 a.m. to 4 p.m. Tuesday through Saturday. The museum includes two Victorian homes furnished in period pieces plus an outbuilding with historical exhibits. A small exhibit to Dr. Biber displays original patient notebooks, prescription pad, stethoscope, and the camera he used to take 'after' photos of his handiwork. Stop between the exhibit building and Bloom Mansion to read the monument to **Buffalo Soldier Cathay Williams**. In 1866, former slave Cathay Williams disguised herself as a man and served in the all-Black 38th U.S. Infantry. She was the first known African-American woman to enlist in the U.S. Army, and lived out her final years in Trinidad. Denied an Army pension once her gender was revealed, she died in poverty. Ironic much?

If you love grand and historic architecture, the Trinidad **National Historic District** is a real treat. The **First National Bank Building**, where Dr. Biber examined patients for decades, is restored to grandeur at the corner of Main and Commercial. It was designed in 1892 by Isaac Hamilton Rapp and C.W. Bulger and was constructed of rough-hewn limestone with arched windows and incised faces. The **Carnegie Library**, 202 N. Animas, is one of the 2,500 libraries built by Andrew Carnegie between 1883 and 1920. **Temple Aaron**, built in 1889 at 407 S. Maple St., is the oldest continuously-used synagogue in the mountain west. All of this and more can be seen on a leisurely walking tour. Maps are available at the Trinidad History Museum or the **Colorado Welcome Center** at 309 Nevada Avenue. **Historical markers** along Main and Commercial relate the town's history. If you'd rather ride than walk, a **free trolley ride** leaves from the Welcome Center on the hour.

Colorado Phantasmagorias

A gorgeous ceramic mural depicting the history of Trinidad can be admired at **Mount San Rafael Hospital** at 410 Benedicta Ave. The mural was designed by Sister Augusta Zimmer of the Sisters of Charity, took four years to complete, and was officially dedicated in 1980, when Dr. Biber was chief surgeon.

Dr. Biber originally came to Trinidad as the official doctor for the United Mine Workers of America (UMWA), so he would have been very aware of the **Ludlow Massacre Memorial** northwest of Trinidad. See a beautiful sculpture of a miner with his wife and toddler. Interpretive signage tells the story: With mine fatalities ten times higher than the national average and pay of pennies a day in scrip (accepted only at the company store), coalminers struck in 1913. Evicted from their homes, they and their families survived in tent cities. On April 20, 1914, the day after the Greek miners had invited miner families of all ethnicities to celebrate Greek Orthodox Easter with feast of lamb and a baseball game, Colorado militia in service to the mine owners opened fire. The tents went up in flames. Four men, two women, and 11 children suffocated in an underground pit where they had taken refuge. Sixty-three people died before the violence stopped. The miners lost the strike, but it's considered pivotal in the movement toward labor reform. The incident enraged Margaret Brown, also profiled in this collection. Take Exit 27 off of I-25 and head a mile west.

You can **fish** for trout, bass, catfish and crappie at **Trinidad Lake State Park** on the Highway of Legends that loops west of Trinidad to Walsenburg. Or **hike** one of the seven nature trails, including the handicapped accessible Sunset Point Trail. There are also trails in **Spanish Peaks** Country. Visit https://spanishpeakscountry.com for maps.

Fisher's Peak will become Colorado's forty-second state park in 2021.

John Denver
1943 – 1997
State Songwriter

"Banned?!"
John Denver's tenor twangs like a broken guitar string.

"Some station owners think 'Rocky Mountain High' is about drugs," says his manager, "so they won't let the DJs play it."

"Geez, have they never left their soulless offices? Never gotten high from nature?" The songwriter is frustrated. Without air play, the song dies. "It's about a meteor shower on a moonless night. Experiencing the Perseids first-hand at twelve-thousand feet. That's the high I'm singing about."

"If you say so, John."

"Come on, Jerry. What good is this sparkly, cute-boy image if the stations ban my song just because I use the word 'high'?" John shakes his head, his longish blond bob swishing side to side, his wire-rim granny glasses slipping down his nose.

"You wanna trade gee-whiz for bad-boy-rocker so the stations have even more reason to ban your music?"

"I probably couldn't pull that off if I tried," he sighs, pushing his glasses up his nose.

"No shit," says Jerry. "Listen, we'll get ahead of this. It's not like all the stations have banned it. I'll get you some interviews. Go on TV and talk all about your meteor shower. Get all passionate about the mountains and nature and all that. The rednecks will come around. It's a great song."

Jerry reaches for the phone on the hotel room desk. "I'll make some calls right now."

John is unconvinced. A joint would be just the thing to calm him down. The irony doesn't bother him that much, but there's none at hand.

As Jerry dials some numbers, John goes to the window of his hotel room, hoping for a beautiful view to soothe himself. All he sees is an office tower and a billboard.

He fidgets with a geode in the pocket of his denim jacket. He'd bought it at a shop in Aspen, brought it on the road in case he got homesick. The peaked crystals inside the two broken halves remind him of the mountain paradise outside his new house in Starwood. He takes it out, jiggles it open, touches the purple tips.

All of a sudden he feels super buzzed. The office tower seems to have developed a golden dome. *That's really weird.* He's not high, and that beer, just one, maybe two, was a while ago. Then the billboard is transformed into a flag, the Colorado flag with its bright yellow middle, flapping in the sunshine and the wind. *Where are these hallucinations coming from?*

And voices? Jerry's conversation on the phone is drowned out by the sound of thousands—maybe millions—of voices. It's like the whole world is singing his song. Or at least the whole state of Colorado.

Jerry puts the telephone receiver back in its cradle and John stuffs the rock back in his jacket. The illusions disappear.

"You know how I've told you I'm clairvoyant sometimes?" John says.

His manager rolls his eyes.

"I'm serious, Jerry. I just experienced something out of the ordinary, really far out. I think I saw the future."

"Yeah?"

"The song's gonna do all right."

༄

Red Rocks Amphitheater
August 9, 1973

"Faaarrrr out!"

John Denver looked out from the stage, humbled by the grandeur of Red Rocks. Glorious red Creation Rock jutted into the sky on his right, Ship Rock to his left. In between, in rows rising to the setting sun, nine thousand fans listened to him sing. Among them were a bunch of disabled guys in wheelchairs, brought there by that long-haired hippie Presbyterian pastor Wade Blank. So far out. How the dude got them here was unbelievable.

John picked out the first notes of his anthem, a love song to his adopted state. His crystalline tenor articulated clearly. The intensity would build. By the chorus, he was singing from his toes, pulling out every feeling from within. The fans joined in. They knew the words. All the words. How could they not? Every radio station in the country was playing 'Rocky Mountain

High.' Pop, rock, country, easy listening. All the stations, or so it seemed, all the time.

Blinded them with his sunny smile and the story of the shooting stars at midnight. The stations saw the light. They played the song. And everybody sang along.

He'd deny to his dying day the song was about pot. Life offers lots of natural highs. The glow of a campfire, surrounded by friends. A meteor shower. Eagles soaring. The view from a mountaintop. Schussing fresh powder. The warmth of a woman. Simple sunshine. And this, the greatest joy of all, thousands of friends listening to him sing and play guitar in the world's most stunning amphitheater.

A real Rocky Mountain high.

AIRPLAY BROUGHT ATTACKS. There was nothing the music critics hated more than cheerfulness. They slammed his music. 'Vapid' they wrote, about songs that incited intense reactions, both negative and positive.

Then came assaults from environmentalists and anti-environmentalists both. 'Eco-twerp' the boosters and developers called him. Bitter after losing the fight to bring the Olympics to Colorado, state promoters hated the line about tearing down mountains to build more. But how else could he describe their Olympic proposals? Shaving Mt. Sniktau to steepen it for Alpine, dynamiting slopes to flatten them for Nordic, encasing Bear Creek in concrete for a ski jump run-out. Incomprehensible.

His fellow environmentalists were just as hostile, often worse. Their jeep bumpers sported 'John Denver Go Home' stickers. They complained his music was attracting 'hordes' of 'nature spoilers' to Colorado. As if Colorado's beauty could be kept a secret if he just shut up about it. He sang to inspire people to protect the wilderness; they would come to Colorado regardless.

He deflected it all with an impenetrable shield of relentless cheerfulness. Critics and cranks couldn't take him down. Radio station rednecks couldn't either. They had to play his songs or lose listeners. He was committed to making other people feel good. And it was working. Millions bought his records and concert tickets.

Aspen
1976

SOME DAYS, OPTIMISM was a heavy burden. Cheerfulness was his professional image, but damn it, life and the world just wore a guy down.

How do you go on the road singing a love song for a wife whose heart you broke when you left her for the road? How do you sing about hope for the future when nukes could blow the whole planet to smithereens? Sunshine can make you happy, but a starving child in Africa needs food.

And what if my music really is attracting hordes to Colorado? Will they destroy our paradise? Could it be I really am creating more problems than solutions? Maybe I am a goddamn eco-twerp.

Surrounded by mountain majesty, he sat morose in his Starwood mansion. An ashtray held the last smolders of a joint, its lemony smoke dissipating. He took a slug of Coors.

"What the hell is the matter with me?" he asked his friend, Tom Crum, licking a bit of foam off his lips. "I have everything I ever dreamed of, a beautiful wife, great kid, fantastic home in the mountains, fans all over the world, more money than I can count. A Learjet for chrissake."

"It's like coming down from a high," his friend mused. "You've been intoxicated with success, but you know that's gonna fade. What's your legacy gonna be?"

"My music is my legacy."

"Hmmm," said Crum, "sing me a Glenn Miller song."

"What?" He opened another can. His second? Third? Maybe fourth?

"Back in his day, Glenn Miller was the biggest musician Colorado ever produced. He was the most popular bandleader in America in the Forties. Big as the Beatles. Surely you know one song."

John hefted his guitar onto his lap, picked out a couple chords, and mumbled a few words of 'Chattanooga Choo Choo' before giving up.

"See? Music popularity is fickle," Tom continued. "Glenn Miller died in a plane crash thirty years ago. If you died in a plane crash, how many people would still know your songs thirty years later?"

"You're saying music is not enough. A legacy is immortality. I can't deny I want some of that."

"Damn straight, you do, and you're willing to build one. I'll pitch in. We'll build something real, but idealistic too, like your music."

JOHN SANG about getting high on sunshine, dancing with the wind. Could there be hope for the future? He ached to make a contribution to the wider world. On the road, he and Tom used travel hours to compose a plan they called Windstar. John would buy a thousand acres and build a place for people to reflect on nature and learn ways to live in harmony with it. Save nature from nukes and coal. But even that wasn't enough. What about all the starving kids?

Those rare days he was home in Aspen, he played with his children, Zak and Anna Kate, and watched them thrive. But all their giggles couldn't drown out his despair over injustice. Why do his own children have plenty of healthy food while other people's kids scrounge for scraps and find not enough? No child deserves hunger when the world is full of food, and here he sat, sitting on a mountain of cash.

He couldn't just stack blocks and spoon oatmeal to his own kids when he had the resources to build something real. He had to save the planet, feed more kids.

JOHN'S AMBITIONS for the world grew as his record sales slumped and his marriage fell apart. Crum had his plate full putting together Windstar, but John's friends Robert Fuller and Werner Erhard wanted to help him end starvation and malnutrition. They put together an organization and called it The Hunger Project.

One morning at home he spotted that old geode he'd bought back when radio stations were still banning 'Rocky Mountain High.' He took it down from the mantel above the fireplace. It occurred to him the rock was symbolic. Perhaps split apart, he and Annie would be more beautiful than they were together.

He opened the two halves, running a finger over the purple crystals inside. All of a sudden he felt spaced out, even though he hadn't yet taken a drink or a toke. He felt dizzy, buzzed, just like he had back in the hotel room with Jerry years ago.

∽

A STRANGE MAN stands next to the fireplace. *How did he get in? Sneaked past the gate?* Fans trespassing has become such a nuisance. *Or is he one of Annie's friends?* She has so many friends he doesn't know. So much time on the road means separate lives, a big part of their problems.

"I'm Mancio," says the man. "I'm a prophet, released from your geode, to reveal your legacy, the future."

It's too early in the morning for nonsense. He hasn't even had breakfast yet. "I don't know who the hell you are, but I'm too busy for any shit today. State your business and get out. Or I'll call the Sheriff."

"The Pitkin County Sheriff doesn't have jurisdiction where we're going," chuckles Mancio, clearly unintimidated. "Come on, of all the people I've visited, I figured you'd be the most open-minded. I know your songs. Hope for the future. What's the future holding in store? What about our dreams? If ever there was a person yearning for a visit from the ol' prophet Mancio, it's you, Mr. Denver."

As he listens to the weird man ramble, the walls of John's house dissolve before his eyes. The mountains disappear. He finds himself magically transported to the flat, sage-studded, wind-whipped prairie. Grasses shuffle around his feet. Giant wind turbines circle slowly above their heads, silhouetted against the bright blue Colorado sky. Mancio stands beside him.

"Pretty desolate," John says. This experience is out-a-sight, especially considering no booze, LSD, or marijuana are involved. But he's had clairvoyant experiences in the past; this is just a particularly vivid version.

"OK, we're not in the part of Colorado you sing about," says Mancio, a little apologetically. "We're on the eastern plains, at the Colorado Green Wind Farm, pretty close to Granada, where the Japanese internment camp used to be."

John turns around, scanning the horizon, so very far off. "Reminds me of Oklahoma, like Grandpa Deutschendorf's farm." He breathes in the smell of dust and trampled grass, remembering. "I drove tractor in the wheat fields when I was a kid."

"This is not your past. It's the future, the twenty-first century."

John pulls his collar close against the wind. "You're telling me humans make it past the millennium without nuking the planet?"

"Yes, John, we do."

"That's great news." His mouth broadens into his famous smile, as wide as the Colorado prairie they stand on.

"I'm glad to see your positivism, but the future has its own challenges. Not that nukes aren't still a danger, but climate change is an even bigger existential threat."

John feels his smile disappear, as if blown away by the wind.

"Drought leads to war," the strange man continues. "War destroys crops, farmers are displaced. By this time in the future, The Hunger Project and other organizations have reduced starvation deaths by half, but that trend starts to reverse. Climate change could undo it all. Not to mention kill off the whole planet, even the wealthy parts."

What a freaking pessimist! What's the point of this bummer news, or prediction, or hallucination, whatever the hell this Mancio is saying?

John's voice takes on an edge he never uses in his music. "Why are you telling me this? Do you want me to give up? Want to convince me it's all hopeless and I may as well go home and drink myself to death? For god's sake, man! Pessimism is pointless. We need to carry on."

"Truly, it's not my goal to discourage. Quite the opposite."

"Well then, stop dwelling on the shit. There are enough people doing that. We *can* end hunger. We *can* live together as human beings on a planet that travels through the universe. If what you say is true, twenty-first century people need my songs more than ever. They gotta hear that in the midst of an insane world, with all its terrors and problems, life is worth living. Music is the best means of speaking to the future."

Mancio interrupts. "Exactly! Don't get me wrong. I mean to inspire your music and activism. The future needs positivism, craves solutions. Look up. The energy being created over our heads is one solution. That's the Windstar legacy. What was taught there showed what is possible."

"Showed? Past tense?"

Mancio ignores the question. "By the time this wind farm is commissioned in 2003, Colorado's population is double what it was when you moved here. And the population just keeps growing. And no, they aren't all coming on account of your songs.

"But they come nevertheless, and keep on coming, and a lot of people require a lot of energy. This is an industrial-scale producer of wind energy. Over a hundred turbines churn out power to Colorado's largest utility company. It's just the beginning."

John gazes up at the turbines, shielding his eyes from the sun with his hand. "All right! Finally some good news outta you. Gotta love the wind. What about the sun? Solar power? Sunshine on my shoulders and all that?"

"Coloradans put solar panels on their roofs, and industrial-size solar farms are in the works. Starting here, out on the plains, Colorado's energy provider reduces carbon emissions forty percent by 2018, aiming toward eighty percent by 2030, a hundred percent by 2050. Some dismiss

Windstar's goals as pipedreams, but they eventually compete head-on with fossil fuels. It may not be enough, or soon enough, but it's an effort. You and Crum are energy pioneers, but you're not living forever and you're not saving the planet all by yourself."

John sees the brightly shining sun against the clear blue sky, hardly a cloud anywhere. Breezes scrape his cheek. Softly, he sings about dancing with the west wind, hope for the future, reaching for all that he can be.

When John's voice fades, trailing off onto the prairie, Mancio grabs him gently by the arm and, faster than a Learjet, transports them both to Denver. *Far out.*

John recognizes the golden dome, the red, white, blue, and yellow flag flying from a tall flagpole. Mancio leads him inside the marble halls. John strides up to the guard by a metal detector, but Mancio pulls him away. "No need for all that. You're not really here, so the guard can't see you."

Music streams out of the rotunda. John hears a guitar, and loud singing, a lot of voices out of tune, the song intimately familiar nevertheless. Legislators in blue suits, men wearing ties and women standing in high heels, all belting out 'Rocky Mountain High.'

What the hell? Wait a minute. This is kind of like that hotel hallucination again. The golden dome. Singing. The voices grow in volume. *It's like the whole state is singing.*

Mancio interrupts his thoughts. "In 2007 'Rocky Mountain High' becomes Colorado's second State Song."

No way. Really? John can't help himself. "Far out!"

Mancio chuckles. "People don't say that much these days."

"A State Song? Like official? There was a vote? It passed?"

Mancio nods.

"All right! And nobody got worked up? Nobody claimed the song was about drugs?"

"Well, a few worry about that. But by 2007 not that many care anymore, and soon care even less."

"Stop being so damned obtuse."

"Well, if you promise not to call the Pitkin County Sheriff, I'll take you back to Aspen and you'll see my point."

Mancio's magic doesn't land them back at his home in Starwood, but in Aspen's downtown business district. Mancio leads him on a walk down streets that are somewhat familiar.

"This is what it looks like when one city runs entirely on renewable energy," Mancio enthuses. "In 2015 Aspen becomes the third city in the U.S. to run entirely on water, wind, solar, and landfill gas. You inspire Aspen and Aspen inspires other cities."

"Fantastic!"

Things around town do not look terrifically different, not really. Skiers clunk around in unclasped ski boots, as usual, going in and out of bars and shops. *But what's with all the green crosses?* And the weird business names—Best Day Ever, Native Roots, Euflora, Green Dragon, Green Joint.

John's eyes widen. His mouth drops open just a bit. "My god, Mancio, are they selling weed in *stores*?"

"Remember what you told *Playboy*? 'Just like alcohol, marijuana should be handled responsibly, or like driving a car, and kids shouldn't be involved with any of them until they can handle them.' That's what you said. And that's the legal deal now."

"Incredible, just incredible! Stores!"

They walk inside a dispensary. A security guard is checking IDs, but just like the guard at the capitol, she can't see them. Bright lights showcase rows of buds in jars, packaged edibles, colorful pipes. A faint but familiar skunky lemon perfumes the air. John gawks.

"Medical marijuana is legalized first," explains Mancio. "Then recreational. Colorado was the very first state to do it. Voters said yes in 2012 and sales began January 1, 2014. For adults only, like you said."

What else was there to say? "Far out!"

"There's even a chain of four dispensaries called 'Rocky Mountain High.'"

"The song's not about pot!"

"If you say so, John. And with that I bid you goodbye."

IN THE SPEED of a sixteenth note, John finds himself at his home in Starwood, the fire in the hearth slowly dying. He considers a beer or a smoke, but the day has been enough of a trip already. Annie is banging around in the kitchen, but he doesn't need to investigate.

All he needs is in front of him: Goals for Windstar, plans for The Hunger Project, and, of course, his guitars.

Epilogue

John Denver died in a plane crash off the coast of Monterrey, California, in 1997. His ashes were scattered over Colorado's Rocky Mountains. He left three children (Zak, Anna Kate, Jesse Belle) and two ex-wives. His Windstar Foundation continued inspiring and educating about environmental caretaking until it was dissolved in 2012. The thousand acres it sat on were sold to a private owner, although a conservation easement protects it from development.

Colorado is the only venue that rejected the Olympics after having won the approval of the IOC. John Denver and then-future-governor Dick Lamm (pictured above with John) both opposed it.

John Denver's hunger work garnered bipartisan recognition during this lifetime. He served on President Carter's Commission on World Hunger and President Reagan honored him with the Presidential World Without Hunger Award. The Hunger Project continues to work to reduce hunger throughout the world. In 2019, it held a five-star rating with Charity Navigator. To learn more, their website is https://www.thp.org/.

John Denver made twenty-one gold albums and thirteen platinum. When he died, legal music sales were still in the CD era, but his Colorado's State Song, 'Rocky Mountain High,' continues to sell into the iTunes era, certified Gold for digital sales in 2017. Forty years after it was written and twenty years after his death, Coloradans still know the words.

Just the Facts, Ma'am

Is the 'Rocky Mountain High' that friends experience around the campfire about pot? To his last breath, John Denver denied it. In 1985 he opposed a censorship bill, testifying before Congress that the banning of the song "was obviously done by people who had never seen or been to the Rocky Mountains and also had never experienced the elation, the celebration of life, or the joy in living that one feels when he observes something as wondrous as the Perseids meteor shower on a moonless and cloudless night."

Interestingly, though, in his autobiography he confesses that another line in 'Rocky Mountain High,' the one about getting 'crazy' and trying to touch the sun, describes an LSD-fueled motorcycle trip up Red Mountain Pass.

John's 1994 autobiography, ***Take Me Home,*** written with the help of his friend, Arthur Tobier, is a very readable story of his life and more self-reflective and less self-congratulatory than you might expect. The in-depth ***Rolling Stone*** interview from 1975, 'John Denver: His Rocky Mountain Highness' by Chet Flippo can be read online at https://www.rollingstone.com/music/music-news/john-denver-his-rocky-mountain-highness-168837/. Another biography, *John Denver: Mother Nature's Son* by John Collis, is a rehash studded with snarky music criticism. A short biography for young readers is ***John Denver: Man for the World,*** by John Stansfield.

The BBC-produced ***John Denver Country Boy*** documentary is available on DVD and via Amazon. Very much produced by and for fans, it includes spectacular footage of soaring eagles, tumbling rivers, bright wildflowers, and interviews with both ex-wives, his son Zak, plus his managers and fellow musicians. The best bits are the hilarious clips from the variety show he did for the BBC in 1973.

Just for Fun

A Perseid meteor shower at **Williams Lake**, between Mt. Sopris and Capitol Peak in the Maroon Bells/Snowmass Wilderness area west of Aspen, was John Denver's inspiration for the Colorado state song, 'Rocky Mountain High.' The four- to ten-mile hike (there and back, depending on where you park) is a difficult uphill climb, but a memorable experience, particularly if you can do it during the annual summer Perseid shower. There are informal campsites and trails along the shore. More information on the hike can be found at https://www.protrails.com/trail/793/aspen-snowmass-williams-lake. To time your trip to coincide with the annual **Perseid Meteor Shower**, check out the American Meteor Society calendar (https://www.amsmeteors.org).

The gorgeous cover art for the album *Rocky Mountain High* was photographed at **Slaughterhouse Falls** near Aspen. The most popular way to experience the falls is on a whitewater raft. The falls are part of a half-day, Class IV rafting experience, not for the faint of heart. But if you're into excitement and are experienced with a paddle, Aspen area rafting companies will take you through the falls from about May through mid-August. For a fee, of course.

A far mellower experience of nature can be had at the **John Denver Sanctuary** nestled in the heart of Aspen, next to Rio Grande Park. Located near the Roaring Fork River, it's ideal for quiet meditation or a family picnic. The Song Garden features many of Denver's lyrics etched into native river boulders. (If you know the words by heart, you'll notice that lines suggesting sex or drugs were left off. It's a controversy.) The man-made wetlands and winding streams work as an innovative storm water filter system, cleaning water before it drains into the Roaring Fork River. Within the Sanctuary, you will find one of the largest perennial flower gardens open to the public, which adds to the friendly atmosphere. These beautiful gardens start blooming late May/early June. TripAdvisor gives it a 'Certificate of Excellence.' There's no admission fee, but plan to pay for parking.

Every October Aspen hosts a week-long **John Denver Celebration**, with sing-a-longs, concerts, songwriting workshops, storytelling and so on. The Aspen Chamber of Commerce has the details. Check out https://www.aspenchamber.org/.

John Denver was an avid skier and famously wrote 'Annie's Song' in ten minutes riding a ski lift to the top of **Aspen Mountain**. There's a memorial to him located off of the Bellisimo Trail. One of the blue (intermediate) ski runs at neighboring **Snowmass** is named Rocky Mountain High. For information on tickets, trails and all things ski-oriented in Aspen, go to https://www.aspensnowmass.com. It's probably no coincidence that Aspen Skiing Company committed to 'going green' in 1997, immediately after John Denver's death. The resort is powered by solar, waste methane, and hydroelectric.

Aspen has one of the highest densities of **marijuana dispensaries** in the state. If you're interested in passing a pipe around, and are over twenty-one years old, there are a number of options. Just walk around. Or ask the Google for recommendations.

John Denver was the first inductee into the **Colorado Music Hall of Fame** located in the Trading Post at Red Rocks Park near **Morrison**. His statue welcomes visitors. Sculpted by Sue DiCicco, it shows him with a guitar slung over his back and an eagle clutching his hand. Inside is an exhibit with some of his concert costumes, custom guitar, the gold record for the *Rocky Mountain High* album, and a yellowed copy of the original *Rolling Stone* interview.

Colorado has produced a lot of popular music. The Hall of Fame spotlights the careers of Colorado musicians **Glenn Miller**, Judy Collins, Nitty Gritty Dirt Band, and many more. Other exhibits tell the stories of non-musician contributors to the Colorado music scene, including the Caribou Ranch recording studio where Elton John, Chicago, Michael Jackson, and many other famous musicians cut records in the 1970s and 1980s. You'll be surprised how much music comes out of Colorado.

Complete **lyrics** to 'Rocky Mountain High' and other songs by John Denver are can be found online from various lyrics websites.

Author Notes and Bibliographies

About Historical Accuracy

My goal for this book is to introduce you to some interesting people and show how our state is shaped by the things they did. I tried to make these stories as accurate as possible within an imaginative framework.

Nobody ever knows what 'really happened' in the past. Two friends relating a shared experience will tell very different stories of the exact same thing, even when it happened just yesterday. News reports and historical accounts relate known events, but also reflect the culture of the times and the resources available to the writer.

Recognizing this just made the countless hours of research more enjoyable. As a journalist myself, I love reading old newspapers and magazines. I also relish the hours I spend in history museums throughout the state. Original papers, when available, are fascinating. But I couldn't have done this without the work of real historians who put original research into context in serious nonfiction.

Occasionally I found inconsistencies in historical accounts, which means one or the other historian or journalist got something wrong. I tried to avoid repeating mistakes and misinterpretations, but I'm sure I made some of my own.

Time travel and hallucinations notwithstanding, I limited my imaginings to things that were probable or at least possible. Inner thoughts and most dialogue are made up, but I tried to stay true to the person's character and style of speaking. In many cases I incorporated actual quotations.

The epilogues, Just the Facts Ma'am, and Just for Fun sections are all based on research and personal observation.

The bibliographies are in a simplified format that should nevertheless provide enough detail for you to find the source online or through a Colorado library. Old newspapers can be read at the Denver Public Library Western History Department or the Hart Library at History Colorado.

Felipe Baca

Key to the Visions
Men in black suits and high collars: Legislators in the Colorado Territorial Legislature
Two-story house: The Baca House in Trinidad
Blur of shiny metal: Cars and trucks on I-25
Otherworldly conveyances: Modern cars and trucks

What's Fact? What's Fiction?
History counts Felipe Baca as the founder of Trinidad, although of course he didn't do it all by himself. He was part owner of the town general store, in addition to farming, ranching, and running a lumber mill.

The riot of 1868 is an infamous event in the history of early Trinidad.

La geoda is Spanish for the geode (but you guessed that, right?) *Los idiotas* is Spanish for the idiots (you guessed that, too). *El vertigo* means the vertigo or the dizziness. *Las ilusiones* means the illusions. *La violencia* means the violence. All these are cognates, words similar in two languages because they were either inherited from the same parent language or borrowed from the other language.

Gracias a Dios means thank God. *La pelea confusa* means the confusing fight.

General stores of the time displayed small wares on shelves behind a counter. Large barrels of flour and such sat on the floor in the middle of the store. Self-serve wasn't a thing back then. The storekeeper retrieved items for shoppers.

Baca was elected to the Colorado Territorial Legislature in 1870. Colorado became a state in 1876. The state Constitution was originally published in three languages, the Spanish version entitled: *Constitucion Estado de Colorado*.

In Baca's day, Trinidad's business district was constructed of adobe and wood. The beautiful brick and stone architecture it's known for today was mostly built in the first decade of the twentieth century (1900-1910).

The famous two-story Baca House on Main Street in Trinidad was built after the riots. At the time of this story, the family lived in a single-story adobe hacienda near the river.

Black powder indeed smells like sulfur.

Colorado Phantasmagorias

Felipe Baca's race toward home and concern for his family are what any husband and father would feel, punched up with a bit of nineteenth century *machismo*.

Luis is described playing with building blocks because he grew up to be an architect. The girls' cooking and weaving activities are typical of what girls would do back then, particularly if their family farmed and raised sheep, as the Bacas did. Churro was a common breed of sheep in that area at the time.

The eldest, Juan Pedro, was the child in charge of the Baca sheep.

The riot of January 1868 is described as it happened. Hispano is a term for early settlers who came to Colorado from New Mexico. Whether the riot was race related or just a bunch of hotheaded drunks having it out remains a matter of historical controversy.

Felipe Baca was known as a peaceful man, but he would certainly have been concerned that his eldest son might get caught up in the violence, not only because that's what young men tend to do, but Juan Pedro in particular was prone to it. Juan Pedro eventually died by gunfire.

The family meeting relates the true story of the settlement of Trinidad by the Baca family and their friends from New Mexico.

The negotiation of the truce is described as it happened and the names mentioned were all real people.

The party was an actual event. *Los judios* means the Jews. Maurice Wise was a resident at the time. Trinidad had a substantial Jewish population at the time, and the temple in Trinidad is the oldest continuously operating temple in Colorado. The women's clothing, Anglo and Hispano, were the fashions of that time period. Sheep ranchers would have served mutton in January, and of course everyone ate spiced beans. Plums were a fruit common to the area, and were dried or preserved for consumption throughout the winter.

The governor and the *Rocky Mountain News* were both present at the party.

Los Hermanos Penitentes were religionists living in the Trinidad area at the time.

Un Profeta means a prophet and *Las fantasmagorias* means the phantasmagoria, more cognates.

The genie Mancio describes Baca's legacy as it is related by historians today, a businessman and cultural peace-broker. The children's futures are fact.

The two-story Baca house is a strange affair combining traditional southwestern building materials with an architectural style imported from the east. Baca famously bought it with 22,000 pounds of wool and he is recorded as saying the trade was clever because sheep grow new wool every year.

Baca fought for the rights of Spanish speakers in the territorial legislature. I can't swear that he also fought for the rights of German speakers, but he would have known the German rancher William Hoehne of Trinidad. At any rate, the original state Constitution was indeed published in all three languages, although the English version was the 'official' one.

St. Christopher, patron saint of travelers, was known at the time. Baca, a Catholic, would have known of him and, time travel being a rather scary thing, would probably have said a prayer.

Trinidad thrived from trade going through the area on the famed Santa Fe Trail. The railroad replaced the trail, then the highway more or less replaced the railroad. Trinidad keeps reinventing itself in spite of the changes. For example, it thrived on the business of gender confirmation surgery in the era of Dr. Stanley Biber, another chapter in this collection.

And, yes, the town still enjoys a good party.

Bibliography

9News, 'A Look at Colorado's Three Versions of the Constitution,' Feb. 18, 2019.
Chronicle-News, 'Felipe Baca: Trinidad's Pied Piper,' Cosette Henritz, undated.
Colorado Encyclopedia, 'Don Felipe Baca,' coloradoencyclopedia.org.
Colorado Encyclopedia, 'Hispano Settlement in the Purgatoire Valley,' coloradoencyclopedia.org.
Colorado Experience, 'Trinidad,' Rocky Mountain PBS, 2016.
Colorado Heritage, 'El Patron de Trinidad,' Paul D. Andrews and Nancy Humphrey, Winter 2004.
Colorado Heritage, 'Hispanic Pioneer: Don Felipe Baca Brings His Family North to Trinidad,' Luis and Facundo Baca, 1982.
Colorado Magazine, 'Trinidad and Its Environs,' A.W. McHendrie, September 1929.
Colorado Virtual Library, 'Colorado's Constitution,' Amy Zimmer, July 5, 2012, coloradovirtuallibrary.org.
De Busk Memorial, Volume 2, 'Trinidad War,' 1933-1934.
Denver Post, 'Colorado's Constitution Has Strengths, Quirks, Too,' Ray Mark Rinaldi, June 21, 2012.
Felipe and Dolores Baca: Hispanic Pioneers, E.E. Duncan, Filter Press, 2013.
La Gente: Hispano History and Life in Colorado,' Vincent C. de Baca, Colorado Historical Society, 1998.

Colorado Phantasmagorias 223

Rocky Mountain News, 'From Trinidad: Full and Interesting Particulars of the Troubles There,' Jan. 6, 1868; 'The Trinidad War: Interesting Particulars by a Special Correspondent,' Jan. 13, 1868; 'A Meeting at Trinidad: A Series of Resolutions,' Jan. 15, 1868; The Anti-State Convention,' Jan. 9, 1869; 'The Sheep Farms of Colorado,' April 16, 1873.
Trinidad Enterprise, April 16, 1874.
Trinidad History Museum: Capsule History and Guide, Colorado Historical Society, 2002.
Trinidad, Colorado Territory, Morris F. Taylor, Trinidad State Junior College, 1966.

Chipeta

Key to the Visions
The Bear Dance: Modern bear dance

What's Fact? What's Fiction?

Chipeta's artistry with beads was appreciated during her lifetime and in the years since. In her last years, she lost sight and her hearing. She spent her last years living on a reservation in Utah, but often travelled to Colorado.

The song 'America the Beautiful,' originally titled 'Pikes Peak,' by Katherine Lee Bates, was inspired by a trip to Colorado and written in a room at the Antler's Hotel in Colorado Springs. By the time Chipeta was an old woman, Bates's song was very popular.

The Utes were and are known as the People of the Shining Mountains.

In the days before "No Smoking" laws, hotel rooms probably all stank of cigar smoke. The nicer burning sage, however, is the scent of the Utes' traditional spring Bear Dance, which is to this day accompanied by the music of sticks rubbing against notched morache sticks.

In 2019 History Colorado in downtown Denver created a large exhibit of Ute history. Aided by the knowledge and wisdom of traditional Colorado Ute people, one theme of the exhibit was 'We're still here.'

The traditional Ute Bear Dance is still held at various locations in Colorado in the spring, in the out of doors, within a corral constructed of freshly-cut twigs and branches.

Chipeta was bilingual or multilingual. Throughout the years, people who know only a single language have deliberately or ignorantly misinterpreted and misused examples of rough syntax to belittle bilingual and multilingual people. Chipeta was obviously intelligent, but that does not shine through in the records of her English. Rather than risk fueling false interpretations, I avoided quoting her words of record and instead paraphrased, constructing the fluidity of thought that a complex thinker like she would have.

Chipeta did, in fact, meet President William Howard Taft, renowned for his magnificent heft (that's putting it nicely) and shaggy mustache, at the ceremony opening the Gunnison Tunnel. Bison is the more modern, proper term for the animals hunted by Native Americans, but buffalo was the colloquial term common at the time.

Water is revered by Native Americans. The government had promised to bring water to the Ute reservation in Utah and by the turn of the century had, in fact, made little to no effort to make good on that promise.

Laws banned the Tabeguache Utes from visiting Colorado, but after 1881, when Colorado author Helen Hunt Jackson stunned the nation's conscience with her book *Century of Dishonor*, some of the most unjust laws against Native Americans were left unenforced, even as they remained on the books.

Chipeta's husband, Ouray, travelled to Washington D.C. by train many times to negotiate treaties of peace. Chipeta did not accompany him in the earlier years, but did so as his health failed. She met President Hayes at the invitation of Secretary of the Interior Schurz.

Although the Ute people did not typically permit women at chief councils, history documents that Chipeta participated in councils after Ouray died. Perhaps because she was Ouray's widow, and probably because she was respected for her own wisdom.

The trip to the tunnel with Taft is described as it happened.

Chipeta's blue dress with its bodice sewn of elk teeth is in the collection of History Colorado. It's stunning.

The story of Ouray, Black Mare, and baby Pahlone is historically accurate. Ouray was multi-lingual, Jesuit-educated, and a successful rancher. Pahlone means 'apple-faced.'

Ute women were responsible for setting up and taking down the teepees. The traditional foods and cooking practices are based on historical descriptions, as is the description of how hides were tanned for clothing.

History records that Chipeta's husband Ouray did listen to his wife's counsel. Photographs show that he was very handsome.

Who knows if Chipeta envisioned the coming of white people as an 'avalanche,' but it's an apt description. The constantly changing demands of the white invaders were a challenge for all Native Americans.

Colorado Phantasmagorias 225

Photographs show Chief Ouray wearing Chipeta's handiwork on official visits to Washington. Historians relate that Chipeta was quite delighted with the shopping on Pennsylvania Avenue, that she gave testimony to Congress, and that Ouray's health was failing fast on that last trip.

The difficulty the Utes had obeying the terms of the treaties is documented by history. The ever-shrinking lands, disappearing game and exile to Utah are all true.

Ouray's Pahlone was kidnapped and never returned.

Ouray consulted every kind of doctor there was at that time, to no avail.

Chipeta did not birth her own child, but she did adopt and raise many orphans.

The description of Ute hunting trips is based on historical accounts. And, yes, hot springs were sacred to the Utes. They soaked to ease sore muscles, just as we do today.

The organizers of the Gunnison Tunnel Grand Opening did rig out a motorcar with a huge banner proclaiming her name. See the photo.

The Meeker Massacre and Pueblo Riot of 1879 are described as they happened. Ouray rode to rescue the kidnapped white women and children, and Chipeta harbored them in their home. Nevertheless, "The Utes Must Go!" became a rallying cry both in protests and on newsprint.

Eugene Field was a wildly popular poet at the time. His poetry is also featured in the chapter about Margaret Brown in this collection.

The description of the Bear Dance is based on modern videos and my own visit.

Although sweat ceremonies are typically considered to be a Lakota practice, Ute people also participate in sweat ceremonies, including women.

Ute artisans continue to create symbolic bead art in the twenty-first century.

Fry bread is delicious. If you've never tried it, you're missing out.

The Native American gaming industry was created out of the 1987 Supreme Court decision, *California v. Cabazon Band of Mission Indians*. The Sky Ute Casino and Hotel outside Ignacia is really magnificent, and a great local getaway whether you gamble or not. The Colorado Ute tribes are also involved in ranching and oil and gas production and exploration.

The description of the hot spring experience is based on my own indulgence in various hot springs around the state. It was a Ute practice to leave a few beads by the pool in payment. Today you pay money before you enter. A shared love of hot springs connects her to Carl Howelsen, also profiled in this collection.

Bibliography
Chief Ouray: Ute Chief and Man of Peace, Steve Walsh, Filter Press, 2011.
Chipeta: Queen of the Utes, Cynthia S. Becker and P. David Smith, Western Reflections Publishing, 2003.
Chipeta: Ute Peacemaker, Cynthia S. Becker, Filter Press, 2008.
It Happened in Colorado, James Crutchfield, Falcon Publishing, 1993.
Remarkable Colorado Women, Gayle C. Shirley, Globe Pequot Press, 2012.
Searching for Chipeta, Vickie Leigh Krudwig, Fulcrum Publishing, 2004.

John Brisben Walker

Key to the Visions
Never-ended snake of vehicles: Red Rocks concert traffic
Ear-splitting music: Red Rocks concert
Flashing lights and whiff of beer: Atmosphere at a Red Rocks concert
Impossible glass tower: Downtown Denver skyscrapers
Ferris wheel and towers of no discernible use: Elitch Gardens, Denver

What's Fact? What's Fiction?

Laudanum is a tincture of opium that was a very popular treatment for all manner of maladies during Walker's lifetime. Hashish was also known and widely used for medicinal and nonmedicinal purposes. Both were legal, although the Food and Drug Act of 1906 required they be labeled by dosage.

Photographs show developer John Brisben Walker as a tidy dresser. Stiff collars were a mandatory part of the businessman's attire of the day, which most certainly had to chafe in the heat because there was no air-conditioning.

This description of Denver's Sixteenth Street is set when motor vehicles were gradually replacing horse and buggy transportation, but it was not yet clear whether gasoline or steam engines would become more popular. John Brisben Walker placed all his bets on steam. He was heavily invested in the Stanley Steamer company. Sixteenth Street became a pedestrian mall in 1982.

Colorado Phantasmagorias

Bouquet Nouveau was a popular fragrance in 1912. Walker's second wife, Ethel, had been his secretary in New York. He left his first wife, Emily, for Ethel.

Newspapers of the day record Walker's big ideas about creating full-size dinosaur sculptures at Red Rocks like the ones in Germany. Not a sculptor himself, he would have had to engage an artist. The details of this meeting with the sculptor are imagined, but the developer would have had to have had meetings of this sort.

The bones of Stegosaurus were first discovered at Morrison, near Red Rocks Park in 1876. John Brisben Walker owned the park in 1912. A grandiose thinker, Walker called it Garden of the Titans, although it was also known as Red Rocks even then.

Walker's donation of land for Regis College, and subsequent disaffection with religion and God, are known from historical sources.

He did have a lot of children by his first and second wives. He built a mansion on Mount Falcon, where Ethel presided.

Joslin's and Daniels & Fisher were department stores on Sixteenth Street. All that remains of Daniels & Fisher is the tower. The Joslin's building is now a hotel.

A ride in a Stanley Steamer required a long warm-up period, which probably explains why the steamers eventually died out, in spite of their advantages. The description of starting the car is based on videos of antique but still operable Steamers. Internal combustion gasoline engines were derided as 'explosion engines' by fans of steam.

The story of Walker's drive up Pikes Peak is taken from historical records.

Walker was obsessed with the need for modern roads, and lobbied for a thoroughfare to his park. We now know it as Morrison Road.

Brisben's back history is factual. He did believe in making money from amusement. River Front Park along the South Platte in Denver was quite the attraction in its day. Elitch's was its competition. River Front Park was long gone by 1912 when Walker was focused on developing Red Rocks.

The description of the tour of Red Rocks is based on photographs from the time. Except for Stage Rock, the names of the monoliths now called Ship Rock and Creation Rock were still in flux at that time.

Famous singers Pietro Satriano and Mary Garden had performed in front of Stage Rock before 1912, even though the amphitheatre we know today wasn't completed until 1941. Mary Garden predicted that 20,000

Colorado Phantasmagorias 228

people would come for concerts. Whether she meant all at once or over time is not clear. Today Red Rocks seats about 9,000 per concert and a million over a season. John Denver, also profiled in this collection, performed there 16 times.

The mansion on Mount Falcon is described based on photographs exhibited at Mount Falcon Park.

The name of Walker's valet is fictional, but plans for his park were printed in a Sunday *Denver Post* that somebody would have had to retrieve from a news seller in Morrison. Walker did believe strongly in the power of the press and got his name in print often. The *Denver Post* that advertised his plans had a story about the Custer pageant on the front page and the headline about poor children inside. Foozlers was slang used in the day. The quotes are rendered word for word as they were printed.

Walker understood it was just as effective to make a fortune from a lot of people paying a little bit than a few people paying a lot. His success with that strategy at *Cosmopolitan* magazine ended with the profitable sale of the magazine to William Randolph Hearst.

Egyptology was a fad at the time.

The idea for building a Summer White House earned a full page spread in the *Denver Post*. Only the cornerstone and a couple partial walls were laid.

The ruins of Walker's mansion and the views from the windows are as they look today.

For a proper dresser such as Walker, today's hiking attire would appear to be miner's clothing. Denim was limited to laborers' workwear and children's playwear until the 1960s, when it was first popularized as leisurewear for adults.

Walker's road, now known as the Castle Trail, makes a popular hike for families today, because it's wide, not steep, and impossible to get lost on. The quote from Walker is accurate.

Walker got architect Jacques Benedict to work for free and successfully solicited donations for his proposed Summer White House from bankers and children.

Walker and President Wilson were pacifists at this time, but the country sent soldiers to fight in World War I regardless.

Fritchle was a brand of electric car that was manufactured on Colfax in Denver. Margaret (Molly) Brown drove one. See the Margaret Brown chapter, also in this collection.

The "invigorating atmosphere" etc. are Walker's actual words.

Colorado Phantasmagorias

The quote about sex and liberated women is made up. However, Walker's third wife was a famously liberated woman, so it's plausible.

Cities near the turn of the nineteenth to the twentieth centuries would have been very stinky. Coal burning in the winter, and horse manure all year long.

Walker would have been familiar with the luxurious Inter-Ocean Hotel that Barney Ford built (another chapter in this collection.) That hotel stood at Sixteenth and Blake until the 1970s. The first glass skyscrapers did not appear anywhere until the 1920s.

The funicular cog railway is long gone from Red Rocks, but you can, in fact, see the scar from the Upper North Parking Lot.

In 1912, Walker would not have been shocked or even surprised by the smell of cannabis. It was legal and not even regulated until 1906. The first serious restrictions on cannabis were put in place in 1937. It was made illegal throughout the U.S. in 1970.

Coors beer was popular then as now. Adolph Coors' story is another chapter in this collection.

Walker eventually sold his park to the City of Denver. Denver Parks Manager George Cranmer was the force behind building the amphitheater, which he achieved with the help of the federal government's Civilian Conservation Corps during the Great Depression. See the Carl Howelsen chapter in this collection for more on Cranmer.

Bibliography

Charleston Gazette, 'John Brisben Walker, 84, West Side Founder, Dies,' July 8, 1931.

Colorado Encyclopedia, 'Fritchle Electric Automobile,' coloradoencyclopedia.org.

Colorado Gambler, 'The Magnificent John Brisben Walker, Father of Denver's Entertainment Industry,' May 9, 2010.

Colorado Heritage, 'Architect J.J. Benedict and His Magnificent Unbuilt Buildings,' Dan Corson, Summer 1997.

Colorado Heritage, 'Making Our Mountains Available for the People,' Wendy Rex-Atzet, July-Aug. 2013.

Denver Business Journal, 'The Failed Dream of a Colorado Summer White House,' Mark Harden, July 7, 2014; 'The World's First Stegosaurus Fossil Was Found in This Colorado Town,' Caitlin Hendee, April 26, 2017.

Denver Post, 'A Summer Palace for Our Presidents,' Nov. 5, 1911; 'How Denver Could Attract Every Visitor to Frisco Show,' John Brisben Walker, Aug. 25, 1912; [entire edition] Dec. 8, 1912; 'Government Makes Town,' John Brisben Walker, Dec. 29, 1912; 'Dream Unfulfilled: Walker Saw Colo. Retreat,' Aug. 21, 1975; 'The 10 Most Memorable Concerts in Red Rocks History,' John Wenzel, June 3, 2016

Denver Public Library, 'The Brief, Brilliant Reign of the Fritchle: Colorado's First Electric Car,' Ariana Ross, June 11, 2017, history.denverlibrary.org.
Denver Times, 'Children Hear Mary Garden Sing on Natural Stage,' May 11, 1911.
Happy Home Chats, June 22, 1936.
Historically Jeffco, 'John Brisben Walker: The Man and Mt. Morrison,' Sally L. White, 2005.
History of Red Rocks Park, Nolie Mumey, Johnson Publishing Company, 1962.
Morrison History, 'John Brisben Walker: A Man of Ideas,' Edna Fiore, Nov. 6, 2010.
New York Times Archives, 'John Brisben Walker Dies at Age of 83,' July 8, 1931.
Rocky Mountain News, 'First Automobile Ascends Rugged Pikes Peak,' Sept. 9, 1900; 'Great Say Denver Men After Trip to Mountains; Foothills Park Sure,' April 9, 1911; 'Diva Amazed at Natural Auditorium,' May 14, 1911; 'The Idea Man,' Frances Melrose, June 13, 1948; 'Dreams Led to Red Rocks Services,' Catherine Dittman, April 6, 1982; 'Denver Businessman First to See Potential of Unique Red Rocks Park,' Frances Melrose, Aug. 5, 1990.
Sacred Stones, Thomas Noel, Denver Division of Theatres and Arenas, 2004.

Golda Meir

Key to the Visions
Scratch of tulle: The feel of the evening gown she wore to dinner with President Richard Nixon when she was Prime Minister of Israel
Sand storm: Palestine and Israel
Glittering Lights: The atmosphere at the White House dinner
Almonds and lemons: Agricultural products of Palestine and Israel
Bursts of light: Media photographers taking her picture

What's Fact? What's Fiction?
Fact: the first thing Golda Mabovitch (later known as Golda Meier) bought with her own money was a plain woolen coat. The chinchilla coat is Margaret (Molly) Brown's famous coat, which she wore for years. The famous Titanic survivor is the subject of another chapter in this collection.

Golda did in fact run away from home in Milwaukee, at fourteen years old, to live with her sister in Denver. She talked of owning a single blouse that she cared for every day. She had an after-school job at her brother-in-law Shamai Korngold's Wisconsin Cleaners next to the Brown Palace after school. Through her work, she would have been aware of the fancy fabrics worn by the society ladies who stayed at the Brown. Margaret Brown, the famous Titanic survivor, lived at the Brown Palace at the time, having rented out her home on Pennsylvania Avenue. Although I don't have the dry-cleaning receipts to prove it, it's highly probable that Margaret Brown took her clothing to Shamai Korngold's shop while Golda worked there.

Mrs. Brown was inclusive of all races and religions and, specifically, always invited the participation of the Leadville and Denver Jewish communities in her various charity projects. Juvenile justice reform was one of those projects.

Golda Meir, nee Mabovitch, met her future husband, the father of her children, in Denver. His name was Morris Meyerson.

Slicing lemons for tea was, in fact, Golda's chore at her sister Sheyna's home on Julian Street in Denver. Shamai and Sheyna were highly involved in the politics of the time and often invited like-minded friends to their small house on Julian Street.

Golda had a fraught relationship with her mother, whose idea of marrying her off to a much older man precipitated her escape to Denver. Mrs. Mabovitch was disappointed in the United States, which was not uncommon among older immigrants, and yearned for her home in Russia. Not so the young Golda.

Lemons were imported to Denver via rail. Cold cars for transporting perishables were a relatively new modern advantage. The lemons would have come from Florida or California, but Golda was aware that citrus and almonds were major agricultural products of Palestine. The country of Israel was not founded until 1948, but Jewish immigrants to Palestine had begun setting up communal agricultural communities known as kibbutzim. Golda did dream of marrying Morris, having children, and living and working on a kibbutz. Eventually, she did all three things.

Tuberculosis was epidemic throughout the United States in the late nineteenth/early twentieth centuries. Golda's sister caught the disease in Milwaukee. Denver was a major destination for tuberculosis patients. Before the discovery of antibiotics, treatment consisted of moving to a place with dry air. Most of today's hospitals in the Denver metro area began as tuberculosis sanitariums. Antibiotics were not discovered until 1929 and their potential not understood until the 1940s.

When Golda lived in Denver there were two Jewish sanitariums, the Jewish Consumptive Relief Society (JCRS) on the west side of town, and National Jewish on the east. We know Sheyna was a patient of JCRS; her medical records are on display at the Golda Meier House on the Auraria Campus. According to History Colorado, Sheyna was a patient at both.

Sheyna's illness and courtship and the story of Golda running away from home are told in Golda Meier's autobiography and other historical sources. Union Station's *Mizpah* arch was a famous welcome for years until 1933, when increased traffic made it a hazard and it was torn down. Sheyna and Shamai's house was tiny, but modern. Golda attended North High School, and did well. And yes, she was in love with Morris Meyerson.

The issues listed (exploitation of workers, anti-Semitism, pacifism, etc.) were the burning political ideas of the day. Golda worried about speaking up, particularly for women's rights. The words she uses here are made up, but based on her ideas.

Her conviction that she was unattractive is based on her own reminiscences, and typical of all teenage girls.

The words of the argument over the motives of Margaret Brown are fictional, but Mrs. Brown's wealth and progressive ideals made her a famously confusing and controversial figure. Historians attribute her liberal politics as one cause of her separation from her husband, J.J. Brown.

The Mabovitch family had witnessed *pogroms,* campaigns of ethnic cleansing of Jewish people, when they lived in Russia. The phrase 'never again' came to be associated with the most heinous *pogrom* of all time, the holocaust in Germany, but the nightmares predated Hitler.

The quote about suffering is an actual quotation from Morris Meyerson. He was not nearly as keen on Palestine as Golda was.

Denver Parks hosted free concerts in 1913. Classic operas would have been played. Morris did read poetry to Golda and he would have been familiar with the meaning of *Tannhauser*. It tells the story of the struggle between sacred and profane love.

Luna Park was an amusement park on Sloans Lake. Boats were rented for those who wished to pull oars. Golda's thoughts on board the boat are the teenage confusions she actually faced at the time. The mountains and JCRS water tower were visible from the lake then and still are.

The Korngold's Julian Street house was moved to the Ninth Street Historic Park on the Auraria college campus in the 1980s to save it from demolition by the Boys' and Girls' Clubs, which purchased the property.

The description of Golda's eventual marriage and political career in Palestine and Israel is factual. The house interior described is the Golda Meir Center, with its exhibits from her political career. It is interesting imagining how a young girl would react to pictures of herself as an old lady. Most likely she just wouldn't believe it.

Bibliography

American Experience, 'The Forgotten Plague,' Chana Gazit, PBS, 2015.
Colorado Encyclopedia, 'Tuberculosis in Colorado,' Mary Swanson, Aug. 9, 2018, coloradoencyclopedia.org.
Colorado Experience, 'Jewish Pioneers,' Rocky Mountain PBS, Jan. 8, 2015.
Colorado Matters, 'How Tuberculosis Fueled Colorado's Growth,' Colorado Public Radio, Feb. 10, 2015.
Denver Public Library, 'Sloan's Lake Neighborhood History,' history.denverlibrary.org.
Golda Meir Center, 'Golda Meir: An Outline of a Unique Life,' and 'In the Shadow of Washington', Metropolitan State University of Denver; www.msudenver.edu.
Golda: The Romantic Years, Ralph G. Martin, Charles Scribner's Sons, 1988.
My Life, Golda Meir, Dell Publishing, 1975.

Margaret Brown

Key to the Visions
Crowd of people: Tourists at the Molly Brown House Museum
Pink hats: So-called 'pussy hats'
Sea of Women: Women's March at Civic Center Park

What's Fact? What's Fiction?

Margaret Brown loved her coffee, and poison was a common fixation back in the day. Being poisoned, intentionally or unintentionally, had been very common in the recent past. Food and drug regulations enacted in 1906 reduced accidental poisonings. The plots of Agatha Christie murder mysteries, popular in the 1920s (and now), often revolve around poison.

The Browns called their house on Pennsylvania Avenue 'The Lion House' on account of the two lion statues guarding the front steps. The porch is still floored in its original green and red mosaic tile.

The Brown Palace still publicizes its 'artesian' water from a well beneath the hotel. You can sample it at a drinking fountain just off the lobby.

Margaret Brown suffered increasingly violent headaches toward the end of her life. She eventually died of brain cancer.

She did have naturally auburn hair before it went gray. The description of her flapper style dress and beadery is based on an old photograph.

The Brown Palace is still illuminated by a skylight, as it was in her day, and the same railings rim the corridors. Guests are encouraged to touch the upside-down griffin for luck.

Margaret (aka 'Mrs. J.J.' during her lifetime and 'Molly,' after her death) Brown is one of the most famous people in these volumes. Stories of carrying on in Leadville, battling Denver society ladies, and surviving the Titanic have been told and retold often enough already. Her passion for social justice and affection for the poems of Eugene Field are less known. She personally saved Field's house from demolition.

Helen and Lawrence were the names of her children. They grew up in Leadville.

The actual program for the dedication of the Eugene Field home museum lists a poetry reading by school children from the Woolston School. Was the poem Fields' *Wynken, Blynken and Nod*? Quite probably, as that was his most famous. Did Margaret actually make the connection between this famous poem and her harrowing night on the lifeboat after the Titanic sunk? It seems impossible that she wouldn't have.

Lucy is an imaginary little girl. Their words are also made-up, but the tone reflects Mrs. Brown's slangy style of communication, as preserved in her informal writings and remarked upon during her lifetime. Her lecture to Lucy is consistent with her ideas about women's rights and knowledge of the very real dangers of mining.

Colorado women gained the right to vote in 1893. Margaret Brown ran for Congress in 1914, although she withdrew long before election day. Even though she always had the right to vote in Colorado, Margaret agitated in favor of nationwide women's suffrage and participated in protests in New York. The Nineteenth Amendment, which granted women the vote throughout the United States, was ratified in 1920.

Margaret was multilingual and French was her favorite foreign language. Her husband did disparage the language, although the comparison to potatoes is my own. The League of Nations was the predecessor to the United Nations. In addition to her concerns for women's rights, Mrs. Brown also fought for labor rights and against child labor.

She also loved drama, both the kind on stage and the style of life she lived.

The Fritchle electric car was manufactured on Colfax Avenue in Denver. Margaret was, in fact, the most famous driver of one. It is featured in the chapter on John Brisben Walker, also in this collection.

After her separation from her husband (they never divorced), Margaret rented out the House of Lions. Mrs. Grable minded the house when it was inhabited by boarders. During those later years, Margaret lived in the Brown Palace, when she wasn't traveling to New York or Florida or Europe. Henry Brown financed the Brown Palace Hotel; he was no relation to Margaret's husband J.J. The hotel is both grand and sturdy as described.

The summary of Leadville's gold and silver mining is historical, as is the story of the Brown's move to Denver, their summer house (in what is now Lakewood), and J.J.'s reputed 'skirt chasing.' Brown money helped fund the cathedral on Colfax. Her other philanthropic activities are based on historical records. River Front Amusement Park is also mentioned in the John Brisben Walker chapter in this collection.

She worked with Judge Ben Lindsey to reform juvenile justice. He is also mentioned in the Stanley Biber chapter in this collection.

It's true and tragic that her relationship with her children was strained by fighting over J.J.'s estate.

Trinity Methodist Church, catty-corner from the Brown Palace, built in 1888, was thickly coated in soot from years standing in air polluted from coal furnaces and dirty vehicle exhaust, and stayed that way until its sandstone was restored to its original, beautiful pink in 2004.

Margaret wore her famous chinchilla coat for many years. The coat also appears in the Golda Meir chapter of this collection.

Margaret talked about running for president during her lifetime, but never did.

Margaret wrote and spoke about her experience on the Titanic, never holding back on her disgust for the man on Lifeboat Six who refused to row. The words 'shivering like an aspen' were quoted by the *Rocky Mountain News*. The comment about Lucy is fictional.

Margaret's horror at seeing the site of the Ludlow Massacre is accurate. The quotation damning Rockefeller is word for word what she wrote in the press. Ludlow is also mentioned in the chapter on Dr. Stanley Biber in this collection.

Reuben was reportedly her favorite sandwich. Today's Ship Tavern at the Brown Palace has the Reuben on the menu. Margaret lived at the Brown during Prohibition, when taverns were prohibited. Ship Tavern opened after the repeal.

She was known during her lifetime as 'the iron hand beneath the glove of glistening silk.' She was friends with Alva Vanderbilt, who advocated for women holding office. Margaret served in the Ambulance Corps in France

Colorado Phantasmagorias 236

and later argued for women serving in combat, too. She was nothing if not passionate and consistent in her advocacy of fairness and equality for all.

Bibliography

Colorado Encyclopedia, 'Ludlow Massacre,' coloradoencyclopedia.org.
Denver Post, 'Carrying Out Mrs. Brown's Plan for Denver Carnival of Nations,' June 27, 1906; 'Mrs. J.J. Brown Scales Denver's Social Pinnacle,' May 2, 1912; 'Mrs. J.J. Brown Writes Own Story of the Titanic Disaster,' Mrs. J.J. Brown, May 19, 1912.
Denver Public Library Western History Department, Margaret (Molly) Tobin Brown Papers, C MSS WH53.
History Colorado Hart Library, Margaret Tobin Brown 1898-1934, MSS #763.
Ladies of the Brown, Deborah Faulkner, The History Press, 2010.
Molly Brown: Unraveling the Myth, Kristen Iverson, Johnson Books, 2010.
Rocky Mountain News, 'The Social Side,' August 19, 1900; 'Mrs. Brown Tells Story of Titanic in Graphic Style' May 19, 1912.

Ralph Carr

Key to the Visions
Fluffy-haired fellows: Governors Dick Lamm and Roy Romer
Younger man with peaked eyebrows: Gov. Bill Owens
Man with friendly wrinkles about the eyes: Gov. Bill Ritter
Lanky man with scraggly hair: Gov. John Hickenlooper
Man with pudgy cheeks: Gov. Jared Polis (my apologies, Governor!)

What's Fact? What's Fiction?

Examples of hate mail sent to Governor Carr are displayed at the museum at the Ralph Carr Judicial Center.

He looked to President Lincoln as an example of courage and integrity. Lincoln did famously counsel 'malice toward none' in his second inaugural address.

Scar-Faced Mag was a real woman who lived in Cripple Creek when Carr grew up there. He was a curly-haired boy who got teased. Carr used the term 'race hatred' in his public writings.

The hospital in Pueblo, known as the state asylum in Carr's day, is now called the Colorado Mental Health Institute.

The marble rotunda outside the Executive Chambers does feature the plaque described.

Colorado Phantasmagorias

The men described are the Colorado governors who served after the plaque was installed. See Key to the Visions, above.

Carr was diabetic and a practicing Christian Scientist. Although Christian Scientists generally avoid all drugs and medical interventions, he took insulin for his condition.

The quotations from Gov. Carr's radio address after Pearl Harbor and his letter to the *Pacific Citizen* are verbatim.

The Denver Post did deride him as 'Mr. Softy' and a 'sappy sentimentalist.'

His childhood and early career are described as history records, as is the mayhem at the State Republican convention in 1938.

The original plan for relocating Japanese Americans was to encourage them to move voluntarily. Many moved to Colorado to join friends and family before the forced evacuation, to the consternation of Coloradans who did, in fact, call them a 'yellow horde.'

Japanese Puebloans actually signed a real loyalty pledge and Japanese American Citizens League of rural Blanca collected scrap metal for the war effort.

Carr would have been familiar with Japanese farmers from his years practicing law in Antonito. And, yes, there was a Buddhist temple in La Jara funded by Japanese Coloradans with some donations from non-Buddhist neighbors. Carr's friends in Antonito nicknamed him Rafaelito because he spoke Spanish. The rest of the quote is made up.

The federal government eventually decided to force the incarceration of innocent immigrants and American citizens in just as shameful a manner as described. Carr's position can be confusing to people nowadays. He opposed the federal government's plan because it imprisoned citizens who had done nothing wrong. The quote is accurate. However, he concluded that if it was to happen anyway, he would welcome the Japanese to Colorado in order to protect their rights and dignity as much as he could. Ironically (or not, you judge), governors in other states enthusiastically embraced the plan to lock up Japanese Americans, just didn't want the camps in their own states.

Carr was famously confident and optimistic. He believed he could turn the tide of public opinion in his favor. The excerpts from his radio address are accurate. The 'enemies' to which he referred would have been those sent here as prisoners of war. Colorado hosted a number of prisoner of war camps for captured German and Italian soldiers. The P.O.W. camps for enemy combatants were not the same as the concentration camp for

Japanese American evacuees. Carr always stood up for the constitutional rights of citizens.

The quotation about rats comes from an actual letter sent to Carr. He employed the term 'race hatred' rather than racism. He did get support from the Council of Churches, head of Agriculture, and CFL. The head of Agriculture surely had an eye out for protecting the sugar beet harvest. The *Rocky Ford Gazette* actually suggested a draft exemption for all farmers.

The meeting at the Brown Palace happened and the quote is what he actually said.

Carr's receptionist was an African-American gentleman, Mr. George Robinson. At one point, Carr was under such duress he went to Robinson's home in Five Points in Denver to hide out for a while.

Carr was a widower. His concern for his two children was the reason he took insulin even as he remained a Christian Scientist.

The view out the governor's office window is as the Civic Center Park appears today. The Ralph Carr Judicial Center is catty-corner from the Capitol.

Colorado's Japanese community donated the plaque in 1974.

The original estimate was for 3,500 evacuees at the Amache Relocation Center in Granada. Amache eventually housed more than double that number.

This scene on the eastern plains is called up again in the John Denver chapter of this collection.

The description of the internment camp is based on historical records. Governor Romer did play football for Holly High School against the Amache High School team.

The camp buildings were hauled away or torn down almost immediately after the war. One barracks has been rebuilt.

Ralph Carr was governor when both Winter Park Ski Area and Red Rocks Amphitheatre opened, connecting him to ski pioneer Carl Howelsen and developer John Brisben Walker, also profiled in this collection.

Bibliography

Amache, Robert Harvey, Taylor Trade Publishing, 2003.

Associated Press, 'Japanese-American Internment Camp Opens Forgotten History,' Russell Contreras, Oct. 19, 2015.

Colorado Encyclopedia, 'Ralph Carr,' coloradoencyclopedia.org.

Colorado Experience, 'Amache,' Rocky Mountain PBS, 2013.

Colorado Virtual Library, 'Ralph Carr: Defender of Japanese Americans,' coloradovirtuallibrary.org.

Colorado's Japanese Americans from 1886 to the Present, Bill Hosokawa, University Press of Colorado, 2005.

Crestone Eagle, 'The History of Japanese Settlers in the San Luis Valley,' Mary Lowers, Oct. 29, 2015.

Denver Post, 'In Gov. Ralph Carr, Colorado Has a Shining Light in the Painful History of Japanese Internment,' Jesse Paul, Dec. 6, 2016; 'Japanese-Americans in Denver Remember Incarceration of 120,000 During World War II,' Tom McGhee, Feb. 20, 2017.

Denver Public Library, 'Ralph Carr (1887-1950),' history.denverlibrary.org.

Discover Nikkei, 'Japanese Americans in Colorado,' Daryl Maeda, Jan. 30, 2008.

Granada Pioneer, 'Letter to the Editor,' Kau Kau Lane AC, Jan. 14, 1943.

National Park Service Sites of Shame, 'Confinement and Ethnicity: An Overview of World War II Japanese American Relocation Sites,' J. Burton, M. Farrell, F. Lord, and R. Lord, nps.gov.

Principled Politician: The Ralph Carr Story, Adam Schrager, Fulcrum Publishing, 2008.

Ralph Carr: Defender of Japanese Americans, Jamie Trumbull, Filter Press, 2011.

Wade Blank

Key to the Visions
Humidity, sweat: The Wheels of Justice ('Capitol Crawl') protest in Washington, D.C.
Child's voice: Jennifer Keelan
Video cameras, flashbulbs: Media coverage of protests
Chains, singing: Protest inside the Capitol Rotunda in Washington, D.C.
Suits, spray, roses, applause, pens: Signing ceremony for the Americans with Disabilities Act (ADA)

What's Fact? What's Fiction?
Michael Patrick Smith was a real person, a poet, and an inspiration to Wade Blank. The quote about Wade being rough outside and beautiful inside is fictional, but based on how friends described Blank.

The excerpt from the poem was penned by Mike Smith while he lived in a nursing home before dying of muscular dystrophy.

Wade Blank was an ordained Presbyterian pastor. He had led a church in Ohio, and would have known and worn the liturgical colors. Purple symbolizes repentance. His radical fight for social justice cost him his church in Ohio. He came to Colorado, but never took a church job while here, although he remained ordained clergy. He was known for 'swearing like a sailor.'

Blank is almost always pictured wearing a t-shirt and jeans and his hair was long, lanky and blond.

If you know much about traditional Presbyterians, divine visions aren't really their thing.

Blank founded the Atlantis Community, one of the country's first independent living communities to free people with serious disabilities from having to live in the restrictive environments of nursing homes. And he organized the bus protest described here.

The names given are those of the protestors, known as the Gang of Nineteen, who participated in 1978.

Derogatory words for disabled people (gimp, cripple) were commonly used at that time period. Blank used these words himself, not thoughtlessly, but on purpose for radical effect. He wanted to shock nondisabled people and make them feel uncomfortable about their own prejudices.

It used to be universally assumed that people with disabilities wanted to stay at home or in a nursing home and wanted never to go out in public. Often it was true, because their families were ashamed of them. Hard to believe we used to think that way, and the main reason it's hard to believe is that Wade Blank and others were so successful in changing attitudes.

Deinstitutionalization of disabled people was a major trend in the 1970s and 1980s. Before then it was commonplace for disabled people to be sent to a far-away state institution to live their whole lives. Deinstitutionalization sent people back to their home communities, but when their families couldn't handle their needs, nursing homes (formerly known as 'old folks homes') leaped in to fill the need. And, yes, Wade Blank began his fight for disability rights with such simple efforts as getting Heritage House, a real nursing home, to allow disabled residents to watch TV, listen to music, eat pizza, and write poetry. The menu is copied from an old Heritage House handout. 'Drug-induced bedtime' refers to the practice of forcing sleeping pills on young residents, who would otherwise have naturally stayed up later than the old residents.

Wade Blank did go out seeking young people for the Heritage House youth wing. In the beginning he saw this as a mission to free young people from institutions, but later came to realize Heritage House wanted young residents for profit.

Colorado Phantasmagorias

Memories of the Heritage House youth wing under Wade's supervision often compare it to a college dorm. Wade took the residents camping, to wrestling matches, ice cream parlors, and concerts, specifically including both John Denver at Red Rocks and the Grateful Dead at the Denver Coliseum. The Red Rocks concert is revisited in the John Denver chapter of this collection.

Wade Blank came to see any nursing home as a prison for the innocent, and understood there was no way to make such a life acceptable, certainly not for young people.

The founding of the independent-living Atlantis Community is factual, as well as the big transportation roadblock. The phone calls are fictional, but based on the actual, historical frustrations, e.g. long lead times, limited routes and times, and judgmentalism.

RTD executives argued that their wheelchair ban was for 'the good of' disabled people, as well as to prevent inconvenience to nondisabled riders. Atlantis's campaign is factual. They lost their lawsuit in federal court right before the bus protest in 1978.

The Gang of Nineteen blocked two buses and screwed up traffic at Colfax and Broadway for 24 hours July 5-6, 1978. "We will ride!" was their chant. Wade Blank often compared this protest to Rosa Parks (whose refusal to change seats in a bus sparked the civil rights movement).

Wade Blank despised pity.

The sentence about disabled people being able to pursue their happiness is a paraphrase of words actually said by Wade Blank. The line about the jail not being wheelchair accessible is made-up, but also true.

The names are accurate, as is the nickname 'Jet Set.'

Most of the dialogue with RTD is fictional, but the gist of it accurately portrays the negotiations that went down at the time. The quotation "We have been unable to ascertain where the handicapped people want to travel to and from" is, unfortunately, verbatim from then-RTD director John Simpson. Simpson is also reported to have issues with lift usage upsetting schedules and noisy hydraulics. Bus drivers not wanting to operate lifts remained a big problem for years.

The Gang of Nineteen did sing "Ain't Gonna Let Nobody Turn Me Around."

They also slept in sleeping bags in the streets. Really. See the photo.

U.S. Representative Pat Schroeder really did bring doughnuts.

'Shot heard around the world' is how the 1978 Denver bus protest came to be known. ADAPT was known as 'Hell's Angels of the disability movement,' and still is, by some.

The 1990 Wheels of Justice demonstration on the steps of the Capitol building in Washington D.C. attracted disabled people from all over the U.S. Wade Blank brought a group, including eight-year-old Jennifer Keelan, who became the star of the day. She was not yet born in 1978. Videos show her colorful headband and record her fighting words. Video from the time also shows people scooching backwards, and whatever else they needed to do to get up the steps, of which there are, exactly, 82.

"F . . . freak." These words are fictional. Wade Blank was well known for full-throated swearing and I'm sure he used the actual obscenity in private, among friends. But remembering how it used to be, before stand-up comics and others made the 'f-bomb' ubiquitous, it seemed to me that an ordained pastor would avoiding using the f-bomb in front of a stranger such as Mancio. But, I could be wrong on that.

The description of the Wheels for Justice demonstration and the ADA is based on historical records. There's some controversy over whether the ADA would have passed intact without the protest. The ADA had a lot of provisions, just a few of them set forth here. Until the ADA, disabled people were sometimes banned as 'fire hazards.' I wish I'd made that up, but I didn't.

At the ADA signing, remarks about sunstroke and the right to sunstroke were overheard in the crowd.

In 1978, where Wade Blank 'time traveled' from, George H.W. Bush was most well known as head of the C.I.A. He did not become vice president until the presidency of Ronald Reagan in 1980. He was elected president in 1988 and signed the ADA (which he supported) in 1990.

Mancio's recitation of ADAPT protests and successes is factual history, including the thwacking of curbs with sledgehammers.

Wade studied Psalm 46 in seminary. His essay on it is in his papers stored at the Denver Public Library. The quoted verse is Psalm 46:5 as translated in the New Revised Standard Version, which wasn't published until 1989, but it's more apropos to this story than the translation Wade would have known, and since he just came back from time traveling anyway . . .

The excerpt from the poem by Mike Smith is as he wrote it.

Bibliography

Congressional Record, Feb. 16, 1993.

Denver Post, 'Having Made Public Aware, Disabled End Bus Barricade,' Fred Gillies, July 6, 1978; 'Disabled Renew Protests of RTD Policy,' John Morehead, July 13, 1978; 'Disabled Demands RTD Meet Topic,' July 20, 1978; 'Disabled Tell Official of RTD to Resign,' July 26, 1978; 'Handicapped Protesters Forcibly Ejected from RTD Offices,' Brad Martisius, Sept. 14, 1978; 'The Full Ride Not for All,' Max Woodfin, Sept. 23, 1978; 'Charges Dismissed in Bus Barricade,' Howard Pankratz, Jan. 9, 1979; 'Handicapped Test RTD Bus Lifts, Sept. 23, 1979; 'Threat of Sit-In Over RTD Lift Plans Dissolves,' George Lane, Nov. 20, 1981; 'Disabled Bus Riders' (editorial), Dec. 8, 1981; 'Handicapped Will Protest RTD Wheelchair-Lift Ban,' George Lane, Dec. 18, 1981; ''Johnson is New RTD Chairman, Jan. 11, 1983; 'Disabled Protest to Governor,' Neil Westergaard, Oct. 4, 1983; 'Own Home At Last,' Fred Gillies, April 28, 1987; '104 Held in Protest by Denver-Based Disabled Group,' March 14, 1990; 'U.S. to Mandate Bus Service for Disabled,' March 23, 1990; 'Arsonist Sets Wheelchair Ramp on Fire,' Aug. 29, 1990; 'Champion of Disabled, Son Drown,' Feb. 17, 1993; 'Meet the Disabled Activists from Denver Who Changed a Nation,' Danika Worthington, July 5, 2017.

Denver Public Library Western History Department, 'Wade and Molly Blank Papers,' 13 boxes, WH 2283.

Denver Public Library, 'We Will Ride! The Origin of the Disability Rights Movement in Denver,' Katie Rudolph, May 18, 2015, history.denverlibrary.org.

Disability Rights Movement: From Charity to Confrontation, Doris Fleischer and Frieda Zames, Temple University Press, 2011.

Enabling Acts, Lennard J. Davis, Beacon Press, 2015.

Health Affairs, 'Rebalancing Medicaid Long-Term Services and Supports,' Jennifer Ryan and Barbara Coulter Edwards, Sept. 17, 2015.

Lives Worth Living, film by Eric Neudel, 2011.

Westword, 'Remembering Gang of 19 Forty Years After Denver Protests Changed Accessibility,' Conor McCormick-Cavanagh, July 4, 2018.

Barney Ford

Key to the Visions
Puffy jackets and clunky shoes: Modern ski jackets and downhill ski boots
Long Boards: Skis and snowboards
Golden dome, radiator heat, onyx and marble: Colorado Capitol building
Woman at lectern, man of their race: Any of the members of the Colorado Black Legislative Caucus
Golden glass: Stained glass window portraying Barney Ford in House Chamber of Colorado Capitol

What's Fact? What's Fiction?
Barney Ford was a well-known citizen of Breckenridge. The description of eighteenth century winter attire is accurate.

Slavery, the practice by which one person owns another person's body, was legal throughout the southern United States prior to the Civil War. Men, women, and children were bought and sold and treated as property. They were put to work at whatever task the owner (master) ordered, and were not paid. Children born to enslaved women were born the property of their mother's master. They had no freedom. Barney Ford was born into this system.

Skiing was a means of transportation in the mountains for miners, postal carriers, and itinerant pastors in the nineteenth century. The idea of skiing for recreation wasn't introduced until the early twentieth-century, popularized by Carl Howelsen, also profiled in this collection.

Barney Ford opened, owned, and sold many successful restaurants throughout his life. His last was the one named Saddle Rock in Breckenridge. He enjoyed hosting children's parties there, where he served popcorn and apple cider. Julia urged him to return them to Denver due to the strain of thin air on her lungs.

He learned hospitality via forced labor for the man who, by law, owned his body, beginning when he was a small boy. As a young man, he escaped to the northern United States, where slavery was illegal.

The man in the top hat is fictional. Barney Ford did own shares in a gold mine and a mining company called The Oro Group that he sold for a profit during his last years in Breckenridge. Although their conversation is imagined, some kind of meeting would have to have been held to transfer ownership.

Colorado Phantasmagorias

Ford was well-known and widely respected. He was frequently mentioned in the *Rocky Mountain News*, which identified him as B.L., while he called himself 'the Old Caterer.' I don't know how he got that nickname or why, but it does seem like good advertising.

Sluice mining for gold was practiced in Georgia before the Civil War and Barney Ford reportedly did that work under orders from his master. The description of him being scrubbed down is based on common treatment of slaves at that time, not on any specific report of Ford's experience.

The story of his experience on and escape from *The Magnolia Blossom* comes from biographies, as is the description of his barbering business. History also reports that H.O. Wagoner recruited Ford for the Underground Railroad and introduced him to Julia.

The memories of his gold chasing and the hotel in Nicaragua are also from his biographies. The quotation from Julia is made up, but summarizes her reported ideas. Their customers were nicknamed '49ers' and 'Go Backers.' Their return to Chicago is accurate per the historical record, as is his participation in the Underground Railroad. The freeing of eleven from Missouri is the same raid that Margaret Brown's father participated in. See her chapter in the first volume of this collection. Ford made the acquaintance of John Brown and Sen. Charles Sumner.

His 1858 trip to Colorado is told factually as is, sadly, the end of his first foray into mining.

The shanty restaurant next to the gambling hall on Blake Street was a real place. The part about the Blake Street fire and rebuilding also comes from historical sources.

The details of the campaign for Colorado statehood are cobbled together from reputable histories, although there are inconsistencies in the historical record. What's irrefutable is that Ford was deeply involved, that the issue of race played a role in delaying statehood, and Pres. Johnson vetoed it using the quotation cited. Also in this collection is a chapter on Felipe Baca, who fought for equal representation for Latinos during the run-up to statehood.

Ford's Inter-Ocean Hotel on Blake Street in Denver was absolutely fabulous, by all accounts. In another chapter of this collection, Ora Chatfield and Clara Dietrich elope to Denver where they stay in 'a hotel;' the exact hotel is not reported in history but it could have been the Inter-Ocean.

Ford's return on investment is sourced from nonfiction histories.

The current Colorado Capitol Building opened in 1894, so it would look unfamiliar to Ford in 1889.

Mancio's recital of the accomplishments of African-American leaders in Colorado is all true, but of course incomplete. A lot changes in politics in a hundred years. In Ford's time, African Americans sided with the abolitionist Republicans, but that changed in the mid-nineteenth century. In 2020 the Colorado legislature had eight Black members, none of them Republican. Julia was the first African-American woman on the Denver Social Register.

Lastly, Barney Ford did die shoveling snow.

Bibliography

Barney Ford, Governor Alexander Cummings, Negro Suffrage and the Colorado Statehood Bill of 1866, Eleanor M. Gehres, University of Denver, 1971.
Barney Ford: Black Baron, Marian Talmadge and Iris Gilmore, Dodd Mead, 1973.
Barney Ford: Pioneer Businessman, Jamie Trumbull, Filter Press, 2010.
Black Democratic Legislative Caucus of Colorado, http://blackcaucusco.com.
Black Past, 'Barney L. Ford (1822-1902), Moya Hansen, undated.
Black Past, 'John H. Stuart (1854-1910), Moya Hansen, Jan. 21, 2007.
Black West, William Loren Katz, Broadway Books, 2005.
Denver Post, 'Gold for Colorado Capitol Dome Back from Italy,' June 17, 2013.
DenverUrbanism, 'Denver's Historic Inter-Ocean Hotel,' Shawn Snow, March 11, 2012.
History Colorado, 'Barney Ford: African American Pioneer,' Feb. 8, 2017.
It Happened in Colorado, James Crutchfield, TwoDot, 2016.
Michigan State University, 'The Great American Oyster Craze: Why 19th Century Americans Loved Oysters,' Feb. 23, 2017.
Mister Barney Ford: A Portrait in Bistre, Forbes Parkhill, Sage Books, 1963.
Rocky Mountain News, Aug. 20, 1863; Aug. 25, 1863; advertisements, 1863; Sept. 21, 1865; June 8, 1866; June 29, 1866; June 30, 1866; June 14, 1867; July 22, 1867; Aug. 9, 1867; May 19, 1869; Nov. 27, 1870; Jan. 22, 1871; July 1, 1871; Sept. 17, 1871; Oct. 12, 1871; Dec. 23, 1871; Jan. 3. 1872; Jan. 6, 1872; May 8, 1872; May 24, 1872; May 31, 1872; June 12, 1872; July 11, 1872; July 26, 1872; Aug. 20, Oct. 2, 1872; 1872; Nov. 10, 1872; advertisements, 1872; Jan. 1, 1873; March 25, 1873; May 30, 1873; June 26, 1873; Aug. 7, 1873; Aug. 10, 1873; Aug 22, 1873; Aug. 23, 1873; Aug. 24, 1873; Aug. 29, 1873; Sept. 6, 1873; Sept. 9, 1873; Jan. 1, 1874; April 8, 1874; April 4, 1880; April 17, 1880; Sept. 25, 1881; Jan. 26, 1882.

Ora and Clara

Key to the Visions
Two men in government office: Gay couple granted marriage license in 1975
Young woman with hoop earrings: Clela Rorex in 1975
Polished pews: Spectator area of Colorado Supreme Court, 1993
Woman in short skirt: Attorney Jean Dubofsky
People on high bench in black robes: Justices of Colorado Supreme Court
Couples: Same-sex wedding ceremonies

What's Fact? What's Fiction?
Lavender was a popular fragrance in the nineteenth century. Queen Victoria of England's wedding set off the tradition of the white wedding gown in 1840. Nibbling mint was a way to freshen breath. Ladies of the era entertained themselves by reading poetry to each other. The poem is by 'Michael Field,' the pen name for poets Katherine Bradley and Edith Cooper. Ora and Clara enjoyed poetry, so they may have read this one, which was published in 1889. The 'Sappho' referenced is the ancient Greek woman who wrote powerfully evocative poetry about other women and lived on the island of Lesbos, from which the English word 'lesbian' is derived.

A bustle is a padded undergarment that gives the illusion of a large posterior. These, like crinolines, held up long, heavy skirts so women could walk. Without a bustle or wire crinoline, the skirt would drag in the dirt and trip the wearer.

Reports from the time are that Clara suggested she was masculine enough to pass as a man.

Girls did not wear corsets until about age fourteen.

The 1880s saw a huge discovery of diamonds in South Africa. Diamond engagement rings were known by 1889, although only wealthy people could afford them. The crystals inside a geode call to mind the facets of a cut diamond.

Magic lantern 'phantasmagoria' light shows were popular entertainment in the nineteenth century. Lanterns were used to project spooky images onto a screen. Phantasmagoria shows were a precursor to movies.

A corset, which cinched a woman's abdomen and lifted her breasts, could constrict breathing and cut off blood flow when pulled too tight. This sometimes led to fainting, and smelling salts were kept handy to revive them.

Bear grease was a common hair tonic ingredient in the nineteenth century.

The rhyme is an excerpt from a poem by Charity Bryant, who lived in a same-sex relationship with Sylvia Drake about a hundred years before Ora and Clara.

Most of the details of their discovery are imagined, but when confronted, Ora did accuse Clara of biting her and squeezing her nearly to death. Clara avowed that she loved Ora more than life itself.

We know from the *Aspen Daily Times* that Clara wrote these verses from Shakespeare's *King Lear* as a love poem to Ora. Women kept their private letters locked in boxes in their bed chambers. A typical punishment for girls who showed any disobedience was to lock them in their rooms.

Maternal mortality was very high in the nineteenth century and did not begin dropping until the twentieth. Contraception was unreliable and abortion was dangerous. Housework was arduous, to say the least.

'Mad Infatuation' was the headline above quotations from Clara's letter to Ora printed in *The Aspen Daily Times*. The plea about 'heart's blood' is verbatim.

Clara got engaged to a man right before eloping with Ora. It must have been a ruse.

Clara's words about horses and silver and sun is imagined, but are based on the ranching/mining culture of 1880s Aspen.

Ora and Clara eloped on the train in the summer of 1889. The tuberculosis deception is made up, although plausible. Tuberculosis was epidemic at the time and Denver had several hospitals and sanitariums specifically for TB patients. See the Golda Meir chapter, also in this collection.

The Colorado Midland train trip is according to historical schedules.

Denver's population in 1889 is from the census. Ora and Clara were reported to have stayed in a hotel. It may have been the Inter-Ocean, which was near Union Station. If so, this ties the women to Barney Ford, also profiled in this collection, who built that hotel. If they had a snack, it probably would have been oysters, the go-to food for all nineteenth century people. Ora signed her letters to Clara, 'Hubby.'

The Denver Times article was printed as described, and reprinted around the country and as far away as Brisbane, Australia.

Colorado Phantasmagorias

The University of Colorado was founded in 1876 in Boulder.

The Boulder County Courthouse was built in art deco style in the 1930s.

The description of Boulder Clerk Clela Rorex's interaction with the gay men is accurate, as is the summary of the 1992 lawsuit to invalidate Amendment Two. Tribade was a word for lesbian in the Victorian era.

Ora and Clara made it all the way to Kansas City, which is where the Pitkin County Sheriff caught up with them.

Bibliography

Appealing for Justice, Susan Berry Casey, Gilpin Park Press, 2016.

Aspen Daily Chronicle, [No headline], Jan. 23, 1889; 'An Aspenite Interviewed,' July 6, 1889; [No headline] March 6, 1890.

Aspen Daily Times, 'Mad Infatuation,' May 11, 1889.

Aspen Weekly Chronicle, 'Emma's Sensation,' July 8, 1889.

Aspen Weekly Times, [No headline], July 20, 1889; 'Fine Entertainment at Emma,' April 25, 1891.

Atlantic, 'But Were They Gay? The Mystery of Same-Sex Love in the 19th Century,' Jennie Rothenberg Gritz, Sept. 7, 2012.

Boulder Daily Camera, 'Boulder Courthouse Up for Historic Designation for Clela Rorex's Same-Sex Marriage Licenses in 1975,' Charlie Brennan, April 20, 2018; 'Boulder County Courthouse Gets Federal Nod for Role in State's LGBTQ History,' Charlie Brennan, July 31, 2018.

Brisbane Courier, [No headline], Sept. 2, 1889.

Charity & Sylvia: A Same-Sex Marriage in Early America, Rachel Hope Cleves, Oxford University Press, 2014.

Chatfield Heritage, 'Clark Samuel Chatfield, Sr. & Mary Elizabeth Morrow,' Catherine Sevenau, Feb. 8, 2011.

Colorado Heritage, 'Why Boulder County Courthouse Is Recognized for Its Role in LGBTQ History,' Winter 2018/19; 'From Hate State to Election of a Gay Governor,' William Wei, Fall 2019.

Colorado's Legendary Lovers, Rosemary Fetter, Fulcrum Publishing, 2004.

Denver Post, 'License Issued in Boulder for 2 Men to Be Married,' March 27, 1975; 'Two Women Receive License to Marry,' April 8, 1975; 'Unisex Licenses at Four,' April 13, 1975; 'Unisex Weddings Held Invalid,' April 25, 1975.

Denver Public Library, 'Luis Rovira (1923-2011), undated.

Denver Times, 'Lovelorn Girls,' July 6, 1889.

Disorderly Conduct, Carroll Smith-Rosenberg, Oxford University Press, 1985.

Documents of the LGBT Movement, Chuck Stewart, Gale eBooks, 2018.

GLBTQ, 'Denver,' Geoffrey W. Bateman, 2004, glbtq.com.

History Channel, 'Women Got Married Long Before Gay Marriage,' Erin Blakemore, June 12, 2019; history.com.

Love Unites Us: Winning the Freedom to Marry in America, Kevin Cathcart and Leslie Gabel-Brett, Lambda Legal, 2016.

Colorado Phantasmagorias 250

NPR, 'Colo. Clerk Recalls Issuing Same-Sex Marriage Licenses – In 1975,' July 18, 2014.

Outfront, 'Our Story: A Curious and Fascinating Timeline of LGBT Denver,' Berlin Sylvestre, June 16, 2015.

San Francisco Chronicle, 'San Francisco Not the First to Marry Couples of the Same Gender,' Suzanne Herel, Feb. 14, 2004.

Strangers: Homosexual Love in the Nineteenth Century, Graham Robb, W.W. Norton & Company, 2003.

Surpassing the Love of Men, Lillian Faderman, William Morrow and Company, 1981.

Washington Post, '40 Years Later, Story of a Same-Sex Marriage in Colo. Remains Remarkable,' Robert Barnes, April 18, 2015.

Westword, 'Clela Rorex Planted the Flag for Same-Sex Marriage in Boulder Forty Years Ago,' Kyle Harris, Aug.13, 2014.

Adolph Coors

Key to the Visions
Women and fruity smell: Women drinking beer in public

What's Fact? What's Fiction?

Verrückt is the German word for crazy. Adolph Coors prided himself on being a law-abiding American. He claimed to support Prohibition, which became law in Colorado in 1916, but of course he thought it was crazy.

He was known for being both tidy and reticent.

The silly headline about 'Mr. Barleycorn' is verbatim from the *Denver Post*.

The reference to the lady who left the geode is an oblique reference to Margaret Brown, another Coloradan featured in this collection. Mrs. Brown may or may not have ever been invited to a luncheon by Mrs. Coors. But it's possible.

'Respectable' women did not drink in public prior to Prohibition. They drank in their own homes or at private parties. *Die Sinnestäuschung* is German for a delusion.

It's documented that Coors dumped 560 barrels of beer into Clear Creek on the eve of Prohibition in Colorado. Whether he stood on the banks personally, I can't attest to, but it makes a vivid picture, and he might have.

He had been brewing beer along the banks of Clear Creek for 40 years before Prohibition. His life story as he remembers it is accurate as recorded by his progeny.

Panschen is German for adulterate.

The temperance movement of the late nineteenth and early twentieth century was primarily led by women, the Women's Christian Temperance Union foremost. Temperance advocates believed that drunkenness was the cause of domestic abuse, child abuse, and poverty. Women had good evidence to believe so. The culture was for men, and men only, to go to a saloon after work and get drunk among their male buddies and prostitutes (as sex workers were known), then go home, penniless, where they'd take out their frustrations on their family. Women, if they drank at all, imbibed at home, sometimes slugging it down while hiding in the outhouse or bathroom. Substituting beer and wine for hard liquor was promoted as a compromise in the early days of the temperance movement when Coors and Jacob Schueler (his original partner) first began making beer.

The details of the early days of Coors Brewing are taken from historical sources. *Der Amerikanischer Traum* is German for the American Dream.

The idea of 'the three places women don't belong' (politics, business, saloons) was commonly espoused back then.

Carrie Nation was a real woman, who did wield a hatchet, ironically, in promoting 'temperance.' Great publicity. The description is from news reports from the time. She visited Denver in 1906.

The goals and tactics of the Anti-Saloon League are factual.

Adolph Coors was known for his gentlemanliness and rectitude and business acumen, so he would have understood that not all drinkers were poor drunks. *Der Selbstbeherrschung* is German for self-discipline. His insight did not win the day.

Dinner at the Coors household was on the dot at 6:25 every evening. That's a fact his children never forgot and often told.

In 1914, Colorado was one of the first states to vote to prohibit alcohol, but the movement was nationwide and gaining momentum. Coors' attempts to keep the family business alive for his sons in the face of Prohibition are factual: near beer (Mannah), malted milk, ceramics.

Coors, a German immigrant, was pro-German until the sinking of the *Lusitania*. RMS Lusitania was a British ocean liner that the Germans sunk in 1915, killing 128 U.S. citizens. It presaged the United States' declaration of war on Germany two years later. *Dummkopf* is German for fool (literally, stupid head), referring to the German Kaiser. (German immigrants had a vocal presence in Colorado prior to World War II. The original Constitution from 1876 was printed in three languages, English, Spanish,

Colorado Phantasmagorias 252

and German. See the Felipe Baca chapter in this collection. Also, Denver Public Schools had separate schools for German children, at the insistence of parents who wanted their children to learn in German.)

Lacherlich is German for laughable. Keep in mind that a majority of Colorado voters, who would be his customers for ceramics and malted milk, supported Prohibition. It would have been good business to respect the voters and protect his remaining businesses.

In the month leading up to Colorado's Prohibition, Wyoming liquor and beer dealers bought pages of advertising in Colorado newspapers, advertising that they would ship to Colorado. Until the whole country went dry, it was legal for Coloradans to buy beer from other states as long as they drank it in private.

Coors was an ardent gardener.

The headline and lead from the *Denver Post* are a hoot, aren't they? Word for word. The press was a little different back then.

The Eighteenth Amendment to the Constitution of the United States, prohibiting 'intoxicating liquors' through the United States, would become the first and only Amendment to be repealed, but Coors did not know that in 1916.

The smell of beer is appropriately pervasive at Coors Field, home of the Colorado Rockies baseball team. Coors Field opened its doors in 1995 on Blake Street in Denver.

Der Wahrsager is German for soothsayer. *Raus hier* means 'get out of here.'

Coors was known to be stubborn.

Den Hintern means the butt or the ass.

The story of the repeal of Prohibition is factual.

John Hickenlooper, governor of Colorado 2011-2019, brewed craft beer at Wynkoop Brewing Company, which he founded with three other guys in 1988.

Bibliography

Coastal Virginian, 'Strange Brew,' Rich Griset, Jan. 2015.
Colorado Encyclopedia, 'Adolph Coors,' Sean Buck, Feb. 16, 2018, coloradoencyclopedia.org.
Colorado Transcript, Feb. 25, 1915; Dec. 28, 1916; Feb. 3, 1916.
Coors: A Rocky Mountain Legend, Russ Banham, Greenwich Publishing Group, 1998.
Denver Post, 'Physicians Offer No Hope for Hon. John Barleycorn and Say Life's Ebbing Fast,' Dec. 26, 1915; 'Do's and Don'ts Under Dry Law Laid Down by State Officials,' Dec. 30, 1915; 'S' Long John, Take Keer of Yourself! Is Farewell Shout in Denver as the Hon. Mr. Barleycorn Packs Grip and Hops Car to Oblivion,' Dec. 31, 1915;

"Brewers and Distillers Worth Millions Locking Up,' Dec. 31, 2015; People Bid John Barleycorn Goodbye with Laugher and Hilarity in New Dry States,' Jan. 1, 1916.
Last Call, Daniel Okrent, Scribner, 2010.
Moffat County Courier, July 29, 1915.
Out Where the West Begins, Philip Anschutz, Cloud Camp Press, 2015.
Rocky Mountain News, 'Coors' New Output to be Malted Milk,' July 18, 1915; advertisements, Dec., 1915; 'Dry Year is Ushered In With Marked Quiet as Bars Close Early,' Jan. 1, 1916; 'Dry Denver Displays No Wet Regret: No Signs of Gloom Seen as Water Replaces Liquor,' Jan. 2, 1916.
Salida Record, July 30, 1915.
The Pre-Prohibition History of Adolph Coors Company, 1873-1933, William Kostka, Adolph Coors Company, 1933.
Wray Gazette, 'What the Liquor People Really Think,' July 2, 1914.

Carl Howelsen

Key to the Visions
Huge tracks like lynx clawings: Downhill ski trails at Steamboat Resort
Seven ski jumps: Howelsen Hill
Colorful contraptions: Painted skis
Monster-sized feet: Modern plastic ski boots
Bald heads of all colors: Ski helmets
Glowing garments: Ski jackets and pants from bright, synthetic fabrics
Cyclops eyes: Ski goggles
Compartments that dangle from cables: Gondola

What's Fact? What's Fiction?
Carl Howelsen coached Steamboat Springs youth in ski jumping at no charge.

He maintained, as do ski coaches today, that learning to fall properly is the first and most important skiing skill.

Ski clothing in the early part of the twentieth century was almost always wool. Although synthetics have advantages, wool is still used for winter outerwear because it's a natural insulator, somewhat water repellent, and wicks sweat from the body.

Pine tar, which was ironed onto the bottom of wooden skis to make them water proof and help wax stick better, does not have that fresh, piney smell we think of from the woods and Christmas trees. It's stinky.

Carl Howelsen performed ski jumps for the Barnum & Bailey Circus until he hurt his back. The slide was covered in petroleum jelly and sometimes he jumped over elephants. His most famous jump was at Madison Square Garden. The quotation is verbatim from the promotional poster.

Carl chewed tobacco, according to his son. Carl was friends with George Cranmer, whom he met in Denver, and who eventually went on to manage Denver Parks, developing both Red Rocks Amphitheater and Winter Park Ski Resort.

A *nisse* is a mythical imp that guards people when it's happy but also plays tricks on people when offended. Sometimes thought of as a goblin, a *nisse* resembles a garden gnome.

Carl Howelsen skied on Rabbit Ears Pass, which has some of the deepest and best powder in the state. He was a champion ski jumper, both in his native Norway and as a professional jumper in the U.S.

Carl stood 5'7" and was renowned for his stamina. He could and did sometimes ski 50 miles.

The conversation about cable cars for skiers is made-up, but of course that's how the ski industry eventually developed. Winter Park Resort had mechanized lifts when it opened in 1939.

George Cranmer was a stockbroker when he and Carl Howelsen became friends. Carl had a friend and employee named Hans Hansen who did somersaults off of Carl's roof. Carl once remarked to a newspaper reporter that he wondered why Coloradans weren't "ski experts." George's words about gold, silver and the winter playground are taken from his speech at the opening of Winter Park. Although that happened years after this, he may well have already been thinking along these lines.

Elk Park was renamed Howelsen Hill in March, 1917. The description of the dedication is based on this type of ceremony held in those days. The article on the christening does not report details. I assume both George Cranmer and Marjorie Perry would have come to the dedication as they were Carl's friends. *Langlauf* means cross-country skiing in German, Norwegian, and even English.

Carl's boyhood and young adulthood in Norway and Chicago were as described by his son, Leif. I imagined him comparing his circus salary to the Prince Regent of Norway, but it's apt. For a young immigrant, two hundred dollars a week was a fortune. In today's dollars, that's almost $300,000 a year (although he got laid up before the year was over).

Colorado Phantasmagorias

The quotation with all its wonderful Ps is verbatim from circus advertising. I couldn't possibly have made that up.

And, yes, Carl called it "a little stunt," because for him, it was. He could jump much higher and farther off of real ski jumps in the out of doors than he could off a jellied ramp inside the circus tent. Even so, he did jump in front of about four million people before hurting his back.

He joined the Denver Local of the Bricklayers and Masons International Union in 1909.

Trains were the primary means of transportation in the early twentieth century and the network was vast. The Moffat Tunnel was not yet complete, but the railroad took the Moffat Road over the pass into Middle Park, when it wasn't blocked by snow, that is.

The story about Carl's trek through Fraser to the Winter Carnival at Hot Sulphur Springs is well-documented by history.

The *Denver Post* published a picture of him on his skis at the State Capitol after a blizzard in 1913. He also met George in a park either on that same day or about then.

Carl was a ski evangelist; when he wasn't working or skiing, he was promoting. Estimates of the spectators at Inspiration Point in 1914 range from 15,000 to 20,000. The quote from the *Denver Post* is accurate.

Howelsen bought a ranch in Steamboat Springs and split his time between Denver and Steamboat for several years. By 1917 he was living and working in Routt County fulltime.

The ski trip to Strawberry Hot Springs is fictional, but something close to it certainly happened. Carl probably also soaked in the hot springs in town, but it's documented that he led ski trips to the Strawberry, sometimes escorting women. There are photographs. Hot springs were sacred to the Utes; Chipeta, also profiled in this collection, may have visited Strawberry.

Carl handcrafted eight-foot-long skis for Marjorie Perry. The sentence about deeper and steeper are her actual words. The Fourth-Annual Winter Carnival is factually described. Carl liked to cook eggs and sausage in the hot springs.

The conversation about ski lifts is imagined, but tells the true story of the evolution of mechanized skier transport. George's comment about buying stock in gloves is my own joke. The sentence about the velocity of the dollar is an actual Cranmer quote, as are the words "wealthy and poor, as well as the vast majority in between." To this day, Winter Park is known as among the least elite of the major Colorado ski resorts. Cranmer is also quoted using the words "thrilling vistas" to describe the views from the chairlifts at Winter Park.

Carl had been awarded the masonry contract for the First National Bank in Craig in 1917. He later also did brickwork for the hospital in nearby Hayden.

The story about the fur trapper really happened, as did going snow blind for three days, which was not uncommon since sunglasses were hard to come by in the west. Steamboat Resort is described as best I could from my own experience there. Carl told people he thought Storm Mountain would make a great ski area.

Mancio's facts and figures are true.

"Once a child gets on skis, it does not take long until they can manage them pretty well," is a documented quotation from Carl.

Governor Carr, also profiled in this collection, came to the dedication of Winter Park.

Carl wrote an article printed in the *Steamboat Pilot*, quoted by Mancio.

I don't know if Carl was at all interested in *nisse* or Norsk gods, but he would have heard of them, and the references are fun. The U.S. had just entered World War I (known then as the World War) in 1917.

Mancio's history of World War II and the 10th Mountain Division and the post-war development of ski resorts is all factual.

Downhill ski resorts get almost all the press, but many Coloradans continue to enjoy backcountry and Nordic cross-country skiing, which involve skiing uphill.

Bibliography

Colorado Business Hall of Fame, George Cranmer, coloradobusinesshalloffame.org.
Colorado Encyclopedia, 'Howelsen Hill;' 'Ski Industry,' Michael Childers; 'The Tenth Mountain Division,' Griffin Noyer; coloradoencyclopedia.org.
Colorado Ski Hall of Fame, 'George Cranmer,' coloradoskihalloffame.com.
Flying Norseman, Leif Hovelsen, National Ski Hall of Fame Press, 1983.
Greenwoodvillage.com, Marjorie Perry: Naturalist, Outdoorswoman, Conservationist,' undated.
History of Skiing at Steamboat Springs, Sureva Towler, 1987.
Just Around Here, George Cranmer, justaroundhere.com.
Lost Ski Areas of Colorado's Front Range and Northern Mountains, Caryn and Peter Boddie, The History Press, 2014.
Middle Park Times, 'Get Your Skis,' Jan. 3, 1912; 'A Carnival of Sports,' Jan. 5, 1912; 'Final Carnival News,' Jan. 30, 1914; 'Steamboat Winter Sports,' Jan. 30, 1914; '4th Annual Winter Sports Carnival a Great Success,' Feb. 19, 1915.

Rocky Mountain News, 'Sport of Skiing in Colorado Mountains,' Menifee R. Howard, December 5, 1915; 'Carl Howelsen Wins National Professional Ski Championship,' Feb. 21, 1921.

Ski Area Management, 'Kottke National End of Season Survey 2018/2019,' saminfo.com.

Ski Style: Sport and Culture in the Rockies, Annie Gilbert Coleman, University Press of Kansas, 2004.

Steamboat Pilot, 'Midwinter Ski Carnival,' Feb. 11, 1914; 'Midwinter Sports Were Enjoyed by Large Crowd,' Feb. 18, 1914; March 13, 1914; March 18, 1914; Oct. 7, 1914; 'Many Experts Coming for Midwinter Ski Carnival,' Feb. 3, 1915; [photograph] Feb. 10, 1915; Feb. 17, 1915; 'Howelsen on the Job,' Nov. 15, 1915; 'Interest in Youngsters,' Feb. 9, 1916; 'The Sport that Makes Clean, Healthful Men,' Feb. 23, 1916; 'Visit Hot Springs,' Feb. 23, 1916; April 5, 1916; July 5, 1916; Jan. 17, 1917; 'Father of Sport Honored,' March 7, 1917; 'Interesting History of Winter Sport,' Carl Howelsen, April 11, 1917; June 20, 1917; Feb. 13, 1918; Feb. 27, 1918; 'Denver Ski Enthusiasts,' Jan. 14, 1920; 'Pleasures Enjoyed by S.K.I. Members, Mrs. F.J. Blackmer, March 10, 1920; March 31, 1920; May 12, 1920; July 20, 1920.

Steamboat Springs Legends: A Centennial Collection, Debora Olsen, Steamboat Springs Chamber Resort Association, 1999.

Steamboat: Ski Town USA, Tom Bie, Mountain Sports Press, 2002.

Vail Daily, 'On Saturday, 5 More Inductees Will Be Enshrined in the Colorado's Ski & Snowboard Hall of Fame in Vail,' Ross Leonhart, Oct. 12, 2017.

Westword, 'How Denver Created Winter Park – And Almost Lost It,' Alan Prendergast, March 21, 2017.

Florence Rena Sabin, M.D.

Key to the Visions
Garden party: A venue she will use to promote her public health initiative
Bonnets, ribbons, lace, silk, embroidered dresses, jewelry: Women's fashions in 1940s
Mortarboards: Headgear worn by female medical school graduates
Lab coats and stethoscopes: Professional attire of female physicians

What's Fact? What's Fiction?
Dr. Florence Sabin worked hard to shepherd her public health initiatives through the Colorado State Legislature. This meeting is imagined, but based on what is known of her fame and status, the behavior of lawmakers throughout all decades, and the status of women in the 1940s.

As a research scientist, Dr. Sabin was exceptionally comfortable with analyzing and understanding data. She had spent all of her career around men and would have felt comfortable among them. The lawmakers, however, would have been less accustomed to meeting with a woman.

Colorado Phantasmagorias 258

There were no women in the Colorado General Assembly (legislature) in 1945.

Stories of Dr. Sabin's childhood in Central City include riding in the ore bucket. She climbed mountains with her sister Mary, although Mary was the more avid hiker of the two.

The exchange about the importance of public health is fictional, but based on facts and attitudes expressed at the time. The perceived burden on cattlemen and dairy farmers was especially controversial. Dr. Sabin expressed optimism that cattlemen and dairy farmers would want to do the right thing.

Dr. Sabin's campaign to clean up Colorado's air, water, and milk was pretty much stymied until she hit on the idea of a public relations campaign directed toward women.

Historians have concluded that Gov. Vivian thought his choosing Florence Sabin to head the public health initiative, which he was not keen on, was a stroke of genius. He was decidedly unenthusiastic about spending state resources on public health, but was feeling pressure to do something. Dr. Sabin—wildly famous, well-respected, beloved by Coloradans—was seventy-four years old. He assumed she'd be a figurehead with little energy to devote to it. Boy, was he wrong!

This particular hike is fictional, but Florence and Mary did some really hardcore hiking as young women, and would have undoubtedly continued to hike as they aged, but presumably shorter and easier hikes such as the one imagined here. 'Tramp' was a popular synonym for hike in the 1940s.

Pictures of Dr. Sabin show her wearing round, rimless spectacles.

The conversation is imagined, but the scene is otherwise accurate as to the beautiful view from Summit Lake, the flora and fauna still found there, and Dr. Sabin's strategy for passing her public health bills.

Every reporter who had ever met Dr. Sabin described her sparkly eyes and friendly smile.

Dr. Sabin often compared the number of combat deaths to deaths from preventable disease.

The comparison of her voice to the actor Katherine Hepburn (1907-2003) is based on my listening to Dr. Sabin's voice on a radio interview.

The description of Dr. Sabin's plain style is based on photographs and historical records. During the years she spent in medical research in New York and Baltimore, she often returned to her home state, giving lectures about science to women's groups. The exact words are fictitious, but

Colorado Phantasmagorias

summarize her plea. The pink leaflet entitled "Basic Health Needs of Colorado" was a real thing she passed out around the state.

Heaven Sent and Chantilly were popular fragrances in the 1940s.

She gave several speeches a day and was adept at adapting her message to her audience. News reports from the day document her presentations in all the cities listed. 'Health to Match Our Mountains' was her slogan. Having little support from the governor, she drove herself and paid for her own gas. She knew how to change a tire and wasn't afraid to drive in the snow.

Her campaign was decidedly successful, resulting in bipartisan support for most of her public health bills. The ones that mandated safety measures by cattlemen took a little longer to pass.

She lived near Cheesman Park with her sister, Mary, and was known to enjoy cooking and throwing dinner parties.

The new governor, William Knous, was a big fan of hers, and he was quoted as calling her both a 'dynamo' and an 'atom bomb.' In these years right after victory in the Pacific Theater of World War II, 'atom bomb' would have had a more positive connotation than it does now. He meant she achieved her objectives in a spectacular manner, not that she annihilated people.

She campaigned for Quigg Newton against Denver Mayor Ben Stapleton, after whom Stapleton Airport was named. Gov. Ralph Carr, also profiled in this collection, introduced Dr. Sabin at a political rally for Quigg Newton. History does not treat Mayor Stapleton kindly. Today he's reviled as a member of the Ku Klux Klan. Newton defeated Stapleton in 1947.

Yellow was her favorite color.

In 1947, televisions were known but not yet ubiquitous. Computers had also been invented, and a scientist such as Dr. Sabin would know about them, but they were very rare, affordable only by the richest corporations, and one computer would take up an entire room due to the size of their vacuum tubes. That a computer could solve 29 equations at once was touted at the time. A laptop-size computer would have seemed impossible and the internet wouldn't be invented for several more decades.

Sybylla's summary of public health achievements and weakness is factual.

We all still wonder, where are the flying cars? In the 1940s, popular magazines predicted flying cars. We're still waiting.

Before she took up public health in retirement, Dr. Sabin's major area of research was the lymphatic system.

Colorado Phantasmagorias 260

The University of Colorado Medical School used to be at 9th Street and Colorado Blvd. in Denver. Dr. Sabin would have been familiar with Fitzsimons Hospital east of the city. The rest of the current Anschutz medical campus is all new. Dr. Sabin did opine that a woman who works hard can be whatever she wants, and she herself was Exhibit A.

Stethoscopes may disappear from medicine in the near future, but some doctors and nurses today use them for the time being.

As this book goes to press, the end of the coronavirus story is not yet known. I keep picking up the geode on my writing desk, asking Sybylla/Mancio to show me how it turns out. It seems I am not influential enough for their attention. Is our public health esponse to coronavirus too much, too little, too late, or just right? We'll probably never know. What we do know is that public health will always remain relevant and important.

Bibliography

Brush News-Tribune, '13 Polio Cases in County,' Aug. 8, 1946; 'May Delay School Opening,' Aug. 15, 1946.

Colorado Transcript, 'Waring Always Full of Facts,' Sept. 5, 1946; 'Avenue Flashes,' Jan. 13, 1947; 'Why Be Sick?' Jan. 30, 1947; 'Colorado Behind in Health Laws Says Dr. Florence Sabin,' Georgina Brown, Jan. 30, 1947; 'The Wise Dr. Florence Sabin,' March 27, 1947; 'So Near, Yet So Far,' H.F. Parsons, Aug. 12, 1948; 'Why All the Fuss About Socialized Medicine?" July 14, 1949; 'Dr. Florence Sabin Addresses Meeting of Health Council,' March 22, 1951; 'Comes a Great American,' Oct. 8, 1953.

Denver Post, 'Colorado's Greatest Woman Tells About Her Discoveries in Search to Cure Anemia,' Frances Wayne, June 14, 1923; 'Native Colorado Girl Is First Woman in Academy of Science,' May 30, 1925; 'Science Will Go Marching On Despite Anti-Evolution Laws: Dr. Florence Sabin, Visiting Denver, Tells of Progress Made in Medical Research Work toward Curing Chief Ills of Mankind,' Frances Wayne, Aug. 11, 1925; 'One of America's Greatest Medical Scientists Is a Woman,' Feb. 22, 1926; 'Colorado Woman Gains Many Scientific Honors," Louise Lazell, Dec. 17, 1929; 'Dr. Florence Sabin Reviews Progress Against Disease,' July 14, 1931; 'Tuberculosis Association to Convene Monday at Springs,' June 5, 1932; 'Dr. Florence Sabin Is Honored Guest at Numerous Parties,' July 18, 1933; 'Dr. Florence Sabin Given Science Prize,' Frances Wayne, Oct. 17, 1935; 'To Give Speech in Home State,' May 20, 1937; 'Dr. Florence Sabin Gives Up Research to Reside in Denver,' Frances Wayne, July 11, 1938; 'Banquet Honors Florence Sabin, Famed Scientist,' Oct. 13, 1938; 'Honorary Degrees Conferred On Three Woman by Denver U.,' March 4, 1939; 'If I'm elected Governor,' by Lee Knous, Aug. 4, 1946; 'Women Are Urged to Support Proposed State Health Bill,' Robert Vigil, Sept. 22, 1946; 'Health Unit at Denver is Sabin Target,' Oct. 2, 1946; 'Mayor's Stand Called Miracle,' Oct. 16,1946; 'Boy Scouts,' Nov. 3, 1946; 'Asbury-Reynolds,' Nov. 10, 1946; 'Club Activity Calendar,' Nov. 17, 1946; 'Dairymen to Ask Revision in Laws,' Nov. 18, 1946; 'Club Activity Calendar,' Dec. 1, 1946; 'Why the Delay?" Dec. 10, 1946; 'Colorado Health Drive Draws Fire of Farmers,' Dec. 11,

Colorado Phantasmagorias 261

1946; 'Mayor Pledges Health Survey,' Dec. 20, 1946; 'Womans Federation,' Dec. 29 1946; 'Bills Presented on Health Setup,' Bert Hanna, Jan. 8, 1947; 'The Smart Set,' Jan. 11, 1947; 'Rocky Mountain Empire Briefs,' Jan. 24, 1947; 'Running the Gauntlet [editorial], Jan. 30, 1947; 'Club Activity Calendar,' Feb. 9, 1947' 'State GOP Leader Charged With Blocking Health Bill,' Harry Tarvin, Feb. 14, 1947; 'Senate Passes Sabin's Health Bill in Surprise Move Monday,' Feb. 17, 1947; 'State Health Reorganization Bill Creates New Department,' Bert Hanna, Feb. 19, 1947; 'Aid for the Ailing,' Feb. 28, 1947; 'Bang's Disease hits One in Six,' March 23, 1947; 'Means to an End,' March 31, 1947; 'Chest X-Rays Win Praise,' F. Sabin, April 21, 1947; 'Newton Indicts Health Department,' May 9, 1947; 'Take Health Department Out of Politics,' Dr. Florence Sabin, May 16, 1947; 'New Faces in the Post Gallery of Fame,' May 24, 1947; 'Polio Fight Outlined by Kauvar,' June 3, 1947; 'The Right Spirit,' June 5, 1947; 'Add Safer Laws, Says Dr. Sabin,' June 7, 1947; 'Early Polio Fight Urged,' June 11, 1947; 'State Club Elects Littleton Woman,' June 15, 1947; 'Kauvar to Resign Health Job; Sabin May Be Named,' Dec. 2, 1947; 'Dr. Florence Sabin Named Denver Health Manager,' Dec. 23, 1947; 'State Hospital Shortage Relief Seen in Five Years,' March 2, 1948; 'Dr. Sabin Seeks Ranchers' Aid for Bang's Disease Bill,' June 9, 1948; 'State to Free Thirty Tuberculars,' March 6, 1949; 'Colorado May Step Backwards in Treatment of Tuberculosis,' Allan Hurst, M.D., March 13, 1949; 'Model Setup Watches Denverites' Health from Infancy to Old Age,' Edward Lehman, June 5, 1949; 'It's Free, Folks!" June 21, 1949; 'Joint Committee Meets on Bang's Disease Curb,' Feb. 19, 1951; 'State Water Board Chief Hits Anti-Pollution Bill,' Robert Staff, Feb. 28, 1951; 'Christmas Seal Sale Backed by Dr. Sabin,' Nov. 25, 1951; 'Mary Sabin Honored by Hiking Club,' Nov. 25, 1952; 'Dr. Florence Sabin, Noted Scientist, Dies,' Oct. 4, 1953.

Denver Public Library Western History, Interview with Florence Sabin (audio), C610.92 S116rad CD.

Eagle Valley Enterprise, June 21, 1946.

Florence Sabin: Colorado Woman of the Century, Elinor Bluemel, University of Colorado Press, 1959.

Florence Sabin: Teacher, Scientist, Humanitarian, E.E. Duncan, Filter Press, 2014.

Hidden from History, Kim Zach, Avisson Press, 2002.

Life of Florence Sabin, Judith Kaye, Twenty-First Century Books, 1993.

Little Kingdom of Gilpin, Alan Granruth ed., 'Dr. Florence Sabin,' Linda Jones, Gilpin County Historical Society, 2000.

National Institutes of Health, 'Changing the Face of Medicine: Dr. Florence Rena Sabin,' https://cfmedicine.nlm.nih.gov.

Palisade Tribune, 'Stockgrowers and Feeders Convention in Boulder,' June 18, 1948; 'Colorado TB Association Holds Meet,' March 25, 1949.

Probing the Unknown, Mary Kay Phelan, Thomas Y. Crowell Company, 1969.

Remarkable Colorado Women, 2d Ed., Gayle Shirley, Globe Pequot Press, 2012.

Rocky Mountain News, 'Women in Clubdom,' Jan. 6, 1895; 'High Honor Bestowed Upon a Denver Woman,' June 30, 1905, 'Mountaineering in Colorado,' Mary S. Sabin, Nov. 5, 12 and 19, 1911; 'Midsummer Finds All Resorts of Colorado Crowded,' July 22, 1917.

Smithsonian, 'Florence Sabin Pioneered Her Way in Medical Science, Then Made Sure Other Women Could Do the Same,' Eliza McGraw, July 6, 2018.

Colorado Phantasmagorias 262

Steamboat Pilot, 'Health Problems to be Discussed at Meeting Here: Dr. Florence Sabin Will Be Speaker Here on May 10,' May 2, 1946; 'Dire Need for Health Program Told by Speakers: Colorado Said to Be Lagging Other States,' May 16, 1946; Senate Maps War on Bang's Disease,' March 6, 1947; 'Governor Knous Congratulates 36th General Assembly as It Completes Its Work After 108 Days of Labor,' Alva Swain, April 24, 1947.

Time, 'Medicine: Colorado Crusader,' Oct. 28, 1946.

U.S. News, 'The 10 Healthiest States,' Casey Leins, May 20, 2019.

Up the Gulch, Cathleen Norman and Linda Jones, Gilpin County Historical Society, 2005.

Westminster Journal, 'X-Ray Locations,' July 22, 1949.

Women Pioneers of Science, Louis Haber, Harcourt, 1979.

Women You Should Know, 'Lymph, There It Is: Florence Sabin, Pioneer Woman of Medical Research;' Dale Debakcsy, Aug. 22, 2018, womenyoushouldknow.net.

Wray Gazette, 'Dr. Florence Sabin to Speak at Yuma,' Oct. 9, 1947.

Stanley Biber, M.D.

Key to the Visions
Mirage of women (and a few men): Transgender women and men

What's Fact? What's Fiction?

Sex change operation was the term in use during Dr. Biber's practice, but more accurate terminology includes gender reassignment, genital reassignment, genital realignment and the current preferred term, gender confirmation.

In addition to his doctoring, Stanley Biber was a cattle rancher. His ranch was near Hoehne, northeast of Trinidad. Whether or not he could see the Spanish Peaks back dropped from his property, I don't know, but it's probable and the image is perfect, because the Utes called them 'breasts of the earth.'

His life story and description of his physique are accurate. He was a very interesting guy.

Was Dr. Biber's first transgender patient named Ann? He never referred to her by name in interviews. He told reporters that she was a social worker, had been living as a woman, and they were acquainted before she came to him for the surgery. Reporters sometimes referred to her as 'Ann,' but it's unclear if that was her real name, a pseudonym, or if the reporters conflated her with a later patient named Anna Louise Jenkins. Virtually all of Dr. Biber's patients came from elsewhere and returned home, but Anna

Colorado Phantasmagorias

Jenkins settled in Trinidad after the surgery and became known by the locals as 'Trannie Annie.'

The conversation is imagined. However, Dr. Biber was quoted as speaking in enthusiastic exclamations such as "Great! Just great!" He wasn't humble. He was proud of his MASH experience in Korea and related that it gave him confidence to do any surgery.

He was very short and quite stocky, but his patient Claudine Griggs described how he appeared taller than he actually was.

Reddish hair, medium build, is how he described his first transgender patient. That first patient had been under the care of Dr. Harry Benjamin (1885-1986), who had been friends with Judge Ben Lindsey (1869-1943), who was friends with Margaret Brown, also profiled in this collection. We have no documented words from this first patient, but Claudine Griggs published her diary, and I have conscripted her words and thoughts for 'Ann.' For example, the 'dirty trick' sentence is paraphrased from Griggs's diary.

The first Nazi book burning torched medical texts describing the sex change surgical procedure. Although the inner thought is imagined, Dr. Biber was Jewish and he had to have been incensed by this.

Christine Jorgensen (1926-1989) was the first transgender woman to become famous. All that is true.

Dr. Benjamin's book was the primary text describing transsexualism in the 1960s. Dr. Biber never mentioned reading it, but he had to have. Dr. Biber did report writing a letter to Johns Hopkins and getting hand drawings in response.

The conversation about suicidal thoughts is also based on Claudine Griggs's diary.

Dr. Biber did the first surgery under the maxim of 'it's better to ask forgiveness than permission.' Obviously, the nuns who attended the surgery could tell what he was doing.

The compassion of the Sisters of Charity at San Rafael is noted by everyone who ever wrote about Dr. Biber's surgeries. A daughter of Felipe Baca, also profiled in this collection, was one of Trinidad's first Sisters of Charity, although she was deceased by Dr. Biber's time.

It's commonly accepted that Dr. Biber's gender confirmation practice saved Mount San Rafael Hospital when other rural hospitals closed.

Casablanca and Tijuana had been popular destinations for transgender people seeking surgery.

Estimates of the gender confirmation surgeries done by Dr. Biber range from 5,000 to 6,000. He was busy. His practice was initially built on word of mouth, his patients praising his skills and integrity, the compassion of the hospital staff and community. He got media coverage in the 1980s and 1990s.

Dr. Biber's first transgender patient, Ann if you will, was reportedly very pleased with the results, even if Dr. Biber wasn't. His skills became refined with practice, and eventually there were reports of gynecologists who could not tell the difference.

The description of his patient Georgina Beyer is based on video of her speaking to the New Zealand Parliament. Her words are an exact quotation.

Mancio's facts and figures are accurate. Drop City was a commune outside of Trinidad from 1965 to the early 1970s.

Chastity Bono was a baby in 1969. Dr. Biber would have known of her because her parents, Sonny and Cher, were famous. Chastity transitioned to Chaz in 2008. Bruce Jenner did not compete in the Olympics until the 1970s, but it's possible that Dr. Biber had heard of him. Jenner transitioned to Caitlyn in 2017.

Brianna Titone was elected the first transgender legislator in the Colorado General Assembly in 2018.

Even as his gender confirmation practice grew, Dr. Biber continued to perform all the other surgeries needed by his patients in Trinidad.

Fisher's Peak is the dominant geological feature in Trinidad.

Bibliography

Being Transgender, Robert Rodi and Laura Ross Broomall, Mason Crest, 2017.
Chronicle News, 'Dreams Come True for Transsexuals Who Come to Trinidad, Biber Very Popular,' Jan. 28, 1985.
Colorado Experience, 'Trinidad,' Rocky Mountain PBS, 2016.
Colorado Heritage, 'Making the Journey to Trinidad,' Madupe Labode, Winter 2004.
Denver Post, 'Health Officials Brace for Stormy Trinidad Hearing,' Donna Logan, Dec. 4, 1968; 'Trinidad Is Sex-Change Surgery Capital,' John Boslough, April 18, 1976; 'Small Town Medical Care Problems Can Be Fatal,' John Boslough, May 31, 1976; 'Fear, Humor in the Gender Cross-Over,' Carol Kreck, March 2, 1980; 'Starting Over,' Karen Evans, July 10, 1983; 'Sex Change Surgeon Bids for Office,' Bruce Finley, Dec. 16, 1990; 'Sex Change Surgeon Gains Office,' Bruce Finley, Dec. 19, 1990; 'Letter to the Editor,' Yetta Cibull, Dec. 27, 1990; 'Pioneer Sex-Change Surgeon Dies at 82,' Claire Martin, Jan. 17, 2006; 'Well-Known Trinidad Sex-Reassignment Doctor Leaves,' Karen Augue, May 4, 2016; 'Privately Owned Fisher's Peak Set to Become 42nd State Park,' Judith Kohler, Sept. 12, 2019.
Gentlemen's Quarterly, 'Meet John, er, Jane Doe,' John Tayman, Dec. 1991.

Colorado Phantasmagorias 265

Georgie Girl, Annie Goldson and Peter Wells, A Women Make Movies Release, 2001.
Healthline, 'What to Expect from Gender Confirmation Surgery,' July 16, 2019.
How Sex Changed, Joanne Meyerowitz, First Harvard University Press, 2002.
Insurance Journal, 'Colo. Sex-Change Surgeon Retires After Losing Malpractice Insurance,' Jan. 3, 2005.
Journal of a Sex Change: Passage Through Trinidad, Claudine Griggs, Berg, 2004 [aka *Passage Through Trinidad,* Claudine Griggs, McFarland & Company, 1996].
Los Angeles Times, 'The Body Builder,' Michael Haederle, Jan. 23, 1995.
New York Times, 'Stanley H. Biber, 82, Surgeon Among First to Do Sex Changes, Dies,' Margalit Fox, Jan. 21, 2006.
NPR, 'Sex-Change Pioneer, Dr. Stanley Biber,' Jeff Brady, Jan. 19, 2006.
PRS Global Open, 'Trends in Gender-Affirming Surgery in Insured Patients in the United States,' Megan Lane et al., April 16, 2018.
Rocky Mountain News, 'Sex-Change Pioneer a Beloved Friend, Mentor,' Deborah Frazier, Jan. 19, 2006.
San Francisco Examiner, 'Gender Bender,' Bill Shaw, July 26, 1984.
Transgender History, Susan Stryker, Hachette, 2017.
Transsexual Phenomenon, Harry Benjamin, M.D., Julian Press, 1966.
Trinidad, Matt Dentler, New Day Films, 2009.
Washington Post, 'Transgender Surgeries Are on the Rise, Says First Study of Its Kind,' Amy Ellis Nutt, Feb. 28, 2018.
Westword, 'Boys Will Be Girls,' Laura Misch, Sept. 27, 1988; 'Genital Hospital,' Harrison Fletcher, Sept. 2, 1998; 'Sex Change,' Nov. 27, 2003.

John Denver

Key to the Visions
Golden dome: Colorado State Capitol
Millions of voices: Fans singing 'Rocky Mountain High'

What's Fact? What's Fiction?

The conversation is imagined, but some radio stations did ban 'Rocky Mountain High' at first, even as John explained he was inspired by a meteor shower. Jerry Weintraub was his manager.

In the 1970s, John's trademark look was long hair and granny glasses. He got contacts later.

John Denver had a high tolerance for irony. He told music reporters he got stoned and even toked in front of at least one, but even so vehemently insisted his most famous song had nothing to do with marijuana. He also opposed the Winter Olympics even as he sang about skiing at the highly-developed Aspen Resort, opposed fossil fuels even as he piloted airplanes for fun, and lectured against wasting water even though he was a golfer.

John told *Playboy* he'd experienced clairvoyance.

According to a plaque at Red Rocks Park, John Denver performed there 16 times. One of those concerts, August 9, 1973 is within the time period that Wade Blank (also profiled in this collection) was taking Heritage House residents to concerts.

'Singing from his toes' is the way John described his intensity. Words and phrasing attributed to him here are mostly imagined, but drawn from interviews and paraphrased from his songs.

John Denver partnered with then-future Governor Dick Lamm (pictured with John) in opposing the Olympics. The dynamiting, shaving and encasing were all real proposals that incited fierce opposition. 'John Denver Go Home' bumper stickers were a thing.

He said his philosophy of singing to make people feel good was inspired by his Uncle Dean.

In spite of his cheerful public persona, John Denver had a dark side. His relationship with his first wife was fraught. His second marriage lasted just a few years. He developed a drinking problem.

Glenn Miller died in a plane crash during World War II. It's interesting that the two most famous musicians from Colorado both died in plane crashes.

John's friend Tom Crum worked with him to found Windstar, an environmental research and education foundation. Robert Fuller and Werner Erhard helped with The Hunger Project to reduce starvation throughout the world.

Colorado Green Wind Farm is a project of Xcel Energy located about 40 miles northwest of Granada, which was the location of the Amache Internment Camp, the subject of the Ralph Carr chapter in this collection.

John grew up an Air Force brat, but shared fond memories of driving tractor at his grandparents' farm in Oklahoma.

Mancio's facts about energy and hunger are based on research.

The Colorado General Assembly made 'Rocky Mountain High' Colorado's second state song in 2007. The votes were 50-11 in the House and 26-8 in the Senate.

The *Playboy* quote is verbatim. Mancio's dates regarding state legalization of marijuana are accurate.

Colorado Phantasmagorias

Bibliography

Aspen Times, 'Why the World Still Needs John Denver,' J.P. McDaniel, Oct. 10, 2002; 'It's Rocky Mountain [Expletive Deleted] Colorado,' Charles Agar, Oct. 13, 2007; 'Aspen Is Third U.S. City to Reach 100% Renewable Energy,' Erica Robbie, Sept. 1, 2015.

Colorado Virtual Library, 'John Denver: Singer and Songwriter,' Arian Osborne, Aug. 26, 2016, www.coloradovirtuallibrary.org.

Denver Post, 'Evergreen Due Consideration,' Joanne Ditmer, Aug. 16, 1970; 'Olympic Plans Draw Fire,' John Toohey, Oct. 25, 1970; 'Denver's Olympic host Role Opposed,' March 31, 1971; ''76 Ski Sites Still in Doubt,' Charlie Meyers, Dec. 30, 1971; 'Letter to the Editor,' Frank Ashley, Sept. 3, 1972; 'Rocky Mountain High Now Second State Song,' Jennifer Brown, March 12, 2007.

Denver Public Library, Olympic Games (Winter) 1976 Clipping file,

Energy News Network, 'Xcel Energy Works to Meet Aggressive Clean Energy Goal,' Allen Best, March 9, 2019.

Green Operations, aspensnowmass.com.

John Denver Country Boy, BBC, 2015.

John Denver: Man for the World, John Stansfield, Filter Press, 2008.

John Denver: Mother Nature's Son, John Collis, Mainstream Publishing Co., 1999.

Minneapolis Star, 'My Songs Touch Me; I Try to Touch People, Peter Vaughan, Nov. 19, 1970; 'John Denver: Critics Only Country Road Bump,' John Bream, April 23, 1976; 'John Denver Sings a Song of Himself,' John Bream, March 6, 1979.

Minneapolis Tribune, 'Can Critics Spoil His Success? Heck, No,' M. Howard Gelfand, May 11, 1975.

New York Times, 'Colorado Has Song in Its Heart, and Not Drugs on Its Mind,' Kirk Johnson, March 13, 2007; 'Commotion Over the Sale of John Denver's Sanctuary,' Jack Healy, June 19, 2013.

Newsweek, 'John Denver: The Sunshine Boy,' Dec. 20,1976.

Orlando Sentinel, 'A New John Denver, Richard Defendorf, Sept. 29, 1985.

People, 'John Denver's Unsung Story,' Frank W. Martin, Feb. 26, 1979.

Playboy, 'Playboy Interview: John Denver,' Marcia Seligson, Dec. 1977.

Rocky Mountain News, 'Snags Arise in Olympic Site Selection,' Richard O'Reilly, April 6, 1971; 'Olympic Alpine Site Conflict Brewing,' Richard O'Reilly, April 7, 1971.

Rolling Stone, 'John Denver: His Rocky Mountain Highness,' Chet Flippo, May 8, 1975.

Statement to Senate on Censorship, John Denver, Sept. 19, 1985.

Take Me Home: An Autobiography, John Denver with Arthur Tobier, Rocky Mountain Merchandise, LLC, 1994.

Westword, 'Is John Denver's Rocky Mountain High about Marijuana, or Is It a Big Myth-Understanding?' Josiah M. Hesse, Dec. 27, 2013.

Xcel Energy, 'Building a Carbon-Free Future,' xcelenergy.com.

Acknowledgments

I am grateful to all historians and librarians, but especially those from History Colorado and the Denver Public Library Western History Department.

Special thanks to my proofreader, Carolyn Reed, the RMFW critique groups at Belmar and Littleton, and all my sensitivity readers:
- Adrian Miller, author of *The Presidents' Kitchen Cabinet* and *Soul Food*, and poet Greg 'Seth' Harris read Barney Ford.
- Diana Biggs and Ute Elder Austin Box read Chipeta.
- Helen Trencher, author and performer of *Golda Meir: Choices & Chances*, and Robin Springer read Golda Meir.
- House District 32 Representative Adrienne Benavidez read Felipe Baca.
- Kathy Larsen Bruner read Ora Chatfield & Clara Dietrich.

I'm also grateful for Don Rosenberry, Kris Monshaugen, Cathy Pierson Mabry, Brenda Bronson, Paula Stacey, and Stephen Hart for reading drafts and giving me the courage to continue.

My research companions Anne Allen, Donald Rosenberry, and Ellen Theis made tripping around Colorado fun. Thanks to Cindy Bosco and Don Campbell for Steamboat Springs accommodations.

Thanks to Jeff Simley for sharing his train schedules, Carrie Makenna for photo assistance, and last but not least, Craig Rouse for the beautiful cover.

About the Author

Joan Jacobson adopted Colorado as her home state over thirty years ago. She's a history lover, journalist, paralegal, and author of a literary novel entitled *Small Secrets*. Joan is a member of History Colorado and The Denver Woman's Press Club.

Did you enjoy this book?

Please post a review on Amazon.com or Goodreads.com and recommend it to your friends. Thank you!

Made in United States
Troutdale, OR
07/04/2024